# HOWARD HUGHES

—— AND ——
## THE CREATION OF MODERN HOLLYWOOD

# HOWARD HUGHES

## AND

## THE CREATION OF MODERN HOLLYWOOD

## JEFFREY RICHARDSON

AMERICA
THROUGH TIME®
ADDING COLOR TO AMERICAN HISTORY

America Through Time is an imprint of Fonthill Media LLC
www.through-time.com
office@through-time.com

Published in the United States of America by Arcadia Publishing
by arrangement with Fonthill Media LLC
For all general information, please contact Arcadia Publishing:
Telephone: 843-853-2070
Fax: 843-853-0044
E-mail: sales@arcadiapublishing.com
For customer service and orders:
Toll-Free 1-888-313-2665
Visit us on the internet at www.arcadiapublishing.com

Published in the United Kingdom by Fonthill Media Limited
Stroud House
Russell Street
Stroud GL5 3AN
www.fonthillmedia.com

First published 2019

ISBN 978-1-63499-145-2

Typeset in 10.5pt on 13pt Sabon
Printed and bound in England

# CONTENTS

*For Giovanna, Milford, and Willow*

# Introduction:
# Everything there is to Tell

Howard Hughes was an industrialist, aviator, and eccentric, but he was also the most important movie producer during the golden age of cinema. At a time when filmmaking was tightly controlled and highly formulaic, Hughes used his enormous wealth to challenge the dictates and restrictions that defined the motion picture industry. Tackling subjects that were explicitly forbidden, he pushed the boundaries of onscreen sex and violence. He also pioneered production and marketing techniques that were revolutionary, including the multimillion-dollar blockbuster and the promotion of scandal.

When Hughes became the first person to completely own a major Hollywood studio, he continued his maverick approach to filmmaking as a mogul. Most importantly, Hughes's role in the federal government's antitrust case against the industry led to the collapse of the entire studio system and the transformation of American cinema. Although his contributions are often overlooked, Hughes was instrumental in shaping the motion picture industry that exists today.

A biographer of Hughes once wrote that "virtually no book publisher today will accept a manuscript of a Howard Hughes *biography*, because Hughes simply has been written about too much by too many writers who have told everything there is to tell."[1] In many ways, the author was correct as there is a countless body of literature on Hughes, despite the fact that his penchant for privacy was so extreme it eventually consumed his entire life. The books written about Hughes can be grouped into several general categories.

Biographies are the most common. John Keats's *Howard Hughes* (1966) was the best account of the reclusive billionaire while he was still alive. Donald L. Barlett and James B. Steele's *Howard Hughes: His Life and Madness* (originally entitled *Empire: The Life, Legend, and Madness of Howard Hughes*) (1979) remains one of the best books ever written on the subject. *Hughes: The Private Diaries, Memos and Letters* (2001), by Richard Hack, has added valuable insight and helped tear away the façade that Hughes himself worked so hard to create.

In addition to biographies, there are several memoirs written by individuals who had personal relationships with Hughes or worked directly with him. *Howard: The Amazing Mr. Hughes* (1972), by Noah Dietrich and Bob Thomas, is an inside look at Hughes as seen through the eyes of his longtime financial assistant. Terry Moore's *The Beauty and the Billionaire* (1984), written by one of Hughes's lovers, offers insight into the private side of the man. Finally, *Next to Hughes: Behind the Power and Tragic Downfall of Howard Hughes By His Closest Advisor* (1992), by Robert Maheu and Richard Hack, chronicles the life and business dealings of the man who came to be known as Hughes's alter ego.

Some accounts deal with specific topics or periods in Hughes's life, and they offer analysis beyond the generalities of the first two categories. *Howard Hughes in Las Vegas* (1970), by Omar V. Garrison, details Hughes's reclusive years as a casino magnate and his influence on the gaming industry. Charles Barton's *Howard Hughes and His Flying Boat* (1982) focuses on the controversial building of the HK-1 airplane, commonly known as the Spruce Goose. *Howard Hughes's Airline: An Informal History of TWA* (1983), by Robert Serling, examines Hughes's role in the airline industry. Finally, Suzanne Finstad's *Heir Not Apparent* (1984) chronicles the contentious battle over Hughes's estate after his death.

The works cited are only a few examples of many. When taken together, they describe the numerous ways in which Hughes contributed to life in twentieth-century America. It is nevertheless puzzling, especially given the fascination with Hughes that has extended to different mediums, that his years in the motion picture industry have not been adequately examined.

Some analysts seem to believe Hughes's tenure as a producer and mogul was insignificant given his other accomplishments, while others describe his films as merely the eccentric hobby of a rich playboy. A few books do discuss the topic in more detail, but they have significant limitations, including authors that often hold Hughes in such utter contempt that it clouds their interpretation.

*Howard Hughes in Hollywood* (1985), by Tony Thomas, gives a brief introduction to the movies Hughes produced, but it reads more like an extended synopsis than a scholarly examination. While Hughes's ownership of RKO Radio Pictures is detailed in Betty Lasky's *RKO: The Biggest Little Major of Them All* (1984) and Richard B. Jewell's *Slow Fade* to *Black: The Decline of RKO Radio Pictures* (2016), these two authors discuss Hughes in the context of the studio, which comprised only a few years of his illustrious career. Most recently, *Seduction: Sex, Lies, and Stardom in Howard Hughes's Hollywood* (2018), by Karina Longworth, deals almost exclusively with tabloid gossip.

General histories of the motion picture industry occasionally mention Hughes, but their coverage is often minimal. For example, the massive *History of the American Cinema* series, a total of ten volumes covering thousands of pages, only mentions Hughes approximately thirty-five times, and almost all of these are passing references to *The Outlaw* (1943) and the closing of RKO. Hollywood historians, much like Hughes's biographers, appear content to dismiss Hughes's tenure as inconsequential, especially when compared to the legacy of more distinguished and acceptable producers like Irving Thalberg and Darryl F. Zanuck.

As such, no one has adequately explored Hughes's impact on Hollywood or American culture. This book will be the first to do just that. With the exception of a brief introduction to Hughes's wealth, which is vital to understanding why he was able to operate independently, it will focus exclusively on Hughes's tenure as a producer and studio mogul. Narrowing the scope even further, this book only examines the films and events in Hughes's career that were truly revolutionary. Minor films and unrelated topics, such as Hughes's affairs with starlets, are completely ignored.

A mystique surrounded Hughes during his lifetime, and it has only grown since his death. This has allowed rumor, innuendo, and propaganda to overshadow all things related to Hughes. Hughes himself compounded the problem by seeking both front-page publicity and complete privacy. His penchant to lie, on and off the record, has added to the confusion.

Many authors have thus been guilty of accepting fictitious claims and stories as fact, while others have unknowingly repeating falsehoods that have become gospel. While this book's main objective is to place Hughes in the proper historical context, it also employs meticulous research to tell the story of Hughes in Hollywood accurately for the first time.

To get beyond the myth and misinformation that has led previous scholars to overlook Hughes's contributions to the motion picture industry, this book relies mainly on primary documents (such as letters, telegrams, contracts, production reports, and corporate records) that allow the participants, including Hughes, to speak directly in their own words. Articles in newspapers and trade journals from the period are also used to show how Hughes was able to exploit and manipulate the publicity surrounding himself and his films. Secondary works are cited sparingly and are only employed to help illuminate Hughes's influence and legacy. Again, by concentrating on the historical record, Hughes's accomplishments are better understood and appreciated, as fact is separated from fiction.

Accessing primary documents is often difficult and time consuming. Writing a book is equally challenging. Although it would be impossible to thank everyone who made this endeavor possible, a few institutions and individuals deserve recognition. The staffs at the Film Department at the University of Nevada Las Vegas (UNLV), the Margaret Herrick Library at the Academy of Motion Picture Arts and Sciences, and the Louis B. Mayer Library at the American Film Institute (AFI) were especially helpful in obtaining key materials. The documents at UNLV, which were given to the university by the Summa Corporation, the company that consolidated many of Hughes's business interests in his later years, were particularly noteworthy as they had been previously unknown or overlooked.[2] Craig Roell at Georgia Southern University and the late Hal Rotham at UNLV helped steer the manuscript in its early iterations. And of course, this book would not be possible without the team at Fonthill Media, notably Matthew Rodriguez and Alan Sutton.

Most importantly, I want to thank my wife Giovanna. She has been a vital sounding board and critic throughout this process. She has learned more about Howard Hughes than she ever cared to know. (And she says Leonardo DiCaprio looks nothing like him!) She has also taken on additional responsibilities, including looking after our "kids," Milford and Willow, which has given me the time to focus on this project. Thank you for everything Giovanna. I love you.

Howard Hughes is not deserving of sainthood. In fact, as the record shows, he could be a terrible person to work for and with. He did a lot of things that people, then and now, believe had a tremendously negative impact on Hollywood and society in general. The continuing debate over sex and violence onscreen, especially its effect on children, is a notable example. Hughes might not have been good, he might not have been right, but that does not mean he was unimportant. In fact, as this book will show, Hughes was one of the most significant people in motion picture history.

With a seemingly endless supply of money, Hughes was able to make the type of films he wanted, the way he wanted, with virtually no outside interference. He fought industry norms, censors, and anything else that stood in his way. His tenure was brief, but when Hughes finally left Hollywood, nothing would ever be the same. Having cast aside the shackles that bound previous filmmakers, Hughes revolutionized the motion picture industry. Despite the fact that his legacy has long been overlooked, Hughes had a profound influence on American popular culture and the creation of modern Hollywood. A thorough and proper examination of Hughes's legacy as a producer and studio mogul has finally arrived.

1

# The World's Most Famous Motion Picture Producer

"Who is that bozo?"—Sergeant Peter O'Gaffney (Louis Wolheim) in *Two Arabian Knights*

The story of Howard Hughes in Hollywood, like all aspects of his life, begins with the Hughes Tool Company, "one of the finest money-makers ever devised by the mind of man."[1] Hughes was able to blaze a groundbreaking trail in the motion picture industry because he had the resources to operate outside the studio system that dominated Hollywood for most of his tenure. While there were other notable independent producers, some of whom made great films and accumulated sizable power, Hughes was different because his wealth was different.

Whereas other producers and studio executives were always conscious of the bottom line and their future in the industry, after all their livelihoods depended on it, Hughes ultimately did not care if he upset the most important people. He spent unprecedented sums, and despite his public pronouncements, it seemed like he did not care if his movies made money. Hughes did not need Hollywood.

If he wanted to set a new aviation record or start a multi-million dollar company, Hughes could leave the film industry and reenter at any time. Movies were Hughes's passion. They were not his profession. As a result, he was able to make motion pictures the way he wanted, truly free of outside interference, the consequences be damned. Hughes was many things—determined, visionary, callous—but he could be fiercely independent in an industry governed by conformity because of his wealth.

And despite spending millions of his own money making motion pictures, Hughes's wealth increased substantially during the three decades he spent in Hollywood. It appeared he simply could not spend all of the money he was making. While his financial empire stretched across multiple industries, the centerpiece was always the Hughes Tool Company, a business born out of the ingenuity of his father.

Howard Robard Hughes Sr. was born in 1869 in Lancaster, Missouri. Like many of his generation, he was groomed from an early age to take over the family business, which in this case was the practice of law. He entered Harvard College in 1893, but he did not take to academic life and dropped out a year later. He nevertheless continued on the path set out for him and enrolled at Iowa State University. Determined to get on with his life, even if it was a life only his parents seemed to want, he passed the Iowa bar before graduating, quit school, and took his place alongside his father at a law firm in Keokuk, Iowa.

After a brief period, he finally had enough. Finding the law a "too-exacting mistress for a man of my talent," he quit the family practice and set out on his own.[2] Finally freed from expectations, Big Howard, as he came to be known, was determined to strike it rich and somehow make a name for himself. Seeking his fortune in the earth, he spent two years mining for silver in Colorado followed by another two years in the zinc fields of the Indian Territory (present-day Oklahoma).

Then in 1901, oil was discovered in a place called Spindletop south of Beaumont, Texas. It was the largest oil field ever discovered up to that point, and for Big Howard and countless others, the allure of wealth and excitement was irresistible. Rushing to the area, Big Howard found that the "reek of oil was everywhere. It filled the air, it painted the houses, it choked the lungs and stained men's souls."[3] The only thing missing for Big Howard was a monetary profit.

While he brought in several wells that yielded modest returns, Big Howard's luck and his finances were quickly exhausted. It appeared that Spindletop would be another disappointment on his quest for fame and fortune. But more than simply a monumental discovery, Spindletop was, in the words of Pulitzer Prize-winning author Daniel Yergin, "the training ground for the oil industry of the Southwest."[4] An entire generation learned the science, some would say the art, of drilling while exploring in southeast Texas.

Big Howard was one of the many, and his initial failure ultimately led him to an invention that proved to be far more valuable than any single well. Like so many of his contemporaries, Big Howard was plagued by the inability to access oil that he knew existed below his feet but was protected by a shelf of impenetrable rock. The problem lay in the equipment, and Big Howard was determined to find a solution.

To drill or make hole, the earliest machinery used heavy cable-tool bits that were lifted and dropped repeatedly to pound the earth. Around the discovery of Spindletop, rotary bits with a fishtail design that more effectively ground layers of rock were introduced. Dragging a rotary-fishtail (or chisel) bit, as opposed to pounding a cable-tool bit, allowed drillers to go faster and deeper than ever before, but even fishtail bits slowed dramatically when they encountered harder formations. The bits commonly broke apart, which required them to be changed frequently, and they often failed to reach intended targets. As one journal put it in 1919, "drilling through rock with a fish-tail was a good deal like filing a sewing machine needle with a finger-nail file."[5]

Big Howard, having considered the problem, theorized that a bit with cutters that rolled on the bottom, instead of dragging like the traditional fishtail bit, would eliminate the slow and costly drilling of harder formations. Around 1906, he began working on a new bit that would replace the fishtail. His first wooden model of a roller-type bit with two coned-shaped cutters was produced two years later.

According to legend, when Big Howard first tested the prototype bit in his garage, it tore through a marble slab, destroyed the workbench on which it sat, and was making its way through the concrete floor by the time it was finally turned off.

Emboldened by the bit's initial success, Big Howard and his business partner Walter Sharp formed the Sharp–Hughes Tool Company on December 11, 1908. (Big Howard may have been the inventor of the bit, but Sharp put up most of the initial funds so his name went first.) Early the following year, they tested the bit at an actual well site in Goose Creek, Texas. They were careful to clear the field and attach the bit themselves so no one would see it and attempt to replicate its innovative design. The bit performed admirably, and the results were duplicated upon further tests.

After a few minor alterations, Big Howard received United States patent numbers 930,758 and 930,759 on August 10, 1909. His invention consisted of a bit with two detachable cones each comprised of 166 cutting edges. "The main object of my invention," read the first patent, "is to provide a drill that is compact and strong and which comprises very few parts that are of suitable dimensions to withstand the strains to which they are subjected even when they are embodied in a drill that is used for boring comparatively small holes."[6]

The S-H Rotary Rock Drill Bit—commonly known as the Hughes bit—revolutionized the nature of oil exploration worldwide. The new bit chipped and crushed rock, as opposed to simply grinding it, which allowed drillers to make hole deeper and faster than ever before. In one instance cited by the company, a depth of "four to six inches per day became an average of from 15 to 20 feet," an astounding increase of 4,400 percent.[7]

The bit "made possible the recovery of oil in the great Southwest fields below hard rock formations and at depths previously untapped, making available to a motorized age vast new reservoirs of oil."[8] Not surprisingly, within a few years, the preeminence of the company's product was indicated by the fact that it supplied "over 75% of all rock bits used in the gas and oil industry."[9]

In a stroke of financial brilliance, the Sharp–Hughes Tool Company had the foresight to lease the bits to drillers as opposed to selling them outright. Once a well was gushing, the leased bits were returned to the company where they were cleaned, sharpened, and leased again. The tactic kept competitors from re-sharpening the bits themselves and selling them at a cheaper price. As the company introduced new drill bits, they too were leased. This effectively forced all drillers to work exclusively with Sharp–Hughes. "Sheer genius," proclaimed William Stamps Farish, president of Standard Oil. "It was highway robbery, of course, but genius all the same."[10]

Just as the Sharp–Hughes Tool Company was taking off, Big Howard's partner Walter Sharp died on November 28, 1912, at the age of forty-two. Sharp had more business acumen and resources than Big Howard, and his contributions to the early success of the company cannot be overstated. But from the outset, it was Big Howard that provided the patents and the genius upon which the Sharp–Hughes Tool Company was built. Sharp's fifty percent interest in the company passed to his widow Estelle. Her lawyers cautioned her that the company was still young and might not succeed, so she sold her shares for $50,000 to Ed Prather, an experienced oilman who was friends with both Walter and Big Howard.

Prather sought to influence the direction of the company, but he quickly learned that his new partner had no plans to listen to anyone. Big Howard had assumed complete managerial control of the company upon Sharp's death, and he would run it as he saw fit. Dismayed at the prospect of being a mere investor, Prather sold his interest to Big Howard.

Thus, on January 29, 1913, the company was incorporated under the laws of the state of Texas as the Hughes Tool Company. Commonly known as Toolco, it was headquartered in Houston. Its sole owner was Howard Hughes Sr. As Big Howard later told his only child, "Don't ever have any partners. They're nothing but trouble."[11]

By the time the company was incorporated, Big Howard was married with a seven-year-old son. Allene Gano was descended from a line of French Huguenots that included a chaplain in George Washington's army and a cavalryman that fought valiantly in the Civil War. Her father was a successful lawyer, and by the time Allene was born, her family was well established within the burgeoning Texas aristocracy. Allene and Big Howard were married on May 24, 1903, after a brief courtship.

Their only child, Howard Robard Hughes Jr., was born two years later. "I was born the day before Christmas in 1905," Hughes later recalled, "in a house that you might call a shack, next door to the fire station."[12] The wealth and comfort provided by Toolco were still a few years away, so the family was living outside Houston in the more affordable suburb of Humble, Texas, when Hughes was born.

Under the ownership of Big Howard, Toolco was immensely successful with net earnings increasing annually, going from $422,793 in 1920 to $1,639,487 only three years later. The Hughes rock bit was the backbone of the company, but other innovations followed. In 1919, the company introduced the industry's first fully heat-treated alloy steel tool joint which seamlessly joined together sections of drill pipe making them stronger and longer lasting. Tool joints ultimately became the second bestselling product manufactured by the company. Most importantly, Big Howard acquired virtually every rival patent which gave his company an effective monopoly on roller drill bits until 1936.

Even after the company's success, Big Howard raised his son in a relatively modest fashion. In an interview in 1948, Hughes described his father and his method of parenting.

> He raised me very strictly. I never got into any trouble because he made me toe the line. He treated me fairly and squarely, but never was over-indulgent. He taught me the value of money. I didn't have everything I wanted, by any means. He showed me how to amuse myself with simple things. He explained the value and the need of concentrating my mind and energies. He used to say to me, 'My boy, if you concentrate hard enough you can conquer anything.'[13]

Stories abound of a young Hughes making do with the limited resources provided by his parents. At the age of twelve, he built an amateur or ham radio out of spare parts and got a license to operate it under the call letters 5CY. Not long after, when his father refused to buy him a motorcycle, Hughes built his own out of a bicycle and parts from an old Buick automobile.

One occasion where Big Howard did indulge his son had lasting consequences. Big Howard attended Harvard, and while he never graduated, he bled crimson for the rest of his life. In 1919, while vacationing in Connecticut, Big Howard and the young Hughes attended the hotly contested crew race between Harvard and its rival Yale. Getting caught up in the atmosphere of the contest, Big Howard told his son he could have anything he wanted if Harvard won.

Harvard did win, and when it was time to pay up, Hughes "asked to be permitted to fly with a pilot who had a broken-down seaplane anchored in the river in front of the hotel. My father finally consented. That was my very first contact with flying."[14] Hughes's love of aviation would go on to play an integral part of his life, in and out of Hollywood.

By all accounts, Hughes grew up in a loving and prosperous home. But everything started to unravel when Allene Hughes died suddenly on March 29, 1922. The day before she had experienced abdominal pains and began hemorrhaging. She was rushed to the hospital and died during surgery. Father and son were devastated.

Less than two years later, on January 14, 1924, Big Howard returned to his office after attending a meeting with oil executives. Big Howard was one of the most respected men in his field, and his company was thriving. As he discussed the meeting with his sales manager, Big Howard suffered a massive heart attack and fell to the floor. He was dead before he reached the hospital.

Up until that point, the eighteen-year-old Hughes had grown up surrounded by a loving and prosperous family. He was now alone. Hughes was also, by virtue of his parents' passing, the single largest shareholder of the company that bore his family name.

Big Howard owned 1,500 shares (100 percent) of capital stock in the Hughes Tool Company upon his death. The listed book value was $1,303,205. According to company documents, "the 1,500 shares of Hughes Tool Company in Mr. Hughes, Sr. estate return were distributed 750 shares to Mr. Hughes, Jr. and 750 to other relatives."[15] The shares not passed to the young Hughes were willed to his paternal grandparents and his uncle Felix.

Taking his father's advice on partners to heart, Hughes set about acquiring complete control of the company.

> The thing I knew was that I would never be able to get along with my relations and that's why I was determined to buy them out and go it alone. If I hadn't been a brash kid I never would have had any such idea—and I don't advise other brash kids to do what I did. I'll admit I didn't realize what hazards faced me—so maybe what I didn't know couldn't hurt.[16]

Using his shares as collateral, Hughes received a bank loan and approached his relatives about selling out.

The family was disgusted by Hughes's actions so soon after his father's death, but they nevertheless realized that they would have little actual control over the company and the relationship with the young Hughes was likely to be adversarial. They therefore agreed to sell, and the stock was recorded on the company's books at a value of $368,640.[17]

Eighteen-year-old Howard Hughes Jr. became the sole owner of the Hughes Tool Company on May 28, 1924. However, in the eyes of the state of Texas, Hughes was still a minor until he reached the age of twenty-one. In other words, he owned the company but could not manage it or his own affairs without an appointed administrator.

Taking another step to establish his own legacy, Hughes successfully petitioned Texas judge Walter E. Monteith, a family friend with whom Hughes frequently golfed, to be declared of legal age when he turned nineteen. Thus, on December 24, 1924, Hughes legally assumed ownership and management of the company that he owned completely.

Hughes spent several months at the helm of Toolco learning every aspect of the business. Then, in a decision that would later seem improbable given his tendency to micromanage, Hughes decided to walk away from the company his father founded. "I wasn't building anything myself," Hughes later mused. "My father's ideas were so sound there wasn't much room for any of my own... My father had been a pony express rider; I was being a postman."[18]

Retaining the title of president of the company, Hughes turned the management over to seasoned business executives. They ran the day-to-day operations, and Hughes reaped the rewards. The Hughes Tool Company subsequently became, in the words of *Fortune* magazine, "one of the most profitable operations in U.S. industry," which allowed Hughes to become the "proprietor of the largest pool of industrial wealth still under the absolute control of a single individual."[19]

The continuing growth of Toolco was spurred by the further development of its signature product, the roller bit. In 1925, the Acme self-cleaning cone more than doubled the penetration rate of previous bits. The improved Hughes roller cutter core bit was released the following year, but the greatest innovation since the introduction of the original Hughes bit was the Tricone bit. Entering the market in 1933, it had three revolving cones instead of the two found on the original Hughes bit. With teeth that were farther apart, the Tricone bit cleaned itself and revolved with more accuracy. It cut drilling time in half yet again. The company held a patent-protected monopoly on the Tricone bit until the mid-1950s.

Other innovations followed, with the company ultimately producing some 400 sizes and types of bits, varying in diameter from 3¾ inches to 26 inches. They ranged in price from $150 to $4,300. At its peak, the company was producing four-fifths of all the drill bits sold in the United States, and its products were exported to fifty foreign countries.

Even after their patents expired and others entered the market, the Hughes Tool Company remained the industry leader. One oil executive summed it up best: "There's really no major difference between one make of rock bit and another. But if I had a choice between Hughes and another, I'd choose Hughes."[20]

The accompanying financial numbers were staggering. Sales at the company rose from $2,992,000 in 1924, the year Hughes assumed control, to $117,059,000 in 1956. Estimated pretax profits that year were $59,524,000, which amounted to almost $29,000,000 after taxes. Hughes kept complete control of the Hughes Tool Company for most of his life, and when he finally sold the original drill bit company in 1972 to the investing public for $150,000,000, it was estimated that the "company had provided him with a total of $745,448,000 in before-tax profits."[21] While only taking a nominal salary of $50,000 a year as president, Hughes used the resources of Toolco to expand his business empire.

One of the most notable and lucrative examples was the Hughes Aircraft Company. Founded to handle Hughes's early aviation projects, it grew to become the largest manufacturer in the United States of electronic equipment for the military. Revenue exceeded $500,000,000 annually at its peak.[22]

Hughes also owned, through Toolco, seventy-eight percent of Trans World Airlines (TWA) which he eventually sold in the 1960s for $546,000,000, which was at the time the largest amount ever paid outright to a single individual in the history of American finance. In addition, Hughes Tool owned the Gulf Brewing Company, the largest brewery in Texas. Hughes's personal investments included multi-million dollar stakes in several fields, including finance, oil, and motion pictures.

His wealth, all centered around his ownership of the Hughes Tool Company, grew to the point that *Fortune* declared Hughes a billionaire and the richest man in America in 1968.[23]

Content not to run the wildly successful Toolco, "my father's business" as he would often call it, Hughes was a very young man with seemingly limitless financial resources.[24] In a moment of candor, Hughes outlined his life's ambitions. "My first objective is to become the world's number one golfer," he told accountant Noah Dietrich, who would go on to help run Hughes's financial empire as his right-hand man from 1925 to 1957. "Second, the top aviator, and third I want to become the world's most famous motion picture producer."[25]

As a golfer, Hughes was very good. He won most of his matches and was near the top of the leaderboard in several tournaments that he entered. But despite his best efforts, which included being one of the first people to record his swing with a motion picture camera to see how he might improve it, Hughes was never able to truly distinguish himself as an athlete. Hughes did however achieve his second objective, and his aerial exploits made him a national hero.

Hughes remained fascinated with all aspects of aviation after initially taking to the air in 1919. He took his first flying lessons in 1925 and secured his private pilot's license two years later. He received his transport rating in 1928 and picked up his commercial multi-engine and instrument ratings shortly thereafter. Showing his dedication to add to his aeronautical skills and knowledge, he even flew with American Airways as a copilot for two months in the summer of 1932 using the alias Charles Howard. When the airline discovered his real identity, he was fired not for his performance but for falsifying his employment application. While all of this was going on, Hughes was also tinkering with airplane modifications, some of which he hired others to do at his direction and some he did himself. Hughes Aircraft Company was born out of these efforts.

Then, over the course of three years, Hughes set every aviation record of consequence. The first mark to fall was the world speed record. Piloting the H-1 Racer that he designed, the first airplane to include flush joints and seams (i.e. smooth metal skin) and the first to feature power-driven retractable landing gear, Hughes attained a top speed of 352.39 miles per hour on September 13, 1935, at Martin Field in Santa Ana, California. This shattered the previous record of 314 miles per hour held by Frenchman Raymond Delmotte.

A few months later, on January 13, 1936, Hughes piloted a remodeled Northrop Gamma from Burbank, California, to Newark, New Jersey, in nine hours, twenty-seven minutes, and ten seconds, a new coast-to-coast record. He used the same plane later that year to set the New York to Miami and Chicago to Los Angeles records. He broke his own coast-to-coast record in 1937, cutting the time down to seven hours, twenty-eight minutes, and twenty-five seconds.

Hughes's most celebrated aerial accomplishment took place in July 1938 when he flew around the world in a remodeled Lockheed Loadstar. Averaging better than 208 miles per hour, Hughes and his crew of four completed the journey in a record three days, nineteen hours, and seventeen minutes. The previous record held by American Wiley Post was seven days, eighteen hours, and forty-nine minutes. Upon landing back in New York, Hughes was honored with a ticker tape parade through downtown Manhattan. The New York Sanitation Department "estimated that 1,800 tons of confetti was tossed down upon his car, breaking the 1,600 thrown at [Charles] Lindbergh."[26]

For his accomplishments, Hughes was awarded every aviation award of consequence, including the Harmon Trophy in 1936 and 1938 (presented to Hughes directly by President Franklin D. Roosevelt in the Oval Office) and the Collier Trophy in 1938. He also received a special Congressional Gold Medal, the most distinguished civilian award presented by the American government, in 1939 "for advancing the science of aviation and thus bringing great credit to his country throughout the world."[27]

Because of his aviation exploits, for the rest of his life, every American knew the name Howard Hughes. As *Life* magazine proclaimed, he was now "Hero Hughes."[28] Having achieved his goal of aviation immortality, he was enshrined in the National Aviation Hall of Fame in 1973, Hughes turned to his third and final objective.

Hughes actually had his eye on Hollywood the moment he decided to walk away from Hughes Tool. As his father had done years before, Hughes sought an industry where he could make his mark.

I began looking around for something I could do. I found that I was interested in movies. I went to see them even when I knew they were cheesy. I came to the conclusion I could make better pictures than were being made. What the hell? When you know you can turn out a better product there's only one thing to do—start turning and look for customers.[29]

So Hughes left Houston in 1925 and relocated to Los Angeles, the movie capital of the world. But to become the most famous motion picture producer, he was forced to confront a ruthless and cutthroat business organization.

The nascent studio system was firmly established by the time Hughes arrived in Hollywood. The history of the American motion picture industry, both then and now, has been a continuous struggle for control. In 1925, the industry was still developing, but a few large corporations already dominated all three aspects of filmmaking: production, distribution, and exhibition.

Films basically have always been made the same way. The production company creates the film, the distributor then wholesales the film from a producer to an exhibitor, and finally, the exhibitor presents the film to paying customers. At the outset of the industry, films were treated as novelties, and it was very easy to get into the business. Thousands of small producers, distributors, and exhibitors managed to flourish, and a relatively competitive economic situation prevailed.

Then, in 1908, the leading equipment manufacturers banded together with the biggest supplier of film stock in an attempt to use their monopoly over raw materials to extort fees and dominate the industry. The newly formed Motion Picture Patents Company (MPPC) required individual producers and exhibitors to join the organization and pay significant taxes. Refusing to license any film made outside the trust, the MPPC attempted to completely eliminate competition and exert absolute dominance over its members.

The MPPC ultimately failed in both regards. Despite draconian measures intended to police its members, many producers and exhibitors broke with company policies in an attempt to make greater profits. At the same time, independents (defined as anyone not associated with the MPPC) used the strong antitrust sentiment of the Progressive Era to challenge the MPPC in court. Although the MPPC was declared in violation of the Sherman Antitrust Act (1890) and forced to disband in 1917, the trust had become wholly ineffective by 1914.

Besides using the courts, independents also sought techniques that would allow them to compete directly with the embryonic trust. Although it took several years to develop, Famous Players–Lasky, under the direction of Adolph Zukor, pioneered a system that successfully confronted the MPPC and ultimately came to dominate the entire industry.

Zukor opened his first theatre in New York in 1904, and refusing to give in to the demands of the MPPC, he expanded into production in 1912. Four years later, he merged his production company with a national distribution company to create the largest producer–distributor in the world.

As other companies attempted to limit the increasing power of Famous Players–Lasky by assembling large theatre circuits, Zukor realized that his corporation needed to not only produce and distribute films but also control the sales outlet for these products. With the backing of Wall Street investment house Kuhn Loeb, the corporation expanded into exhibition and assembled the largest theatre circuit in America in only four years.

Successfully integrating all three aspects of filmmaking, Famous Players–Lasky pioneered vertical integration within the industry, establishing the corporate strategy that would dominate Hollywood for decades to come. This form of industrial organization came to be known as the studio system.

In reality, the term studio system was really a misnomer as a more accurate description would have been diversified theatre chains as the bulk of industry venue was in exhibition. But since the general public associated films with the studio that produced them, as opposed to the corporation that financed them, the term studio system was used. Thus, a corporation like Famous Players–Lasky was better known to the public as Paramount Pictures, its production studio.

Following the example set by Zukor at Famous Players-Lasky, several corporations began buying large theatre chains. As a result, a series of mergers during the 1920s produced five vertically integrated companies: Famous Players–Lasky (which changed its corporate name to Paramount Pictures in 1936), Loew's Inc. (parent company of Metro-Goldwyn-Mayer), Warner Bros., Fox (later to become Twentieth Century-Fox in 1935), and Radio-Keith-Orpheum (RKO). They were commonly known as the "Big Five."

Universal, Columbia, and United Artists were called the "Little Three" because they only maintained production and distribution units. Lacking theatre chains, their power in the industry was limited in comparison to the Big Five.

At its peak, these eight corporations controlled ninety-five percent of all industry revenue. Hollywood's Big Five, with the tacit cooperation of the Little Three, came to establish oligopoly control, monopoly power exercised by a small group of corporations, allowing them to dominate the industry. Independents were now defined as anyone not on the payroll of one of the major corporations.

Producer Walter Wanger was only partially joking in 1938 when he said "an independent producer is someone dependent upon the banks, the trade press, the lay press, the radio critics, the theatre men, distributors, and, lastly, upon the public."[30] In reality, independents were especially dependent upon the major corporations who supplied talent (contract actors, actresses, directors, writers, and technicians), sound stages and outdoor lots, technical expertise, and financing. Most importantly, independents needed access to the best theatres, a necessity for financial success, which were owned by the major corporations. If independents wanted access to all of these things, they had to accede to the demands and dictates of the individuals that controlled the industry.

Having established "formidable barriers to entry," particularly the expense of acquiring large theatre chains, the prospect for a truly independent producer working within the system was difficult.[31] It was virtually impossible if that producer sought to work outside the system.

Howard Hughes, with no direct affiliation with a major studio and the resources to do as he pleased, entered the motion picture industry as an independent producer in every sense of the word. While some prominent independent producers had their own production companies, such as Cecil B. DeMille and David O. Selznick, these individuals were financially or contractually tied to a major studio. Hughes had no such connections. Consequently, many people tried to warn him of the challenges he faced upon his arrival in Hollywood.

In a telegram to Neil McCarthy, an industry lawyer who came to work for Hughes, seasoned movie executive Richard Rowland told McCarthy that Hughes was likely to fail. "You know pretty well what chance independent producer has in this market today," Rowland wrote, "and would not want to offer any great encouragement Hughes spend lot money making special pictures taking chances them becoming hits."[32] Rowland worked at the time for First National Pictures, a company that began as an exhibitor but was forced to expand into production and distribution in an attempt to survive in an industry dominated by vertically integrated corporations. Recognizing that the experienced Rowland knew what he was talking about, McCarthy responded simply, "Appreciate your suggestions concerning hazard of independent production and as you know I agree with you entirely."[33]

Whether these concerns were relayed to Hughes is unknown, but records do indicate that Hughes made inquiries into the idea of a permanent alliance with at least one major studio.[34] Hughes however decided to remain independent, indicating he was either unaware of the challenges he faced trying to break into the industry, or he simply did not care. Either way, as soon as he arrived in Los Angeles, he set about becoming a motion picture producer.

As the old saying goes, the only job in Hollywood that requires no qualifications is that of a producer. All a producer needs is money. And money was certainly one thing Hughes had.

According to a popular story, one which is probably apocryphal, Hughes set up a meeting with Louis B. Mayer when he arrived in Hollywood. Mayer ran Metro-Goldwyn-Mayer (MGM), the production studio of Loew's Inc., one of the Big Five. When Hughes asked Mayer how to go about making movies, Mayer answered that you get an idea, a camera, some actors, and start shooting. Mayer also said there were a lot of small studios that could be bought or rented to facilitate production. Hughes thought it over a minute and replied, "How much do you want for Metro-Goldwyn-Mayer?"[35] Again, the story is most likely not true, Hughes did not have the financial means to acquire a studio of that size *at that time*, but it highlights the fact that Hughes was not typical as he entered the industry.

There is no record that Hughes even knew Mayer when he first arrived in Los Angeles, but he did know a few lesser characters. One such individual was the actor Ralph Graves. Graves was an acquaintance of Big Howard, and at a low point in his acting career, Big Howard put Graves briefly on the payroll of the Hughes Tool Company. Born in Ohio in 1900, Graves made his way to Hollywood while in his teens. His first screen credits date to 1918. Between 1922 and 1924, he starred in a popular series of over twenty two-reel comedies produced by Mack Sennett. He also worked alongside other silent film luminaries such as Dorothy Gish, D. W. Griffith, Raoul Walsh, Gloria Swanson, and Frank Capra.

Hoping to make the transition to writer and director, Graves began working on a script about a big-hearted derelict that is constantly doing good deeds, like helping orphans. When Graves ran into the younger Hughes on a Los Angeles golf course, he was excited to learn that Hughes was looking to break into the industry. Graves let Hughes know that he had an available script that was sure to be a winner.

"You should have heard him tell that story—and play all the characters, too," Hughes recalled a few years later. "When he got to the scene where the baby died I cried and said certainly I'd invest sixty thousand dollars. The way he told it, it sounded to me like a million dollar picture."[36] With Graves serving as writer, director, and star, Howard Hughes was now a motion picture producer.

Hughes's lack of knowledge about the industry and the mechanics of motion picture production were immediately evident as filming commenced. Whereas a typical producer would provide some oversight, Hughes simply sat on the sideline learning as much as he could while Graves handled virtually all aspects of filming.

The amount of control a producer exerts fluctuates from person to person, even from film to film, but all producers are mindful of a movie's cost. The film must come in on time and more importantly on budget. But when Graves approached Hughes during production needing additional funds, the inexperienced Hughes agreed without giving it a second thought. Hughes's financial assistant Noah Dietrich later noted that the film cost twice what it was originally budgeted.

When the film was complete, Graves once again assured Hughes that it was sure to be a smash hit. Hughes sat down to view the film, entitled *Swell Hogan* (1926), and he thought "it wasn't such a bad picture."[37] Certainly not a ringing endorsement, Hughes's tepid review may have been an attempt to minimize the damage as others were not so guarded. *The Motion Picture Director* noted that "those who had seen the early rushes were extremely skeptical of results."[38]

Jacob Wilk, an experienced industry executive who served during his career in various positions, including publicity director for the World Film Corporation and a story editor at Warner Bros., was consulted about the film's prospects. Wilk said that "in the shape it is in now I cannot see where it can be sold... I know that this sounds rather banal to people who have spent so much money as has been spent on this picture, but I cannot see where anything else can be suggested."[39]

Hughes was unable to find anyone who was willing to distribute or exhibit the film, and it became evident very quickly that *Swell Hogan* was a complete failure. A commentator joked that Hughes would accept any reasonable offer on the film: "Probably $1.25 would interest him if the bidder would pay express charges."[40] With the exception of the few individuals who saw a preview of the film, *Swell Hogan* was never viewed by the general public. The film today is classified as lost, like many others from the silent era, and legend has it that Hughes personally burned all the available prints.

For those watching Hughes intently, including family members still reeling from his acquisition of Hughes Tool and industry insiders curious to see how long he would last, the failure of *Swell Hogan* seemed to indicate that Hughes's career as a producer would end as quickly as it began. But instead of taking the failure as an indication of his future prospects, Hughes was actually emboldened to succeed. "It turned out to be a challenge for me," Hughes said. "I was determined from then on to make pictures that could be released and make money."[41]

Showing his intent to remain in the industry, Hughes amended the charter of a corporation he owned to allow it to produce motion pictures. The Caddo Company was originally incorporated as the Caddo Rock Drill Bit Company, an oilfield service operation, in Louisiana in November 1912. It held the patents to drill bits that competed with Hughes Tool, so Big Howard purchased the company and it became a subsidiary of Toolco. Instead of starting a new corporation to finance and produce motion pictures, Hughes decided to use the Caddo Company, and it was restructured accordingly in August 1926.

Hughes acquired an art deco building at 7000 Romaine Street a few years later to serve as his base of operations. The building, which took up an entire block between North Sycamore Avenue and North Orange Drive on the outskirts of Hollywood, originally housed an early color film company in which Hughes had invested.[42] When the company folded after only a few years, Hughes used the imposing structure to manage all of his varied business interests, including his motion picture activities. Hughes ultimately supplemented the building with a personal office at the Samuel Goldwyn Studios which had an editing bay and screening room.

The first film Hughes produced through the newly reorganized Caddo Company was *Everybody's Acting* (1926). Written and directed by Marshall Neilan, the story centered on a woman working at a stock company who falls in love with a cab driver who is actually the son of a wealthy businesswoman. The mother objects to the union and unearths information on the woman's past in hopes of breaking up the couple. Hughes agreed to finance the film up to $150,000, with Neilan getting paid $10,000 for writing and an additional $25,000 for directing.

According to the film's governing contract, after cost profits were to be split fifty-fifty between Hughes (listed as the producer) and Neilan (listed as the artist).[43] Interestingly, the contract did not specify how credits would be publicly advertised, and while this film is also lost, the surviving ephemera promote it as a Marshall Neilan Production.[44] The movie was distributed by Paramount Pictures, and *Moving Picture World* described it as a "pleasant little comedy drama" with an "exceptionally strong cast."[45]

Things really started to change for Howard Hughes the producer with his third film, *Two Arabian Knights* (1927). Directed by Lewis Milestone and starring William Boyd, Mary Astor, and Louis Wolheim, the film followed two American troops (Boyd and Wolheim) in the First World War who escape from a German POW camp only to find themselves facing life-threatening adventures as they cross the globe. After saving an Arabian king's daughter (Astor) from drowning, both men compete for her affection.

Hughes, as he had done on his previous pictures, quietly absorbed all aspects of the filmmaking process. To some, his lack of knowledge was still shocking. According to star Astor, Hughes "came on the set a few times, and couldn't understand where 'the fourth wall' was."[46] Whatever others thought of his abilities as a producer, Hughes's personal vision was starting to take shape.

When Hughes saw the early rushes of the film, which was supposed to be an epic romance, he could not stop laughing. "Why not let everybody laugh?" Hughes said. "This isn't a romance; it's a comedy."[47] Scenes were rewritten and reshot at Hughes's insistence to shift the focus and alter the tone of the film. When production concluded, the budget topped out at $465,846, a dramatic increase from Hughes's first two productions.

Distributed by United Artists, it appeared Hughes's instincts about *Two Arabian Knights* were correct. Critic Mordaunt Hall of *The New York Times* wrote that the film was a "comedy of a thousand and one laughs" that featured "common-sense direction [and] intelligent acting with genuine humor."[48] The *Los Angeles Times* declared it a "pronounced success."[49] It even made history as director Lewis Milestone went on to win the Oscar for Best Director, Comedy Picture at the first Academy Awards held in 1929.[50]

The award was given to Milestone, but Hughes took it as a vindication of his decisions and talent as a producer. When Hughes sat down twenty-five years later in 1954 for a rare interview with *Look* magazine writer Stephen White, he took offense to an early draft of the author's story that referenced Milestone in conjunction with the film. "Can't you take out Milestone entirely?" Hughes asked. When White correctly pointed out that Milestone won an Academy Award for his direction of the film, Hughes stated matter-of-factly, "What's the award for Milestone got to do with the picture?"[51]

Hughes was taking a more active role as a producer, and he was beginning to believe that he and he alone was responsible for any success, critical or financial, his films received. It appeared Hughes had finally solved the mystery of the fourth wall.

Hughes followed the award-winning *Two Arabian Knights* with *The Racket* (1928). The film, about an honest police captain who attempts to bring down a bootlegger who is protected by powerful politicians and judges, was based on the play of the same name which ran on Broadway at the Ambassador Theatre for over 100 performances from November 1927 to March 1928. Hughes saw the play, and thinking it would make a good movie, he acquired the story for just under $25,000. Hughes obviously did not have an issue with any accolades Lewis Milestone had received up to that point, as Hughes retained his services as director for *The Racket*.

Hughes acquired actor Thomas Meighan for the lead role. Under contract to Paramount, Meighan had completed five pictures of a seven-picture deal, worth a lucrative $1,000,000, when his popularity seemed to fade. Paramount lost confidence in the star, and his career stalled. When Hughes approached Paramount about acquiring Meighan and assuming his contract, "Hollywood snickered. The kid bought a gold brick!"[52]

The story itself was seen as an even bigger gamble than Meighan. Politicians, judges, and even police officers were depicted as corrupt and on the payroll of powerful gangsters. At a time when real-life gangsters were making front-page headlines, the film was one of the first to tackle the subject. Hughes was adamant about how the film would be made.

> I won't tone anything down. I believe the screen is a powerful influence on the thoughts of the average citizen. It's a powerful instrument. It bores through opinions like my father's bits bore through rock... If I have to make silly theatrical movies with pretty little plots, I'll quit. I'm going to make pictures of people as they are. I want them to act as they do in life and I'm going to let people look at the screen and find out what's going on in the world about them.[53]

It was said that many in Hollywood were afraid to make the movie, and Hughes's attitude seemed to reflect his naivety. The movie however turned out to be another critical success for the young, independent producer.

The reviewer for *Variety* commented that *The Racket* "grips your interest from the first shot to the last, and never drags for a second."[54] Meighan was especially showered with praise. The *New York Sun* said he "does his best work in several years," while the *Duluth Herald* said he "has regained his pristine halo."[55] The film was the second Hughes production, alongside *Two Arabian Knights*, to receive recognition at the first Academy Awards. It was nominated for Best Picture, Production but lost to the aerial epic *Wings* (1927).

It appeared that Hughes's judgment as a producer, most notably bringing the story to the screen and casting Thomas Meighan, had proven correct yet again. The movie was the first to features the tag line "Howard R. Hughes Presents," and after a rough start in the industry, "Hollywood was less certain that Hughes would return to Houston in a freight car."[56]

The last Hughes production released in the 1920s was *The Mating Call* (1928). Based on a story by Rex Beach, it addressed another controversial topic, the Ku Klux Klan. Meighan was again chosen to star, the final film in the contract Hughes acquired from Paramount, alongside actresses Evelyn Brent and Renée Adorée. James Cruze was hired to direct.

In the film, a World War I veteran (Meighan) returns home from the battlefield to discover that his marriage has been annulled and his ex-wife (Brent) has married a rich Klansman. The veteran must prove his innocence when the jealous Klansman attempts to frame him for murder. After a string of successes, the film was a setback for Hughes. Meighan's work was praised once more, but the film was described by critics and exhibitors alike as a "dud" and a "flop."[57]

Howard Hughes nevertheless was firmly established as an independent producer by the time the decade came to a close. He knew virtually nothing about making motion pictures when he arrived in Hollywood, and his first experience was a complete failure. But with each subsequent picture, he began to take a more active role in his productions.

When the films were critically successful, Hughes believed it was because of the decisions that he made. Furthermore, Hughes financed each picture independently using his own money, unlike other producers who relied on a studio or an affiliated production company. Without his investment, the movies never would have been made. Like many producers before and after him, Hughes reasoned that this made him primarily, if not solely, responsible for the success of the films.

Not surprisingly, Hughes started to see a more significant role for himself in the industry beyond merely a financier. Having worked alongside skilled director likes Marshall Neilan, Lewis Milestone, and James Cruze, Hughes even went so far as to tell Noah Dietrich, "I can direct as well as those other guys."[58]

Besides his growing belief in his ability as a filmmaker, Hughes also became convinced that making profitable motion pictures was simple. It was frequently reported that "Hughes averaged from 50 to 100 per cent on his investments."[59] Hughes now believed that "if he could make 50 per cent profit on an ordinary picture, he should be able to realize proportionately greater returns with better pictures."[60] But just as he had convinced himself that he was responsible for the success of his initial films, Hughes apparently had also convinced himself and others that his movies had made a significant profit.

Corporate records however state otherwise. The experience of *Swell Hogan* apparently had been forgotten completely, because it was a financial disaster that returned nothing. *Everybody's Acting* cost $150,293 and returned only a small profit of $38,557 or twenty-six percent. His biggest success, *Two Arabian Knights*, cost $465,846, and it gave Hughes a forty-one percent profit of $190,928. *The Racket* and *The Mating Call* lost $25,750 and $45,957, respectively.[61] Since industry watchers and Hughes himself stated that *he* made a fifty percent profit, these numbers are based on the producer's profit and not the total profit.

As an independent producer, Hughes had to split the total profit of each film with the company that distributed it, which was Paramount for *Everybody's Acting*, *The Racket*, and *The Mating Call* and United Artists for *Two Arabian Knights*. The revenue generally was split with seventy percent going to the producer and thirty percent going to the distributor. In the case of *Two Arabian Knights*, Hughes also had to split profits with director Marshall Neilan. As a result, the total profit on each film technically was higher than the numbers given above, but again, Hughes stated *he* had made a fifty percent profit.

No matter what numbers are used, his films were not as monetarily successful as he stated. Nonetheless, Hughes was now convinced that simply by spending more money he would make more money. With his theories about filmmaking established, all Hughes needed was the perfect production to prove his financial theory, and if necessary, demonstrate that he really could direct as well as those other guys.

# Forcing Costs Skyward

"Isn't there any end to this?"—
Monte Rutledge (Ben Lyon) in *Hell's Angels*

Howard Hughes proved that he could survive as an independent producer, but his objective was to become the world's most famous motion picture producer, not simply one that turned out a few minor hits. In order to accomplish his goal, he needed to find a production that would revolutionize the motion picture industry like his father revolutionized the oil industry. As he was searching for the perfect production, he was bombarded with reminders of his other great passion: aviation.

On May 21, 1927, Charles Lindberg successfully piloted the first non-stop solo transatlantic flight in his single-engine plane, the *Spirit of St. Louis*. Considered one of the greatest feats in modern history, the flight caught the attention of the world and captivated an envious Hughes. That same year, Paramount released *Wings*, an epic tale of the exploits of American pilots during World War I. *Wings* turned out to be a critical and financial success, culminating with its win over Hughes's *The Racket* for Best Picture, Production at the first Academy Awards in 1929.

The attention showered on Lindberg, *Wings*, and seemingly everything else related to aviation inspired Howard Hughes the motion picture producer. Realizing he could combine his love of aviation with his passion for movies, Hughes was convinced he could make an even greater air epic. The film would ultimately pit the independent producer against the dictates that governed the studio system, but in the end, Hughes's actions would have a lasting impact on how all motion pictures were produced.

When director Marshall Neilan approached Hughes in 1927 with his latest story idea, it seemed the perfect combination of director and producer. On their initial collaboration *Everybody's Acting*, the production went smoothly, and the young Hughes did not interfere with the more experienced Neilan. The movie was positively received, and after the utter failure of *Swell Hogan*, the film was Hughes's first profitable production, even if only marginally so. More importantly, *Everybody's Acting* proved to Hughes's critics that he intended to stay in the industry.

Having established a successful working relationship, Neilan was more than willing to share the idea with Hughes in hopes of embarking upon a second collaboration. Neilan called his story *Hell's Angels* (1930), and much like *Wings*, it focused on the exploits of aviators during the Great War. Neilan knew that aviation fascinated Hughes, and he correctly assumed the story would be appealing to the young producer. When pitching the idea, Neilan insisted upon directing the film.

Hughes agreed to finance the film independently through the Caddo Company, and he agreed to let Neilan direct. A distribution contract was signed with United Artists in August 1927 which stated the film was to be completed "within Twelve (12) months from date hereof."[1] Given their previous collaboration, Neilan could not have imagined Hughes playing a role in the production beyond that of financier. Unfortunately for Neilan, he had no idea how much had changed, at least in Hughes's mind, in such a short time.

It became clear almost from the outset that *Hell's Angels* was Hughes's movie. Taking an active role in preproduction, more active than he had been on any previous film, Hughes enlisted a group of writers, led by Harry Behn, to expand upon Neilan's original idea, broadening the story to include the exploits of Allied and German pilots. Whereas Neilan had free reign on the set of *Everybody's Acting*, he spent six months of preproduction on *Hell's Angels* disagreeing with Hughes over the smallest details. Hughes ultimately exercised his authority as producer and the movie's sole financier to win the battle for creative control. In response, less than a month before filming was scheduled to begin, Neilan left the production.

According to Caddo attorney Neil McCarthy, "Micky [Neilan] could not seem to agree altogether with Howard on how it should be done and Micky was entirely agreeable to its being directed by someone else."[2] Having brought the story to Hughes with the stated intention of directing, it is fair to conclude that Neilan was not necessarily agreeable to the idea of someone else assuming the role. But Hughes now controlled the rights to the story, and having been in the industry for many years, Neilan knew that he could not work under these conditions.

Luther Reed ultimately was borrowed from Paramount to replace Neilan as director. Reed was rather inexperienced behind the camera, having directed only six films, but as the former aviation editor of the *New York Herald-Tribune*, he seemed a good fit for the production. Filming was less than two weeks away when Reed was hired, and all of the principal actors were in place.

The two lead roles went to Ben Lyon and James Hall. Lyon was a former Broadway star who made the transition to feature films. Throughout the 1920s, he appeared with some of the decade's most famous leading ladies, including Barbara La Marr, Gloria Swanson, Mary Astor, and Claudette Colbert. Hall's short career was still on the rise, and his most notable roles up to that point occurred opposite Pola Negri and Bebe Daniels (the future wife of Ben Lyon). Other notable male cast members included John Darrow and Lucien Prival.

The only female lead of any consequence was given to Norwegian actress Greta Nissen. Born Grethe Rüzt-Nissen, she was a classically trained ballerina who transitioned to acting after being discovered by Paramount's Jesse L. Lasky. Nissen typically played seductive roles, "always obtaining excellent results with an originality rarely beheld on the screen."[3]

With the cast and crew assembled, actual filming began at the Metropolitan Studios on October 31, 1927, with interior and non-aerial sequences. The first month of filming foreshadowed what was to come. In a series of letters, Whitman Bennett, a longtime movie executive who was now the production manager at Caddo, shared his impressions with fellow company officers.

Bennett was cognizant of the fact that Hughes was his employer as his assessments initially were carefully worded. Noting "Mr. Hughes's own persistence and unwillingness to be satisfied with second best," Bennett wondered whether Hughes was experienced enough to make the appropriate production decisions.[4] When Bennett questioned Reed's direction, he was shocked to learn that Hughes believed the film "did not require direction with any special comedy sense, distinction, originality or personality."[5]

As more time passed and his opinions continued to be overlooked, Bennett's cautious approach when discussing his employer began to fade. His frustration was evident when he stated that "Mr. Hughes production habits are most peculiar and his power of foreseeing results not very trained."[6] He went on to say that "Mr. Hughes underestimates the difficulties and costs... we are making preparations as fast as Mr. Hughes will permit... which means that instructions are generally given and countermanded a couple of times before they are really final."[7]

Beyond the astonishing amount of film being used, Bennett was especially concerned at the spiraling cost. The distribution contract with

United Artists stated that a budget of $200,000 was "sufficient money to produce a high-class motion picture," but after only a few weeks, the cost was approaching $500,000, a number Bennett knew was preposterous and unprecedented.[8]

It soon became clear to Bennett that his critiques of Hughes meant his future with the company was in jeopardy, and his words became highly critical. "The one thing that worries me about Mr. Hughes is his unusual self-assurance," Bennett complained. "I feel that he seriously regards himself as a competent script writer and almost a qualified director."[9]

Bennett's apprehension about his job proved to be accurate, and he was removed as production manager in December. Although his comments can be viewed as coming from a disgruntled employee, it does not take away from the fact that the experienced Bennett realized very early on that Hughes's methods were extreme, even in an industry dominated by large egos and eccentricity.

With Bennett gone, the production moved into its second month. The dramatic shots were wrapping up, but the biggest challenges remained, as Hughes knew all along the success of the film depended on the aerial sequences.

Determined to make his film as authentic as possible, Hughes purchased or leased as many vintage warplanes as he could find. The aerial squadron ultimately was comprised of eighty-seven planes, forty of which were used in front of the cameras. The fleet included Fokkers, Sopwith Camels, S.E.5s, Avros, de Havillands, Sopwith Snipes, Curtiss JN-4s, a Sikorsky S-29-A, and a Zeppelin. The cost just to acquire and recondition the planes approached $560,000, and Hughes had the distinction of possessing the "largest air-fleet ever assembled, except by governments."[10]

Eight separate locations were maintained across southern California for the aerial sequences, including the main flying base, Caddo Field, in Van Nuys; a training camp at Inglewood (now the site of Los Angeles International Airport); and a mock German field at Chatsworth. Other locations included Santa Cruz, Encino, San Diego, Riverside, and Oakland. A total of 137 pilots, mainly stunt flyers and veterans of the First World War, were employed along with an equal number of mechanics. Hughes also hired twenty-six aerial photographers to work on the film.

By the time the difficult task of shooting the aerial sequences began, it was clear that Hughes was embarking upon a million-dollar production, a rarity in the early years of the studio system.

The Big Five, using their control over the industry, sought to reduce any unnecessary costs in an attempt to maximize profits. Since exhibition accounting for the bulk of industry revenue, corporate executives came to see production as an "inconvenient necessity."[11] With trade agreements guaranteeing a market for even the most mediocre pictures, high-budget productions carried a substantially higher risk of failure than low-budget movies.

Production costs nonetheless skyrocketed over the years, worrying corporate executives. *Motion Picture Classic* estimated that an average movie cost approximately $41,350 in 1917, but less than a decade later, an industry insider estimated the cost around $250,000.[12] Marcus Loew, the head of one of the Big Five, stated it simply: "The cost of making pictures has got away from us."[13]

Costs got so bad that several studios contemplated halting production temporarily. "Production conditions are and have been outrageously abnormal," lamented R. H. Cochrane, vice president of Universal, in 1923. "It would be a great thing if all studios could close their doors until the people who have been forcing costs skyward have a chance to wake up."[14]

Besides corporate executives, rising production costs also worried bankers who were becoming an important aspect of the industry. The studios needed commercial and investment banks to provide the needed capital for all corporate activities, especially the purchase of expensive theatres. Bankers initially were leery of the industry because of its structure and the intangible nature of motion pictures. "Making motion pictures is not a business," exclaimed one banker, "it's a gamble."[15]

But as production companies began to diversify and establish uniform accounting measures, banks slowly began to invest in the industry. The principal objection bankers continued to have was the failure of producers "to keep within agreed limits."[16] In an attempt to placate these concerns, studios adopted a budget system that sought to limit costs and better manage personnel resources.[17]

At the same time, many producers also turned to smaller, more intimate productions. Speaking on behalf of the industry, Will H. Hays, president of the Motion Picture Producers and Distributors of America (MPPDA), said, "We are particularly engaged right now in an effort to eliminate waste and any unnecessary extravagance in production and distribution."[18] Unfortunately for the majors, Hughes was an independent with seemingly limitless resources that he was willing to spend on his aviation epic.

Less than two weeks into aerial photography on Hughes's million-dollar picture, director Luther Reed finally had enough. Hughes had very concrete ideas about how the outdoor scenes should be shot, and his constant meddling and questioning of Reed became unbearable for the director. One day, Reed reportedly shouted at Hughes, "If you know so much, why don't you direct it yourself?" "It's a good idea," Hughes replied. "I will."[19]

Hughes later told the story much more diplomatically. "Luther's work was entirely satisfactory," he said. "But I have been so wrapped up in 'Hell's Angels' since I first decided to make the picture, that I was constantly interrupting him on the sets—when a scene was not shot to my liking I would have him re-take it—naturally, a director cannot work under such a handicap, so we agreed that one or the other of us would withdraw and Luther bowed out."[20] No matter how it happened, Hughes was now directing the film.

With Hughes at the helm, the Caddo Company issued a press release entitled "Safety First is Slogan for 'Hell's Angels,'" but it became clear almost immediately how difficult and dangerous the aerial sequences would be for everyone involved.[21]

Al Johnson was one of the many pilots employed on the film, and his contract noted that he could "execute certain maneuvers and produce certain effects in flying without any risk or injury to himself." It nevertheless went on to say, as it did in all of the pilots' contracts, that he "agreed to and does assume any and all risk" arising out of "any accident or injury to the Artist, or the death of the Artist on account thereof."[22]

Tragically, this clause became necessary on the morning of December 30, 1927, when Johnson was instructed to transport a converted Jenny from the Kinner Airplane Company in Glendale to Caddo's field in Inglewood. Johnson taxied the plane down the runway, and upon getting airborne, he turned away from the wind. Standard procedure for pilots dictates they turn into the wind because it allows for greater lift. Johnson's method of takeoff became a serious problem when he noticed that he was heading toward high-tension wires hanging between two towers.

Realizing he would not clear the wires, Johnson attempted to dive below them, unaware that heavy cables also hung about 30 feet from the ground. In a last-ditch attempt to make it between the two sets of wires, Johnson's frantic maneuvering caused the tip of the plane's wing to hit the tower on the right. The plane then spun violently striking the left tower before crashing to the earth. Johnson died shortly thereafter. A subsequent investigation of the crash by Caddo concluded it was due to "poor judgment on the pilot's part."[23] The stress filming imposed upon Johnson and other pilots was never taken into account.

A second fatality occurred in October 1928 as the production searched for clouds. In order for the aerial photography to have a feeling of speed and drama, clouds were needed in the background as a visual reference point for the viewer. Without clouds, the action seemed slow and simulated. Hughes initially did not know this, and he shot several thousand feet of film before he realized the importance of clouds. Scrapping the original footage, Hughes was determined to find clouds at any cost.

Ridgeway Callow, an assistant to Hughes on the film, summed up the struggle with the elements. "We used to send our air fleet up and they would chase clouds all over Southern California," he later recalled. "They would hear there were clouds down at Santa Monica, and if there were no clouds they would come back, sit on the ground and play around."[24]

After several fruitless months, Hughes finally moved the entire production to Oakland where clouds were more plentiful. Pilot Clement Phillips experienced mechanical problems *en route* to the city, and despite his best efforts, the plane crashed killing Clement upon impact.

The third casualty of the production involved one of the many planes Hughes acquired for the film, a Sikorsky S-29-A which was modified to look like a German Gotha G. V. bomber. A stunt called for the giant plane to spin in a free fall for several thousand feet before it was pulled up at the last minute.

Famed pilot Roscoe Turner primarily flew the plane during the production, but he refused on this occasion stating the stunt was too dangerous. Twenty-five other aviators on the set also refused, citing the same concern. The situation got so desperate an article in the *Los Angeles Times* pleaded for "a pilot who will attempt the feat."[25]

Al Wilson ultimately agreed to do the stunt for a cash bonus. Mechanic Phil Jones accompanied Wilson in the plane, and his job was to light smoke pots that would give the effect the plane was burning as it spun to the ground. At the height of 7,500 feet, Wilson initiated the spin as Jones lit the smoke pots. The plane started to break apart, and as Turner predicted, Wilson was unable to pull it up.

When the plane crashed, the engine was buried 6 feet into the ground. Wilson safely parachuted from the plane, but Jones never made it out. He died instantly upon impact. The spin, but not the actual crash, was caught on camera and used in the final film.[26]

Despite the three casualties, Hughes issued a press release that stated, "Miraculously, there were no serious accidents," which was especially ironic given the fact that Hughes himself was injured in a serious accident.[27]

Cameras were mounted inside of the planes to capture all angles of the aerial footage, a technique that was employed for the first time, and Hughes used his own plane, a Waco, to direct from the air. Surrounded by some of the most daring aviators in America, Hughes believed that he was capable of performing every stunt he demanded from his pilots. On one occasion, a pilot stalled a Thomas Morse Scout plane upon takeoff. Hughes ordered the pilot out of the cockpit with the intention of showing him exactly how it should be done.

Hughes had very little experience in that type of plane, and he was advised not to take it up himself. Never one to take orders, Hughes jumped in the plane and took off. Unaccustomed to the controls, Hughes had trouble getting the plane level. When he attempted to make a left turn, the plane stalled and fell to the earth from a height of 300 feet. The propeller dug into the runway, the landing gear splintered, and the wings ripped from the fuselage. "My god," someone was heard to remark. "There goes fifty million dollars and my job."[28]

The stunned crew ran to the crash site and pulled a dazed Hughes from the wreckage. Hughes was heard mumbling, "That's another par hole I made; I shot a four on that one."[29] An avid golfer, he clearly was suffering the effects of a concussion. Later reports claimed Hughes "escaped with a few cuts and minor abrasions" and was found "combing pieces of motor out of his hair."[30] In reality, Hughes cracked his skull and crushed his cheekbone. The accident left him in a coma for several days. After a short stay in the hospital, Hughes returned to the director's chair immediately upon his release.

Filming that was supposed to take only a few months seemed to stretch endlessly into 1928. The difficulty of the aerial sequences certainly contributed, but the real culprit was Hughes. In the words of Ridgeway Callow, Hughes was simply "feeling his way. He was insecure."[31] This was after all the first time Hughes had ever directed, and as Whitman Bennett observed early on in the production, an astonishing amount of money and film stock were being used.

Examples of Hughes's excess were numerous. A scene called for a brief close-up shot of a winch pulling a cable. Hughes exposed 18,000 feet of film to get the shot to his liking. A total of 9 feet would make it onscreen. Hughes consumed 20,000 feet of film for a close-up of valves on an airplane engine which amounted to 25 feet in the final picture. Hughes often would shoot a scene over 100 times before he was satisfied. Amazingly, he would remember every one of them. When an assistant once asked Hughes which of the 100 scenes he wanted to use for a particular shot, Hughes immediately responded, "Number one and number sixteen."[32]

As the production continued, the cost rose accordingly. Whereas other producers and directors had to account for every foot of film and every dollar spent, Hughes had no such limitations. It was his money. If he wanted 100 takes, he was going to get 100 takes.

Neil McCarthy summed it up best in a letter to banker A. P. Giannini: "[Hughes] is making some mistakes in the business, but it is necessary for him to do so in order for him to learn, and, as you know, he is just starting." McCarthy went on to state that *Hell's Angels* "will cost a great deal more than it should. It is this additional cost that he will be able to avoid later on as his experience grows and as he develops a better organization."[33]

With the cost escalating substantially every day, the production continued as Hughes tinkered with his masterpiece. Hughes finally felt confident enough in May 1928 to announce that *Hell's Angels* would have its world premiere in September of that year. The date came and went, and the production continued.

In December, Hughes decided to test the film at the Apollo Theatre in Chicago, Illinois. The manager of the theatre noted that his patrons "were more than pleased," and he said the film was a "splendid success."[34]

Well over a year after production began, it appeared *Hell's Angels* would be ready for general release early in 1929. In February, Hughes said the film was on the cutting room floor and should be ready in the fall. The cost stood at $1,532,851.[35] The production had consumed an amazing 1,500,000 feet of film.

In June, Hughes announced the film's premiere date for the second time. It was now set for October 1929, two years after production began. But before the latest premiere date arrived, the industry was shaken by something even more revolutionary than Hughes—sound.

The idea of combining moving images with recorded sound was as old as cinema itself. Photographic pioneer Eadweard Muybridge claimed to have discussed the topic with Thomas Edison in 1888, six years before the first commercial motion picture exhibition. Edison worked on the idea for years, and he successfully managed to bring the two concepts together with the unveiling of the Kinetophone in 1895. The device was basically a combination of his Kinetoscope with a cylinder phonograph that allowed a single individual to view images in a cabinet and hear audio through the use of earphones. Successful film projection ultimately made the device outmoded, but it also highlighted several major problems that plagued sound films for years.

Pictures and sound initially were recorded and reproduced on separate devices that were difficult to start and maintain in synchronization. Even if synchronization was successful, audio technology before the development of electric amplification was not sufficient to fill the large spaces that projection made possible. Finally, recording fidelity of the era was of such low quality that performers were forced to stand directly in front of cumbersome recording devices, such as acoustical horns, thus limiting the sort of films that could be created with recorded sound. Because of these technical challenges, most films were silent during the first few decades of the motion picture industry.[36]

Technological developments of the 1920s ultimately made sound motion pictures commercially viable. Lee De Forest overcame the problem of synchronization with the introduction of the Phonofilm in 1923. De Forest's system recorded audio on the side of a film's celluloid creating a composite print. This sound-on-film technology was guaranteed to playback successfully so long as proper synchronization of sound and picture was achieved in recording.[37]

Around the same time, AT&T's Western Electric manufacturing division overcame the problems of recording and fidelity. The introduction of sensitive condenser microphones and rubber-line recorders greatly improved the recording of audio, and the advent of moving-coil speaker systems allowed for sufficient amplification to fill large rooms. With these developments in place, sound was now practical for motion pictures.

Warner Bros. was the first studio to capitalize on the new technology. The first feature-length film they released that employed synchronized sound throughout was *Don Juan* (1926). The film contained a musical score and sound effects, but it did not have recorded dialogue.[38] Earning $1,693,000, *Don Juan* was the most successful film in the studio's history up to that point.

Then, on October 6, 1927, Warner Bros. released *The Jazz Singer* (1927) starring Al Jolson. The film primarily used a musical score and sound effects, but when Jolson sang his first synchronized song, a new era had begun.[39] *The Jazz Singer* earned $2,625,000, yet another record for the studio.[40]

The following year, Warner Bros. released the first all-talking feature, *Lights of New York* (1928), and it too proved to be wildly successful. Although some in the industry remained skeptical about "talkies," the profits accrued by Warner Bros. erased any lingering doubts. By the end of 1929, all of the major studios were making sound motion pictures.

For Howard Hughes, *Hell's Angels* was supposed to show his critics and the world that he was capable of producing and directing an epic masterpiece. But *Hell's Angels* was now destined to be a silent film in a sound world. In other words, Hughes's masterpiece was outdated before it was even released.

Having proven that time and money were no obstacle, the decision was easy for Hughes. "I made up my mind to remake as much of 'Hell's Angels' as was necessary," he conceded. "It was a problem of risking still more to get back my original investment. Without dialogue I was sure it would fail."[41]

The production would thus continue, and any thought of the film being released in 1929 disappeared. The cost for the completed silent film stood at $1,962,834, and that figure was sure to rise substantially with the transition to sound.[42] Wanting to keep the aerial sequences already shot, Hughes was able to record authentic plane noises to coincide with the footage. Technical limitations however meant the process required significant expenditures.

For the dramatic sequences, writer Joseph Moncure March was borrowed from MGM to work on the story. March thought the film was "depressingly bad" so he decided to rework the entire story "but still manage to have it logically embrace the sequences which were good enough to keep."[43] To help with the actual dialogue, Hughes brought in writer Howard Estabrook. Two years after filming began, the cast was summoned to return to the studio on September 1, 1929, to begin reshooting in sound. There was however one problem.

Norwegian-born actress Greta Nissen originally was cast in the lead female role. At the time, her thick Norwegian accent was not an issue as the film was silent. But when the decision was made to reshoot the film with dialogue, she could no longer believably play the part of the British character.[44] After several months on the film at a reported salary of $2,500 a week, the decision was made to completely recast the role of Helen. While Nissen continued to act into the 1930s, like so many other actors and actresses of the silent era, the conversion to sound effectively ended her career.[45]

Hughes began an exhaustive search for Nissen's replacement. The process was so difficult that Hughes began reshoots before the new female lead was even cast. As Hughes was testing countless girls, star Ben Lyon was visiting the set of another production where he was struck by "the most amazing girl" with "platinum hair" and a "tight-fitting black silk dress that showed every curve of her body."[46] Lyon introduced himself and proceeded to bring her to Hughes to test for the role.

When she appeared on stage for her audition, writer Joseph Moncure March and others in attendance were transfixed by her appearance. "My God," March said aloud, "she's got a shape like a dustpan."[47] Hughes was not as impressed as the others, but he agreed to cast her in the role and signed her to a three-year contract which paid the Screen Actors Guild minimum of $1,500 for the entire production. While she had appeared in a few minor roles using her real name Harlean Carpenter, the world would come to know her as Jean Harlow.

Hughes knew nothing about dialogue, his limited experience came from silent films, and his real passion during the production had been the filming of the aerial sequences. Recognizing his limitations, or simply revealing his lack of interest, Hughes brought in stage director James Whale to supervise the new scenes. The entire cast was experienced actors, and they had little trouble transitioning to sound. The sole exception was Jean Harlow, whom an observer on set described as "one of the world's worst actresses."[48]

Almost all of Harlow's scenes revolved around her sex appeal, but even that was called into question. "Tell me," she said to Whale in desperation one day, "tell me exactly how you want me to do it." "My dear girl," Whale replied, his patience sorely tested, "I can tell you how to be an actress but I cannot tell you how to be a woman."[49]

Despite the difficulties during filming, there seemed to be no denying Harlow's allure onscreen. Her line "Would you be shocked if I put on something more comfortable?" would become infamous.[50] After the movie's release, she quickly came to be known as the "foremost U.S. embodiment of sex appeal."[51]

Filming concluded on December 7, 1929, over two years after photography initially began. The cost stood at $2,511,775.[52] The film still needed to be cut and edited so production rolled into 1930. Postproduction took several months because Hughes shot 2,254,750 feet of film, a staggering number. To put it into comparison, the average director shoots around ten times more footage than they actually use. Hughes consumed over 150 times more footage. Hughes continued to toil on the film and reducing it down to a manageable number proved to be as costly and time consuming as every other aspect of the production.

In late April 1930, the film was finally complete. It stood at 12,909 feet. Corporate records listed the cost at an astonishing $2,808,710.[53] The production had gone on so long that it had become a joke around Hollywood.

A man was discovered who was celebrating his 105th birthday, and it was said that he was the only living person who could remember when *Hell's Angels* was started. It was predicted that airplanes would be as out-of-date as ox carts before the picture was released. They told of young men who went to work on *Hell's Angels* when it started, who were now giving up their jobs to their great-grandchildren.[54]

Even the cast got in on the act. Stars James Hall quipped, "If it isn't finished soon, I'll be playing my own father."[55] When it became known that the film was complete, many still questioned if it would ever be released: "'Well,' say the wise-crackers, 'now that the talkie version of 'Hell's Angels' is finished, they're waiting for television!'"[56]

As the jokes continued, Hughes prepared to premiere the film in Hollywood. He had spent almost $3,000,000 and devoted well over two years to his aerial epic. Expense was never an issue on the film, and Hughes wanted to make sure the opening was equally lavish. Lincoln Quarberg, the publicity director of Caddo, came up with a list of ideas to make sure the film had "a campaign of exploitation more brilliant and spectacular than has been given to any previous film production."[57]

Quarberg suggested billboards and advertisements leading up to the opening that exploited the film's production record with slogans like "At last!" and "$4,000,000—Three Years to Make!"[58] For the opening itself, he recommended stunts for both air and land, ranging from planes flying overhead to mock airplane noises on the streets. Many of Quarberg's suggestions were quite elaborate, but it was exactly what Hughes wanted. Ideas in hand, Hughes announced on March 11, 1930, that the film would make its world premiere in six weeks. And it would take place at the famous Grauman's Chinese Theatre.

Sid Grauman opened the luxurious theatre in 1927, and he hoped his "dream castle" would create the illusion of "entering another world."[59] The theatre's ornate exterior was surpassed only by its decadent interior. When the theatre hosted a major premiere, an elaborate prologue was commonly staged that often rivaled the film itself. The excitement Grauman brought to the Chinese quickly made the venue one of Hollywood's top tourist attractions. Grauman ultimately parted ways with the theatre in 1929, but demanding nothing but the best, Hughes contracted Grauman to return to the Chinese to work on the opening of *Hell's Angels*.

The premiere date was set for April 19, 1930, but a scheduling conflict at the theatre forced Hughes to delay it once again. Despite some talk of moving the premiere to a different venue, a new date was set for May 27. In anticipation, advertisements for the premiere started to appear in the *Los Angeles Times* beginning on May 15. The initial ad proclaimed the premiere would be "the greatest opening the world has ever known." It also cited the film's epic production, noting it was "three years in the making" and done at a "cost of $4,000,000."[60]

Despite a record-setting charge of $11 per ticket, the opening sold out in a few days. On May 21, an advertisement noted "it may be too late for you to secure tickets for the performance but the pre-opening spectacles and Mardi Gras spirit will pervade all Hollywood Boulevard from Vine to La Brea featuring an illumination unparalleled in history."[61] The day of the opening the *Los Angeles Times* warned its audience that streets around the theatre were to be closed and special regulations would be in place because of the "vast throng expected for the spectacular civic and military festivities."[62]

The premiere was a lavish spectacle that incorporated many of Quarberg's ideas. Airplanes flew overhead and furnished a display of fireworks. Hollywood Boulevard was lined every few yards for over a mile with huge sun arc lights. The neighboring hills were dotted with fan-shaped clusters of multi-colored searchlights. In addition to floodlights, over 200 giant searchlights were used in the display. "Never was the sky of Hollywood more brilliantly illuminated," wrote one observer, "never were the white smoke screens made by airmen more lavish and never were the air stunts more brilliantly hazardous."[63] Edwin Schallert of the *Los Angeles Times* said it was "the biggest crowd ever" for a premiere and "more police reserves were required to hold them in check than ever."[64]

Scheduled to begin at 8:30 p.m. sharp, the movie started over two hours late, but it managed to keep the estimated 2,000 attendees in their seats well past one o'clock in the morning. The stars in attendance were thrilled. Mary Pickford said, "Seldom does a moving picture audience have the privilege of seeing such a picture." Douglas Fairbanks declared, "Anybody who doesn't believe that patience is always rewarded should see 'Hell's Angels.' It took Howard a long time to make it, but it will take you much longer to forget its great appeal." Charlie Chaplin exclaimed, "'Hell's Angels' is the most tremendous production since the advent of talking pictures."[65]

When the film premiered in New York a few months later on August 15, 1930, Hughes took the unprecedented step of opening it in two different theatres, the Criterion and the Gaiety, because of the "tremendous New York demand."[66] The film was roadshowed in major cities and then released across the country on November 15, 1930.[67]

The film centers on two English brothers named Roy (James Hall) and Monte Rutledge (Ben Lyon). Roy is in love with Helen (Jean Harlow), a young English society girl, while Monte enjoys the affections of many different women. The lives of all three are disrupted when war breaks out between Germany and England. Roy immediately enlists in the Royal Flying Corps, while Monte is tricked into enlisting with the enticement of a kiss from a pretty girl. At a military charity ball, Monte meets Helen for the first time, and despite Roy's strong feelings for her, the two find themselves attracted to one another. Later that night, Monte and Helen embrace and apparently consummate the relationship.

High above London, a German Zeppelin is making preparations to bomb the city. The English spot the activities of the Zeppelin, and planes are deployed to destroy it. Roy commands one such plane with Monte as his gunner. Most of the British planes are shot down in the ensuing battle. Roy and Monte's plane is hit, but they manage to land safely. One British plane is left to destroy the Zeppelin. Unfortunately, the plane's guns are jammed so the pilot heroically decides to crash his plane into the Zeppelin, destroying it.

Back on land, the two brothers are sent to France where Roy runs into Helen who is flirting with other soldiers. Roy is crushed when Helen confides she never had feelings for him. Later, Roy and Monte are assigned a dangerous mission to enter German territory and bomb an ammunition depot in advance of a British invasion. Monte is scared and wants to disobey orders, but Roy convinces him they must proceed. Roy and Monte successfully manage to bomb the depot, as an amazing dogfight takes place between the British and the Germans.

Attempting to escape, their plane crashes in German territory. Roy and Monte are taken captive and interrogated by the Germans in hopes they will reveal the British plans. Monte seems willing to tell the Germans anything they want, so Roy tricks his captors into thinking he will give them the information. As part of the deal, Roy is given a gun with one bullet presumably to shoot Monte so he will not brand Roy a traitor. In reality, Roy reluctantly uses the bullet to kill Monte to keep him quiet. Roy is forced to take such drastic measures to keep the British plans a secret. The Germans kill Roy for his duplicity. In the end, their deaths are not in vain as the British invasion is successful.[68]

Despite some criticism of the dramatic sequences, the reviewers were almost unanimous in their praise. Prunella Hall of the *Boston Post* said it was the "greatest spectacle the screen has yet seen" and it left her "gasping for air."[69] The reviewer for *Time* magazine said the picture stood "as an astounding achievement."[70] *Variety* said the "spectacular features" make the film "an important box-office entry."[71] Mordaunt Hall of *The New York Times* thought the film was "absorbing and exciting."[72] Harleigh Schultz of the *Boston Evening American* wrote that it "has about exhausted our supply of adjectives."[73]

Maj. C. C. Moseley, an air veteran of the First World War and an early entrepreneur in the aircraft industry, reviewed the picture for the *Los Angeles Times*. "It actually shows you the things the gang who flew at the front has been trying to explain for twelve years," he wrote. "What's more, it gives you a few jolts that can't ever possibly be set down by word of mouth or in writing."[74]

While reviewers and veterans liked the film, Hughes was criticized across the industry for his lavish spending. Joseph Schenck, the president of United Artists, the film's distributor, described the sentiment surrounding Hughes in the aftermath of *Hell's Angels'* release. In a letter to Neil McCarthy, Schenck wrote that because of Hughes "the cost of the negative is entirely too high, in proportion to what you can get back at the box office," and as a result, many producers believed "that Howard is a menace to the business, because he has done a few things that have been detrimental to the picture industry in general."[75]

Schenck went on to say that "the public does not pay enough at the box office for a picture to absorb all these crazy conditions" and the opinion of Hughes would only change if "he is willing to subscribe to the ethics of the picture business."[76] In other words, the studio system was designed in part to keep production budgets arbitrarily low, and unlike other producers, Hughes was not acceding to the demands of the Big Five.

Showing his disdain for the likes of Schenck and Hollywood's unwritten rules, Hughes took out advertisements and gave interviews in which he continued to proudly proclaimed that the "total cost of 'Hell's Angels' will approximate $4,000,000" of his own money, which made it the most

expensive film ever produced up to that point.[77] Hughes even went so far
as to release an itemized accounting of his expenditures. The final cost
he provided was $3,866,475, exclusive of cutting costs, dubbing, and
exploitation. With those expenses added in, it was estimated that the "cost
of 'Hell's Angels' will be over $4,000,000."[78]

No one had ever spent that much money on a film, and Hughes knew it
guaranteed free publicity. In the words of film historian Richard Maltby,
"the reputation of a movie is enhanced by the conspicuous display of its
production budget."[79] Hughes certainly believed this, and he promoted the
film accordingly. But internal company documents show Hughes did not
actually spend $4,000,000.

The final budget report for the film listed a total cost of $2,808,710.[80]
A report on after print costs said the total was $2,879,017.[81] The most
compelling evidence that the film cost less than Hughes stated in the press
comes from a loan application Hughes sought for the Caddo Company
in 1931 from the Bank of America. To secure the funds, Hughes put up
three of his films including *Hell's Angels* as collateral. The bank required
financial statements to prove the films' costs, and Hughes could not
manipulate the figures without suffering serious legal consequences. The
listed cost of *Hell's Angels* on the loan documents was $2,900,000, almost
a million dollars lower than the numbers provided to the media.[82]

Hughes must have known it was better to be thought of as the producer
of the most expensive motion picture of all time, as opposed to the second
or third most expensive, so he manipulated the figures released to the
public. As a result, every subsequent mention of the film cited its supposed
record-breaking cost. Hughes thus came to be known as a visionary who
would do whatever it took to realize his dreams. Money and industry
norms would not stand in Hughes's way of giving audiences the best
motion pictures possible.

*Hell's Angels* certainly was a watershed moment in the history of
Hollywood. "Nothing like it has ever happened before," wrote one
industry magazine, "and probably nothing like it will ever happen again."[83]
And Hughes certainly spent an unprecedented sum of his own money on
his aerial epic, but as the records show, he just did not spend as much as he
led others to believe.

The cost was not the only financial exaggeration Hughes made about
the film. Hughes always claimed that *Hell's Angels* returned a substantial
amount of money. After all, his production philosophy was based on the
simple conclusion that the more money he spent the more money he would
make. Hughes may not have spent as much as he stated publicly, but the
film nevertheless cost a substantial amount. If Hughes's theory held, he
would have made a significant profit.

Hughes certainly conveyed as much to the press. After the film's initial run, reports claimed that the film's earnings were "two million dollars above the investment of four million dollars."[84] It was said to have brought in "a load of money."[85] Years later, after several reissues, the reported profits, which were described as simply "prodigious," rose to $4,000,000.[86] One article on Hughes even went so far as to claim the film "returned dividends of more than ten times its cost."[87] Once again, internal company documents tell a different story.

As early as February 1931, United Artists began to note that they "had many complaints on HELL'S ANGELS engagements" and "the figures indicate that the picture does not hold up to expectations."[88] The financial climate at the time of the film's release surely played a part. As Hughes's lavish masterpiece was making its initial run, the country was in the midst of the worst depression in its history.

The popularity of talkies initially shielded the motion picture industry from its effects, and the 1929–1930 exhibition season saw ticket sales and profits hitting new highs. The growth slowed in late 1930, and the downturn continued until 1933 when the industry began to rebound. Unfortunately for Hughes, his film was released during the worst part of the depression for the motion picture industry.[89] As a result, many theatres sought reductions on their contracts for *Hell's Angels*.

The Wayne Palace in Philadelphia was a typical example. "Due to the business depressions in this section," read United Artists' rental reduction notice for the theatre, "it was necessary to grant above reductions in order to get this picture played."[90] Some situations were even worse as theatres across the country, like other businesses, were forced to close, often unexpectedly. "The reason for this cancellation is that the theatre is closed and the whereabouts of the exhibitor are unknown," stated one of many similar worded notices. "Therefore the amount is uncollectible."[91]

By August 1931, Caddo's application for the Bank of America loan stated the film had a total revenue of $1,474,099. The producer's revenue (seventy percent) was $1,031,869.[92] A listing of after print costs, dated 1935, said the producer's revenue was $1,578,054.[93] In 1949, after the film was reissued several times, an internal audit of the film estimated that its total worldwide gross was $2,633,037. Using their calculations, Hughes's revenue was somewhere around $1,569,000.[94]

Noah Dietrich once joked that he "would hate like hell to have to live the rest of my life on what Howard made out of 'Hell's Angels.'" He went on to say that if the figures often quoted in the media were true Hughes would "have a lot of unpaid federal estate taxes to pay."[95] Dietrich claimed in his book that the film lost around $1,500,000.[96] This figure matches the numbers stated in internal company documents.

From all indications, it seems the film was unable to recoup its large investment. Hughes's production philosophy apparently did not hold up. Nonetheless, the media and many within the industry believed that the film was a substantial moneymaker. In a town based on fantasy, fiction is often more important than reality. Hughes may not have made a profit on his film, but he certainly fooled a lot of people into thinking he did. And the financial numbers were not the only thing people believed about the film.

As he attempted to do with his earlier films, Hughes made a conscious effort to take full credit for every aspect of *Hell's Angels*. In an official biography released by Caddo in 1930, the film was described as "truly a 'one-man picture'—from the outset, from conception and creation of the story, to casting, actual filming, cutting and editing, it is in every sense a Howard Hughes production."[97] An early article on the film said it was "written, produced and directed by one young man."[98]

In an interview in 1932, Hughes made sure everything was about him: "I had to worry about money, sign checks, hire pilots, get planes, cast everything, direct the whole thing." He went on to say bluntly, "All I know is about me. I did everything, because I was new in this business and had no confidence in anybody else and I wanted it done right."[99]

The sole focus on Hughes continued over the years. An article in 1946 said Hughes was "his own director, designed sets, worked on the script, intervened in everything."[100] Stephen White's *Life* article, published in 1954, called the film "the closest thing to a one-man picture ever made in Hollywood."[101] Hughes certainly played a significant role in the film, but once again, the truth was not as Hughes had everyone believe.

There is no denying the fact that Hughes used his own money to independently finance the entire picture. He also directed the dangerous aerial sequences. But as described, many other individuals also contributed to *Hell's Angels*. Marshall Neilan came up with the original story idea and the title for the film. Harry Behn led a group of writers who worked on expanding the story. Joseph Moncure March wrote the story for the sound version of the film, and Howard Estabrook helped March with the dialogue. Director James Whale staged the non-aerial dramatic sequences. Lincoln Quarberg and Sid Grauman worked on the publicity for the film. Many other people helped with editing, photography, settings, music, and sound effects.

Despite what Hughes wanted others to believe, *Hell's Angels* was the result of the combined efforts of many individuals. Nonetheless, Hughes's impact on the film was tremendous. Without his passion and desire, the film never would have been made. Without his money, it never would have been completed. Without his sheer determination, it never would have been as spectacular. It might not have been a one-man show, but *Hell's Angels* certainly was a Howard Hughes production.

With his aviation exploits still a few years away, *Hell's Angels* introduced Howard Hughes to the world. A mystique immediately grew around the young producer, the maker of the "most expensive motion picture ever made."[102] The film was heralded as an "incredible money-maker," evidently proving his production philosophy on spending was correct.[103] A poll from *Film Daily* listed Hughes among the "ten best cinema directors of 1930–1931," confirming he really could direct as well as those other guys.[104]

While *Hell's Angels* seemed to vindicate Hughes, a detailed examination proves that the true story was much more complicated. At the same time, it shows how successful Hughes was at manipulating the media and shaping his public persona. Everything about Hughes ultimately seemed possible because everything was possible for Hughes. The myth surrounding Hughes would reach legendary proportions, and it all began with *Hell's Angels*.

Regardless of the truth, Hughes quickly went from a joke to one of the biggest names in the motion picture industry. At a time when the major studios controlled almost all aspects of filmmaking, Hughes blazed a revolutionary path, as *Hell's Angels* was proclaimed to be "the most amazing thing that has ever happened in a business where odd and peculiar hocus-pocus is no novelty."[105]

The major studios responded to Hughes by focusing more on so-called prestige pictures. *Variety* reported in 1934 that prestige pictures were being made "in numbers so thick as to constitute the champion of cycles since sound came in."[106] Prestige pictures were loosely defined as having a big-budget, a major star, a splashy premiere, and heavy advertisement. With a supposed budget of $4,000,000, Jean Harlow (not to mention Hughes himself), Grauman's Chinese Theatre, and countless newspaper and magazine stories, *Hell's Angels* was all of these things and more.

Prestige pictures ultimately were a small percentage of the actual films produced in the 1930s, but they accounted for a significant share of the major studios' production budgets. They also were the most heavily promoted, discussed, and awarded pictures of the era. Hughes's aerial epic started the cycle, and it was regarded as one of the quintessential films of the 1930s until it was eventually (and permanently) overshadowed by *Gone with the Wind* (1939), one of Hollywood's most celebrated pictures and the film that finally eclipsed the reported record-breaking cost of *Hell's Angels*.[107]

Legendary producer and executive David O. Selznick was the mastermind behind *Gone with the Wind*, and when he opened Selznick

International Pictures a few years earlier in 1935, he announced that "there are only two kinds of merchandise that can be made profitably in this business—either the very cheap pictures or the expensive pictures."[108] Like everyone else in the industry, he was responding to the success of Howard Hughes and *Hell's Angels*. Film historian Tino Balio, confirming Selznick's observations, writes that "the prestige picture was far and away the most popular production trend of the [1930s]."[109] Again, it all started with Hughes and *Hell's Angels*.

The studio system was designed to eliminate outside competition, and the few independents that did manage to survive had no choice but to give in to the dictates of the Big Five. The independent Hughes managed to show what was possible for those who refused to be subjugated. He defied the low-cost production philosophy of the major studios, and he seemed to prove that it was possible to make a profit on a multi-million dollar production. In order for the Big Five to keep pace with the young filmmaker, they had to reevaluate their position in regards to production costs.

It was not the fact that Hughes made one epic film that caused the major studios to worry. It was the thought of Hughes, now a major figure in the industry, making many more extravagant films that horrified the powers that be. After all, the mystique surrounding Hughes made anything seem possible. As one article put it simply, "Mr. Hughes has the picture business guessing."[110]

3

# A Demoralizing Influence

"Your fault, my fault, who cares."—
Tony Camonte (Paul Muni) in *Scarface*

Howard Hughes completed his masterpiece, and he was now a significant force in the motion picture industry. So what would he do for an encore? For one thing, Hughes claimed he would not embark on such a large production by himself ever again. "Trying to do the work of twelve men was just dumbness on my part," Hughes conceded in an interview in the aftermath of *Hell's Angels*. Apparently recognizing his limitations, Hughes went on to profess his latest production philosophy: "If you want a thing done right, go get the man who knows how to do it best, and don't bother him—much."[1]

Hughes was certainly more experienced as a producer and more knowledgeable about the workings of the studio system, including the challenges he faced as an independent, but it was clear he was still defiant and confident in his abilities. "I haven't been wrong in *everything*, though," he was sure to stress. "I've found out that the big guys aren't always right either."[2]

Taking a more hands-off approach to production, Hughes followed his aerial epic with a series of critically and financially disappointing films upon which he played a minor role.[3] The notable exception was *The Front Page* (1931), the story of a newspaper reporter who hides a man convicted of murder in an attempt to cash in on the story. It garnered positive reviews and received three Academy Award nominations, including Outstanding Production.[4] But even this movie did not return a profit for the producer. *The Front Page* cost $539,089 and returned a producer's revenue of only $502,717.[5]

Hughes nonetheless was still convinced he knew what audiences wanted, and he was sure he could make profitable motion pictures. The problem, Hughes believed, were the censors that required him to make changes to his movies. Censors were a powerful lobby in the industry, and even an independent like Hughes was forced to work with them. However, on his next major production, Hughes decided to challenge the censors, which once again put him at odds with a fundamental aspect of the studio system.

The motion picture industry came of age during a time of widespread social activism and political reform commonly known as the Progressive Era. Many apostles of the movement, including the clergy and women's groups, recognized the power and potential of movies to entertain and educate, but they also worried about the potential harm movies could do if left unchecked. Calling for direct government oversight, advocates sought the establishment of censorship boards "to prevent the moving picture show from being a demoralizing influence in the community—and to permit it to be the pleasant, stimulating, and even inspiring form of entertainment that it can be at its best."[6]

Censorship was ultimately implemented at all levels of government. Cities, big and small, passed censorship laws. Seven states, including New York, Pennsylvania, Kansas, Ohio, Maryland, Florida, and Virginia, had official censorship boards by 1922. National censorship boards also existed, with varying degrees of power, and legislation was introduced multiple times at the federal level for even more oversight.[7]

Preferring to keep all aspects of filmmaking in-house, the industry responded by creating the Motion Picture Producers and Distributors of America (MPPDA) in 1922. Led by Will H. Hays, the former chairman of the Republican Party and the postmaster general under President Warren G. Harding, the MPPDA claimed to "foster the common interests of those engaged in the motion picture industry in the United States, by establishing and maintaining the highest possible moral and artistic standards in motion picture production."[8]

In reality, the organization was created by the major studios to reduce the threat of federal censorship and to diminish the possibility of legislation or court action that would impose a strict application of federal antitrust laws against the industry. Avoiding controversy was key to this agenda, and the best way to eliminate controversial motion pictures was through censorship.

According to Hays, who came to be known as the "dictator of the cinema" and the "Little Napoleon of the Movies," "the responsibility for better pictures rest on those who make the pictures," i.e. the producers.[9] The MPPDA thus scrutinized motion pictures at every stage of development, from the writing of the script to the final cut. If the MPPDA thought anything was objectionable, they recommended that the unacceptable word or scene be removed.

As a result, while the MPPDA was involved in matters of arbitration, intra-industry relations, and negotiations with governmental bodies, it primarily came to be known as a censorship organization. But Hays was quick to point out that the dictates of the MPPDA were "not censorship in any sense of the word" because all changes were supposedly made voluntarily in the best interest of all parties.[10]

The advent of sound offered the opportunity to explore subjects the industry previously avoided, which led to further calls for outside oversight, but it also made removing a word or scene after the fact more difficult as cuts could dramatically impact the film's continuity. To eliminate objectionable elements at the outset when it was easier, the MPPDA adopted the Motion Picture Production Code of 1930 to make sure that "no picture shall be produced which will lower the moral standards of those who see it."[11] To remove any uncertainty, the code specifically stated how certain topics should and should not be treated.

Crimes against the law, for example, should never be presented in such a way "as to throw sympathy with the crime" or "to inspire others with a desire for imitation." The code had specific rules governing the treatment of murder ("brutal killings are not to be presented in detail"), methods of crime ("the use of firearms should be restricted to essentials"), and vulgarity ("subject always to the dictates of good taste").[12]

In regards to sex, the code stated that the "sanctity of the institution of marriage and the home shall be upheld" and pictures "shall not infer that low forms of sex relationship are the accepted or common thing." And nudity "is never permitted... in fact or silhouette."[13]

The Big Five, once again acting in collusion, agreed to abide by the requirements of the code because it was in their combined best interest. Unfortunately for the MPPDA, not everyone wanted to avoid controversy.

Whereas the Big Five, the Little Three, and almost every other significant studio and production company were members of the MPPDA by 1930, Hughes and the Caddo Company were not. As such, the MPPDA technically did not have jurisdiction over him. But if Hughes wanted his films exhibited in the best theatres owned by the major corporations, he needed to get the association's approval. Many of Hughes's previous films required some cuts or eliminations, which Hughes reluctantly agreed to make. When those films suffered at the box office, Hughes blamed the MPPDA.

The independent Hughes was looking for the right production to bring him back to the forefront of the industry when he came upon a little known novel entitled *Scarface* (1930) by Armitage Trail. The book was a tale of gangland rule that incorporated many aspects of the life of noted Chicago racketeer Alphonse "Scarface" Capone.

A national figure, Capone's escapades initially appeared to be tolerated by the general public during prohibition, but the bloodshed associated with the St. Valentine's Day Massacre in 1929, the killing of seven rival gangsters reportedly ordered by Capone, led to a general outcry to "end the reign of gangdom."[14] Capone quickly went from a celebrity to public enemy number one.

The change of attitude about gangsters like Capone was seen in the output of the motion picture industry. During the 1930–1931 production cycle, approximately twelve movies dealt directly with gangsters, but they all but disappeared thereafter. Late in 1931, the MPPDA went so far as to pass a resolution banning gangster films, but before such action was taken, production on Hughes's *Scarface* (1932) had already begun.

Hughes believed the way to differentiate his movie from those that preceded it, and the ultimate key to the film's success, was to make it as realistic and therefore as violent as possible. Knowing Hughes could be difficult, the industry's censors kept a close eye on his gangster production from the outset.

The MPPDA was especially worried that highlighting a real-life criminal whom authorities had failed to bring to justice might embarrass the government and lead to increased regulation of the industry as reprisal. "The motion picture industry has for a long time, in spite of strong denunciations and criticism, maintained its right to produce purely fictional underworld stories, provided certain standards were maintained," wrote Colonel Jason Joy of the MPPDA in a letter to Hughes, "but has, on the other hand admitted the grave danger of portraying on the screen actual contemporary happenings relating to deficiencies in our government, political dishonesty and graft, current crimes or anti-social or criminal activities."[15]

Despite such warnings, Hughes proceeded with the intention of making the film as factual as possible. Following his new philosophy of hiring the best people for the job, he surrounded himself with individuals who had firsthand knowledge of Capone and other gangsters. For the screenplay, Hughes chose Ben Hecht, a former newspaper writer who had reported on the activities of Chicago criminals before penning the classic gangster film *Underworld* (1927).[16] W. R. Burnett, another veteran of Chicago who wrote the novel upon which *Little Caesar* (1931) was based, was brought in to work on the continuity and dialogue, along with Seton I. Miller and John Lee Mahin.[17] Fred D. Pasley, the author of *Al Capone: The Biography of a Self-Made Man* (1930), also worked on the film.[18]

With the script in place, the cast and crew were assembled. Many individuals were considered for the title character (whose name in the film is Tony Camonte), but in the end, Hughes decided upon Paul Muni. At the age of thirty-five, Muni was a veteran of the stage, but he had very little experience acting in motion pictures. Nonetheless, his first feature role in the film *The Valiant* (1929) was a critical success, and it foreshadowed his onscreen potential. Osgood Perkins was chosen to play the critical role of his underworld boss. The two main female leads, Camonte's girlfriend and sister, went to Karen Morley and Ann Dvorak, respectively. George Raft and Boris Karloff rounded out the cast. Hughes turned to Howard Hawks to direct the film. Although he was a little younger than Muni, Hawks had already directed ten feature films.[19]

As preproduction continued, the MPPDA continued to worry about *Scarface*. Dr. Carleton Simon, the consulting psychologist and criminologist of the association, had two main suggestions on how to improve the tone of the film. First, he feared that the characters "would be highly objectionable to millions of Italians in this country," so to compensate, he suggested adding a scene where Scarface's mother points out all that Italians have done for posterity and then chastises her son for "bringing odium and shame upon his race." Second, Simon argued that a "great many of the shooting scenes that serve no purpose except to paint the ruthlessness of the gangster can be wisely deleted and fist fights substituted," so as not to allow for a "glorification of the criminal."[20]

Beyond the content of the film itself, which Jason Joy described as the "most harsh and frank gangster picture we have ever had," the MPPDA was also worried that the success of the film, critically or financially, would revive the controversial gangster genre which seemingly had come to an end.[21] The MPPDA's fears were expressed by writer Lee Shippey of the *Los Angeles Times* when he wrote, "If 'Scarface,' which the Hughes organization has spent a lot of time and money on, is a hit it is going to be pretty hard to stop gangster pictures, no matter what they call 'em."[22]

In a series of conversations with Hughes and others at the Caddo Company working on the film, representatives of the MPPDA continued to stress the sensitive nature of the topic in hopes they would abandon the production. "I have been told emphatically by censors, chiefs of police, newspaper editors, exhibitors and leaders among the citizenry," Joy wrote in one such letter, "that there is a vast growing resentment against the continued production and exhibition of this type of picture."[23]

Representatives for Hughes sought to do everything they could to reassure the MPPDA. E. B. Derr, the supervisor on the film, responded to Joy by pointing out that Caddo was "conscious of all recent censorship eliminations" regarding gangster films and they intended to get a lot of scenes "across by impression rather than direct shots."[24] Will Hays noted that he spoke to Hughes directly, and Hughes assured him "he would be very careful of the treatment."[25] Finally recognizing that "nothing I am sure will deter him from making the film," the MPPDA seemed content that at least Hughes now understood the seriousness of the situation, and as the producer, he seemed willing to make the necessary changes.[26]

With the MPPDA apparently feeling a little better about the production, filming began on June 15, 1931. The MPPDA preferred to address controversial issues prior to actual production, but they continued to work with Hughes and others during filming to make sure the changes discussed were actually made. Joy held a conference with Howard Hawks, and he reported that the director "has already taken care of the numerous suggestions which we have made."[27] On June 29, Joy seemed downright jubilant when he wrote that Hughes has "not only incorporated our suggestions but insisted upon our tieing (*sic*) in closely with the director during the picture's production."[28]

Joy's optimism began to fade as he came to realize that Hughes, despite his promises, was not including all of the MPPDA's suggestions. Joy's tone was dramatically different when he wrote "they [still] have everything in the story, including the inferences of incest," and the "picture is beginning to look worse and worse to us, from a censorship point of view."[29]

Despite the constant battle with the MPPDA, filming went smoothly and concluded after three months in September 1931.[30] In anticipation of the film's release, Hughes's Caddo Company signed a contract with United Artists to distribute the film.[31]

Although the MPPDA had many concerns about *Scarface*, they were especially worried about the ending. The original ending had Camonte shooting it out with the police until he ran out of ammunition. Camonte refuses to run, and he continues to brave the onslaught of police bullets until he is ultimately gunned down. The MPPDA thought this made Camonte seem heroic, so they argued for a more suitable ending even before production began. Joy thought Camonte "should be shown as cringing coward and Guarini, the policeman, should be man who is fearless, and who walks into Camonte's blazing arsenal to capture him alive."[32]

When production started, Joy had a meeting with Hawks to discuss the ending, and it appeared the director would consider altering it accordingly. Hughes, on the other hand, was not so willing to concede. At a meeting with Joy, Hughes made it clear that he thought portraying Camonte as a coward would weaken the story, and he was reluctant to make the suggested changes. When production concluded and a rough-cut version of the film finally was screened by the MPPDA on September 8, 1931, Joy was surprised to see that the ending had not been reworked at all.

Continuing to argue for a complete revision, Joy conceded a new ending would "greatly weaken the value of the picture," but he thought it was necessary in order for the picture to comply with the Motion Picture Production Code of 1930.[33] Hughes initially was noncommittal, but Joy impressed upon Hughes that the current version of the film "could not play in more than 50% of the English-speaking territory."[34] Finally, on September 21, 1931, Hughes gave in and agreed to shoot a new ending.

Besides depicting Camonte as a coward, Hughes also added an element recommended by the MPPDA that argued criminals were only powerful as a result of guns and strong firearms legislation would help eradicate the criminal element. The MPPDA thought this message would make the film more appealing to censors. The new ending had Camonte lose his gun in the fight with police, and as a result, he turns into a coward. When the police go to apprehend him, Camonte runs in fear and is shot down. The new ending took four days to shoot and cost Hughes an additional $25,000.

Then, after the new ending was shot, the MPPDA decided it too was unacceptable, and they convinced Hughes to shoot a third ending, which required more time and money. The latest ending had Camonte lose his gun and turn cowardly, but instead of being shot down after running, Camonte is arrested and hanged for his crimes.[35] With the latest ending in place, the picture appeared to be finished.

The film *Scarface* centers on the life of Tony Camonte (Paul Muni), a violent and ruthlessly ambitious gangster. Camonte helps his boss Johnny Lovo (Osgood Perkins) solidify control of bootlegging in the city's south side. Camonte wants to take over the whole city, but Lovo overrules him. Camonte plans to kill Lovo and take over the city himself, along with the help of his faithful lieutenant Rinaldo (George Raft). When Camonte has Rinaldo kill the leader of the north side, Camonte now rivals Lovo for power, which is confirmed when he wins the affection of Lovo's mistress Poppy (Karen Morley). Lovo tries to kill his former underling, but Camonte manages to escape and kill Lovo.

Now firmly established as the undisputed boss, Camonte decides to celebrate and go on vacation in Florida. Unbeknownst to Camonte, Rinaldo has fallen in love with Camonte's sister Cesca (Ann Dvorak). Rinaldo is initially scared to act on his feelings for Cesca because Camonte behaves more like a jealous lover than a protective brother. The relationship between Cesca and Rinaldo intensifies with Camonte out of town.

The two ultimately get married and move in together. When Camonte returns from his vacation and finds the two living together, he shoots and kills Rinaldo. In hysterics, Cesca tells Camonte they were married and planned on surprising him with the news upon his return. Camonte attempts to console his sister, but she pushes him away and calls him a butcher. The police learn of the murder and issue a warrant for Camonte's arrest.

Cesca, intent on exacting revenge, beats the police to Camonte's apartment. With Cesca pointing a gun at him, Camonte successfully convinces her that all they need is each other. The police arrive, and Cesca helps Camonte prepare for the shootout. Shots are exchanged, and Cesca is hit. Camonte expressed his true feelings for Cesca as she dies in his arms. Overcome with sadness, Camonte attempts to flee without a gun. The police ultimately corner him. Camonte tells them he does not have a weapon, and he pleads for his life like a coward. Arrested and found guilty in court, Camonte is walked to the gallows where he is hanged, ending his violent rule.[36]

The new version of the film incorporated many of the suggestions of the MPPDA, and Jason Joy was ecstatic. "Not since my arrival have I met with greater willingness to cooperate than in this instance," he wrote in a letter to Will Hays.[37] In another conversation with Hays, Joy pointed out that Hughes's cooperation demonstrated an honest effort to save "the reputation of the industry."[38]

Besides praising Hughes's efforts, Joy also noted that the picture was excellent entertainment. "I have seen it twenty times," he wrote, "and still it has the power to move me."[39] Others key figures in the industry agreed. Irving Thalberg hailed it as "one of the strongest pictures he has ever seen," while Douglas Fairbanks and Harold Lloyd were on record calling it the "greatest picture of its kind ever made."[40]

Individuals in the motion picture industry were not the only ones who liked the film. *Scarface* was shown to a group of Los Angeles law and enforcement officials who, citing its accurate portrayal of criminals, "unanimously expressed approval" of the picture.[41] Executives at Caddo even contemplated sending a print of the film to President Herbert Hoover in an attempt to get his endorsement.[42] Given Hughes's willingness to cooperate and the initial reception of the film, Jason Joy felt strongly that the MPPDA should do all it could to help get the film passed across the country.[43]

The MPPDA had been worried about how other censors would react to *Scarface* from the outset, and those concerns were communicated to Hughes. Despite the changes already made, the MPPDA knew it would still be difficult to get the film passed by every censorship board. In October 1931, Joy met with several censors and other individuals who had influence in such matters. They promised to keep an open mind about the film, but they were all "pretty dubious."[44] Will Hays held a meeting with notable industry executives, and the consensus was the film was "dangerous" and "simply will not do at all the way it is."[45]

The sentiments were relayed to Hughes who conceded that the film was "full of dynamite," which is likely what he wanted, but Hughes apparently expressed hope that the MPPDA could help him "save it."[46] Nevertheless, Hughes was reluctant to reshoot more scenes, a process that would take more time and money. Hughes thus met with Hays, Joy, and others from the MPPDA to discuss how to proceed. Hughes proposed cutting the film and strengthening the anti-gun propaganda in an attempt to make it more acceptable. Joy reported, in what was to be the final in-person conference on changes, that there was a "complete meeting of the minds and Mr. Hughes is setting about the job of accomplishing the agreements."[47]

One of the changes Hughes finally seemed willing to make concerned the title. The MPPDA never liked *Scarface* as it was associated directly with Capone, so they had sought a change for some time. Hughes was always reluctant to alter the title because he thought the connection with the noted real-life gangster would generate interest and increase the box office potential of the film.[48] The MPPDA was nonetheless adamant the title had to be changed, and Hughes appeared to relent. The alternative titles considered were *Shame of the Nation*, *Yellow*, and *Man is still Savage*. For the time being, Hughes settled on *Shame of the Nation*.[49]

In addition to the title, Hughes also weakened the allusion to an incestuous relationship between Camonte and his sister Cesca. Hughes ultimately made over thirty-nine changes to the original version of the film without shooting more scenes, which significantly decreased the amount of violence shown onscreen. The MPPDA got Hughes to change a lot, and not everyone was happy about it. Lincoln Quarberg, the publicity director of Caddo, believed the changes dictated by the MPPDA dramatically weakened the film.

In a letter to Hal Horne of United Artists, Quarberg argued that the film should initially be released in those areas of the country that did not have censorship boards. Law enforcement and newspapers in those areas would endorse *Scarface*, according to Quarberg, and that support would force censorship boards to pass the film. "As a matter of fact," he wrote, "it will be a page-one news-story after the picture has been shown in Los Angeles and other cities where the censorship problem is nil, if one of these politically-dominated censor boards attempts to ban 'Scarface.'"[50]

Quarberg went on to accuse the censors of owing their jobs to politicians who were funded by gangsters. "They are probably fearful of certain big politicians who in turn are fearful of Mr. Capone himself, or if not fearful, are well-informed as to who keeps the feed-troughs full." As for the idea of adding an anti-gun agenda, Quarberg thought that was "the most asinine idea ever proposed...Who in Hell would believe an argument like that?" he wondered. "How many gangsters give a damn about laws?"[51]

As an independent producer, Hughes was not obligated to abide by the dictates of the MPPDA. He was even convinced that doing so voluntarily in the past had hurt his films. But in a letter to Quarberg, Hughes explained why he was working with the MPPDA on *Scarface*.

> Naturally all of us would like to be able to make and release our pictures just as we wish however unfortunately I dont (*sic*) own my own releasing company and when United Artists tells me they wont (*sic*) release the picture unless passed by Hays and when the Publix Loews Fox and Warner chains of theatres state they will not play the picture unless passed by Hays there is only one thing I can do and that is to get the picture passed by Hays and that I have done with as little damage as possible.[52]

In other words, even a powerful independent like Hughes working outside the studio system was not completely free of the dominance (and therefore the mandates) of the Big Five corporations.

Having sought and received the approval of the MPPDA, Hughes set about releasing *Scarface*. Reports appeared in major cities across the country, including Los Angeles, Chicago, and New York, that the film would be released in the near future. According to *The New York Times*, the film was set to premiere on Broadway sometime in December 1931. But it first had to pass local censorship boards, including the powerful Motion Picture Division within the New York Department of Education.

Upon reviewing the film for the first time in January 1932, the New York censors noted that it was the story of a man who committed "commercialized murder" with "brutal indifference." He escaped punishment "by perjury, vicious coercion of witnesses and corrupt use of the laws of the nation." He also "loved his sister, not as a sister, but as a woman." Despite the changes already made in conjunction with the MPPDA, the film was denied approval in the state because it was "indecent," "inhuman," "immoral," and "will tend to incite to crime & corrupt morals."[53] The film was screened several more times that month by the New York censors as minor changes were made, and the reviewers continued to "unanimously recommend its rejection."[54]

As the film languished in the office of the New York censors, Lincoln Quarberg wrote Hughes a harshly worded letter connecting the film's troubles with a conspiracy against the producer. "As you undoubtedly realize by now, the men who are actually running the picture business, including Will Hays and the Big-Shot Jews, particularly the MGM moguls, are secretly hoping you have made your last picture," Quarberg ranted.

"They are jealous of your successful pictures, and have resented your independence, and your entrance into the industry from the start."[55]

United Artists' Hal Horne was also privy to Quarberg's opinions, and he directly refuted them. "Permit me to again emphasize one thing: that there is no conspiracy against Mr. Hughes," Horne stressed, "for such conspiracy would carry with it organized influence against [United Artists, the distributor], which naturally none of our officials would for a moment countenance."[56] Horne argued the apprehension surrounding the film was due to its association with Al Capone.

Referencing the anxiety the MPPDA had already expressed about a movie based on a real-life gangster, Horne noted "that should Caponi (*sic*) be released from jail, that all that was necessary was to have his lieutenants make a threat against an exhibitor in only one spot and no other exhibitor would dare show it."[57] It was reported that associates of Capone threatened Hughes and Hawks during production, and there was concern that others might be harassed in the future.[58]

Capone was even on record having criticized such films, although the reason for his condemnation was certainly surprising. "I think these gangster pictures should be stopped," Capone said subtly in an interview. "They are bad for the kiddies."[59] Regardless of whether there was a conspiracy against Hughes or a genuine fear for the public's safety, the ultimate status of the film was still in question.

Hughes continued to make minor revisions to *Scarface*, and with each modification, the New York censors screened the latest version. No matter what changes were made, the censors were unrelenting in their opinion that the film should continue to be denied.

United Artists, acting on behalf of the film as its distributor, asked James Wingate, the director of New York's Motion Picture Division, for additional information on the film's rejection. Wingate supplied the company with a copy of the informal notes of the New York reviewers. "There are so many of these," Wingate wrote in a memorandum attached to the notes, "that it is substantially a rejection in toto, and I fail to see how eliminations, if made, could make this picture meet the provisions of the Motion Picture Statute."[60]

It appeared Hughes was never going to get *Scarface* passed in New York, so Joseph Schenck of United Artists wrote to Will Hays in an attempt to salvage the situation. "I don't think it will ever get by the board of censors wherever there is censorship," observed Schenck, "and Hughes should be permitted to get what he can out of the picture in the spots where there is no censorship and where local authorities permit him to run it."[61] Schenck hoped with the blessing of the MPPDA that Hughes could finally premiere the film in certain non-censorship areas.

This endorsement technically was not necessary, but Schenck knew some exhibitors, fearful of incurring the wrath of the Big Five, would be reluctant to show the film without such approval. Although the original, uncut version of the film could be shown in areas without censorship, Schenck assured Hays that only the MPPDA-approved version C would be exhibited. Schenck needed to specify exactly which version would be screened because negotiations over the content of the film had been so protracted and so many changes had already been made three different versions of the film existed.

The original, unaltered version screened by the MPPDA on September 8, 1931, was referred to as version A. The MPPDA deemed this version unacceptable because they felt Camonte was portrayed heroically throughout the film, especially at the end where he braves the police bullets until he is ultimately killed.

Version B incorporated the anti-gun angle and the end was changed to show Camonte turning yellow after his gun is shot out of his hand. Camonte tries to run and is gunned down by the police. This version was also rejected by the MPPDA, and it was the first version rejected by the New York censors.

The heroic nature of Camonte was thus weakened further, the anti-gun angle was strengthened, and the allusions to an incestuous relationship between Camonte and his sister were removed. The ending was updated to show Camonte getting tried, convicted, and executed for his crimes. This version, which incorporated all of the changes, was known as version C. According to the MPPDA, "it was the opinion of the association that the picture then satisfied the Code requirements."[62] Version C was nonetheless still rejected by the state of New York.

Trying to get the film exhibited in those areas without censorship, Schenck assured Hays that "the picture will be released with the eliminations but Hughes insists on releasing it under the title 'Scarface.'"[63] Jason Joy noted that Schenck, in a follow-up telephone conversation with Hays, repeated the assurance that only the edited version would be exhibited. As such, the MPPDA noted in an internal memorandum that version C "is the only version which will be released by the Caddo company."[64]

With this understanding seemingly in place, Hughes premiered *Scarface* in Los Angeles, a city without censorship, on March 2, 1932, five months after filming was completed. The opening took place at Grauman's Chinese Theatre. It was a rather somber occasion in comparison with the premiere of *Hell's Angels* two years earlier. Local newspapers featured no advertisements leading up to the event, elaborate displays heralding the latest Hughes's production were gone, thousands of near riotous onlookers were absent, and there were no celebrities praising the extravagance of the occasion or the film.[65] In fact, the press were the only people invited to the unannounced premiere.

Hughes hoped the support of the media would help in his battle with the censors, so he premiered the film exclusively for the press. Hughes also recognized that releasing the film in a non-censorship locale might upset the censors who were still reviewing the film, so he tactfully did not announce the premiere in an attempt to limit any collateral damage. Edwin Schallert of the *Los Angeles Times* was one member of the press in attendance at Grauman's Chinese, and his review ran the following day.

Schallert thought that the film was by far the "goriest, most machine-gun laden of the epics of the underworld." Schallert liked the movie, especially the "bang-up cast," but he questioned whether gangster films were out of season. "Today 'Scarface' depends on the whims of the public that regulate the timeliness (or untimeliness) of a subject," he wrote. "It will answer the question of whether audiences are still interested in such brutal warfare as it depicts."[66]

Unbeknownst to Schallert, he saw the most violent version of the film. Despite Joseph Schenck's assurance that only the MPPDA-approved version C would be released, Hughes exhibited the original, unaltered version A for the press.

James Fisher of the MPPDA was on hand at Grauman's the night of the premiere, and he reported his findings to Jason Joy. Fisher reported that the "picture he saw is <u>not</u> the picture which we have approved under the Code, but is the original version containing all the shots to which we have objected and none of the re-shots which were subsequently added which, together with the eliminations, made it satisfactory under the Code."[67]

In a telegram to Joseph Schenck, Hughes's rationale for defying both the MPPDA and United Artists became clear.

> Critics saw 'Scarface' in original form praising it to the skies and almost all stating they could see nothing censorable, objectionable, and nothing which should be withheld from public. With this reaction I urgently advise the picture be released in original form in non-censorable territories. If any squawks we can always modify later to present version and show censors or whoever make complaint the many changes we have made, the great expense we have incurred in modifying the original version which they will already have seen... My experience has been censors always want to make cuts so they can show their superiors they are not drawing pay for nothing.[68]

Having made up his mind on how he planned to proceed, Hughes now had to convince Will Hays and the MPPDA.

Hughes called Hays and told him that he delayed the release of the film for several months while working with the censors and nothing happened. Reminding Hays that he "cut up" his past films until they were not "any good in order to cooperate," Hughes said that *Scarface* should be released in the non-censorship areas in its original form with its original title, as "all the newspaper men say it's wonderful and it ought to be shown."[69]

That being said, Hughes nonetheless agreed to release the altered version of the film if he was allowed to keep the original ending which showed Camonte die in a hail of gunfire. "I think if you don't let me show this with the original ending," Hughes argued, "I am discriminated against." Hughes went on to state boldly (and inaccurately), "Nobody ever told me this picture was contrary to the Code, that was never suggested."[70]

Hays replied that the film's violence was "a square violation of one of the very bases of the Code," and despite warnings about its prospects with censorship boards, the MPPDA was doing all it could to get the film passed.[71] Hays stressed that this was based on the understanding that only the MPPDA-approved version C would be exhibited across the country. In a victory for Hughes, Hays agreed to reconsider granting approval to the original ending and title.

Hays hoped the ongoing negotiations would remain private, but the press ultimately picked up on the battle over the different versions of the film. Edwin Schallert, who reviewed the original, uncut version at Grauman's Chinese for the *Los Angeles Times*, informed his readers that version A was used for the premiere in Los Angeles while version C was the one refused by the New York censors.[72]

Schallert described the reaction of the press to the competing versions of the film. "With some reviewers denouncing the Hays's office for not permitting the release of the picture in the form in which it was shown," he wrote, "and others, though not so many, pitted against the picture." Schallert went on to say that Hughes wanted to release the original version of the film and Hughes was "willing to back it against any censor board in the country, even though the Hays office and the producers' committee says 'No go!'"[73]

Chapin Hall of *The New York Times* also described Hughes's willingness to fight the censors. Hall said Hughes was "openly defying the Hays's office and the New York censors" in an attempt to "force a final decision on the power of the censors." Hall noted that it would be a "lone fight" for Hughes because his fellow "producers will not oppose the dicta of Mr. Hays."[74] Despite the fact that both accounts made it seem like Hughes and the MPPDA had reached an *impasse*, the two sides were still trying to find a compromise.

Hughes wanted the original ending, and after Hays reviewed it again as promised, the MPPDA continued to find it objectionable as the association believed it glorified Camonte the criminal. In an attempt to find a solution, Jason Joy and James Fisher of the MPPDA screened the film with ending B (Camonte becomes yellow after losing his gun and is shot down by the police when he tries to run) attached to version C, the one that featured the most cuts. They agreed that this new version was "satisfactory both from the standpoint of the Code and public policy."[75]

With the approval of the MPPDA to remove the hanging sequence (the ending of version C), Hughes had United Artists change all of the distribution prints, including those intended to be shown in areas with a censorship board. Hughes still had to get the film passed in those locales, but his decision to premiere the film in its original version in an attempt to gain leverage on the MPPDA seemingly had worked.

Hughes received more good news about the film later in March 1932 when the National Board of Review finally approved the film. Established in 1909, theatre owners and film distributors created the National Board of Review to combat charges that cinema degraded the morals of the community. Although the stated purpose of the organization was to endorse films of merit, it actually was a censorship body like the MPPDA.[76] Producers routinely submitted their films to the National Board of Review for approval, and the organization refused to endorse a film until all objectionable scenes were removed. And like the MPPDA, the National Board of Review stated all cuts were made voluntarily as the organization was "staunchly opposed to all censorship of the motion picture."[77]

In reviewing *Scarface*, James Shelley Hamilton of the National Board of Review noted there were many different versions of the film and there was no telling what the title ultimately would be: "Whatever the difference between what it is and what it started out to be, as a film it is as good as any gangster film that has been made." Stressing the film's true value, Hamilton wrote, "It is more brutal, more cruel, more wholesale than any of its predecessors, and, by that much, nearer to the truth."[78] As such, the National Board of Review approved the film.

With the latest approval of the MPPDA and the additional endorsement of the National Board of Review, Hughes scheduled the first public screening of the film for April 9, 1932, in New Orleans, Louisiana. New Orleans did not have a censorship board, and Hughes independently contracted the theatre for the exhibition. The screening was successful, and he began preparations to release the film in other areas without censorship boards.

The Los Angeles release was scheduled for April 21 at the Paramount Theatre. The first advertisement ran in the *Los Angeles Times* on April 18, and it proclaimed "a massacre was just another party to him."[79] The criminal nature of the title character was described further the following day. Scarface, the ad proclaimed, was "the leader of America's legion of the damned," who "terrorized a city" and "scared a nation from end to end."[80] The advertising campaign took a different approach on April 20 when the controversy surrounding the film was highlighted: "The picture that powerful interests have tried to suppress—in the uncut, unaltered, original version!"[81] The day of the opening two different ads repeated the claim that the film was in its original, uncut form.

Released as scheduled on April 21, Philip K. Scheuer of the *Los Angeles Times* described the film as "the biggest of the gangland pictures" that combined "sheerly massive, Wagnerian effects" with "considerable dramatic merit." Scheuer noted that Hughes "finally forced it through in a practically intact condition."[82] The management at the Paramount Theatre reported that ticket sales for *Scarface* topped all recent records.

Hughes felt vindicated, but the MPPDA was appalled. The organization was not upset with the success of the film *per se* but rather the advertising used to promote it. Despite the fact that Hughes kept his word and released the latest MPPDA-approved version (version C with the ending from version B), the film was advertised as the uncut, original version. In a letter to Joseph Schenck, the MPPDA noted that "reprehensible phrases of this type of misrepresentation" could cause "potential difficulties to Caddo, to United Artists, to the Industry."[83] The MPPDA also worried that the false advertisements would hamper the ongoing negotiations to get the film released in New York.

The New York censors screened another revised version of the film on April 18, 1932. It was the "unanimous opinion" of the reviewers that there had "not been a substantial revision of the picture," and as a result, their rejection of *Scarface* stood.[84] Hughes finally had enough, so he decided it was time to try a radically different approach in the state.

As early as March, the press began to report that Hughes was willing to fight the censors if they refused to allow the film's exhibition. The *Los Angeles Times* reported that Hughes was now "ready to take the matter to the highest court," if necessary.[85] *Time* magazine also reported that Hughes "planned to argue his rights in court" to get *Scarface* shown in areas with censorship.[86]

To help determine if he could win such a suit, Hughes enlisted the council of Morris Ernst, a successful New York attorney who in 1917 co-founded the National Civil Liberties Bureau, the predecessor of the American Civil Liberties Union.[87] The threat of a lawsuit and the publicity it garnered greatly upset the MPPDA, an organization that was established to avoid such controversy. Echoing the sentiments the organization expressed about Hughes's marketing of the film in Los Angeles, the MPPDA stated that this type of legal action would cause "serious difficulty for the distributor and the Industry."[88]

In a telegram to Hughes, Al Lichtman of United Artists let Hughes know that his tactics were not helping the cause. "You promised to keep attorneys out of censorship proposition and if you do so promise get you results," Lichtman wrote, "but if you get these money hungry attorneys to interfere am afraid results will be disastrous."[89]

Hughes responded that his only desire was to see the original version shown in New York, and the attorneys he contacted, including Ernst, assured him they could win the case. Hughes did not want to further delay the release of the film while the case played out in court, but he felt the "publicity and added value original version would more than compensate."[90]

Hughes also let Lichtman know that he did not appreciate the publicity United Artists put out saying the version released in non-censorship areas had been cut according to the suggestions of the MPPDA. "Even if we had," Hughes conceded, "you know its injurious publicity."[91] Hughes argued that the public did not want to see censored films, so advertising the film as such would have a negative effect on its box office. Hughes ultimately assured Lichtman that he would not do anything without consulting United Artists, but it was clear that Hughes had not abandoned the idea of a lawsuit.

Hughes's threat of a lawsuit intensified when the New York censors denied the film yet again on April 25. Without consulting further with United Artists, as he promised, Hughes released statements to the press describing what he believed to be a conspiracy against the film. "It becomes a serious threat to the freedom of honest expression in America," Hughes declared, "when self-styled guardians of the public welfare, as personified by our film censor boards, lend their influence to abortive efforts of selfish and vicious interests to suppress a motion picture simply because it depicts the truth about conditions which constitute front-page news."[92]

Hughes went on to outline his intentions. "In order to obtain justice in the case of 'Scarface,'" he said, "I intend to file suit immediately in the New York State courts to restrain the New York censors from further interference with the exhibition of this picture in its original version."[93] Taking a shot at the MPPDA, Hughes noted that he expected to have the "support of Will H. Hays, head of the Motion Picture Producers' and Distributors' Association, who has said he believes censorship is un-American."[94] As noted in the press, Hughes's suit would be the "first time that any important film producer has gone to the courts to oppose censorship."[95]

Not surprisingly, the MPPDA was outraged. Frank W. Beetson of the MPPDA wrote candidly that Hughes's highly offensive comments were a deliberate attempt to undermine the association and Will Hays. "The situation," Beetson wrote, "is really hopeless."[96]

In an attempt at damage control, Al Lichtman wrote a letter to Hughes pointing out all that the MPPDA and United Artists had done on behalf of the film. "We have spent more time to get this picture passed," Lichtman observed, "than we have on all the other pictures released through United Artists combined."[97] Lichtman even went so far as to recommend that Hughes apologize to Hays for his recent actions.

Hughes did not apologize, and the threat of a lawsuit remained. But in spite of his posturing, Hughes continued to revise the New York print in an attempt to get the film passed. A new version was screened almost daily, and every revision failed to appease the New York censors. When the censors viewed the film on May 6, it was once again denied approval. It appeared the two sides would never reach an agreement, and a lawsuit seemed inevitable.

However, the censors noted for the first time that the film would be "satisfactory" if certain eliminations were made.[98] Somewhat surprisingly, the film had not been denied in its entirety. Wingate compiled a list of approximately twenty required cuts which he passed along to United Artists. Coupled with the revisions that had already been made during the months of negotiations, the eliminations reduced the violence directly shown onscreen, but it did not fundamentally alter the tone or scope of the movie.

Hughes did not like all of the required changes, especially having to use the ending which showed Camonte hanged for his crimes, but he agreed to make them to get the film passed in the most populous state. United Artists compiled a list of all the eliminations made, and it was agreed formally that they "will not be inserted therein in any exhibitions in New York State."[99] On May 11, 1932, after months of negotiations, the New York censors granted the film a certificate of approval for exhibition in the state.

The unexpected approval of the film came so abruptly that many individuals wondered how it ultimately came about. Chapin Hall of *The New York Times* wondered if the controversy "was noise of a manufactured variety" that was "not quite as deadly as it sounded."[100] Norbert Lusk of the *Los Angeles Times* speculated that Hughes's "controversy with the New York censors suddenly ended, probably, by his threat of a lawsuit."[101] Regardless of the reason, the film finally made its New York premiere at the Rialto on May 19, and it was reported that "the theatre has been packed ever since."[102]

Hughes was triumphant, and he publicly reveled in his success. "I am glad that the New York censors have reversed themselves in the case of 'Scarface,'" Hughes said in a statement released to the press, "as their original decision, if permitted to stand, would have been a serious blow to free and honest expression."[103]

Now that the film had been approved in New York, Hughes wanted to make sure it was marketed in a way he felt was appropriate. In other words, he specifically wanted to make sure that the film was not publicized in such a way that "might give New York public impression they will see a revised version of picture."[104] Hughes thought advertising it as such would result in a "bad reaction at boxoffice (*sic*) and be injurious publicity," so he asked the MPPDA not to make any statements about the required changes. Hughes fought a fierce battle over every single change, but he now argued that the changes did not need to be addressed because they were "minor and harmless."[105]

Will Hays replied that there was no reason for his office to issue any publicity about the film so long as Hughes's advertisements were in accord with the facts surrounding the case. In other words, the MPPDA would not say anything about the cuts so long as Hughes did not advertise the film as being the original, unaltered version. The MPPDA was willing to work with Hughes because they too were happy with the final result. "Never before has so difficult a problem been presented," Jason Joy wrote, "and never before has the result been so complete."[106]

The New York censorship board was the most powerful in the country, and after it approved the film, other censors followed suit.[107] With the exception of the city of Chicago, which was especially sensitive given its association with Capone, Hughes ultimately got the film passed everywhere in the country.[108]

Critics praised *Scarface*. The *Los Angeles Times*, *The New York Times*, *Film Daily*, and the National Board of Review all named it among the best movies of the year. But despite the critical success and the effort that went into getting it approved, the film was not profitable for Hughes. *Scarface* cost $711,915 and returned a producer's revenue (seventy percent of the total revenue) of only $612,788.[109] Interestingly, Hughes spent approximately $100,000 making changes demanded by the censors, an amount which ultimately made the film unprofitable for the producer.

Hughes nonetheless took pride in his accomplishment as an advocate of free speech. "I regard this, not only as a personal victory," he said, "but as a real triumph for the independence of the screen."[110] For Hughes, the battle with the censors was about more than just *Scarface*. The studio system was designed to eliminate outside competition, and as an independent producer, Hughes faced many obstacles. Determined to cement his status within the industry following *Hell's Angels*, Hughes came to believe that the major studios were using the censors to ruin his films and punish him for his independence. Initially resigned to try and work with the censors, Hughes ultimately made the monumental decision to directly confront the MPPDA and other censorship boards.

His threat to challenge the censors in court was unprecedented. Although Hughes did not follow through with legal action, the damage to the uniformity of the studio system was evident. It appeared that Howard Hughes, the independent producer, was once again vindicated in his struggle against the powerful studio system. "Until Howard Hughes brought the censorship crisis into the public limelight by compelling the powerful censor boards of the country to lift the bans on 'Scarface,'" Lincoln Quarberg wrote in a press release, "this sinister form of political regulation of the screen was obtaining a strangle hold on the industry."[111]

The film's violence clearly violated the tenants of the Motion Picture Production Code, but after battling the industry's governing body and the most powerful state censorship board, Hughes was successful in getting *Scarface* exhibited across the country. Hughes had triumphantly returned to the forefront of the motion picture industry, and he expected his victory to have long-term consequences for Hollywood and the American public. "I hope, for the benefit of other producers as well as myself," Hughes said, "that censorship in the future will not be exercised against films of this caliber, as the public is certainly entitled to be entertained, and to know what is going on in this country."[112]

Hughes may have won this round, but when he attempted to push the boundaries of onscreen sex with his next film, "Hollywood's fighting producer" quickly found out that he had inadvertently made the censors even more powerful.[113]

4

# The Picture
# That Couldn't Be Stopped

"The crazier a man is for a woman, the crazier he
thinks, and the crazier he acts."—Doc Holliday
(Walter Huston) in *The Outlaw*

After successfully confronting the censors over *Scarface*, Howard Hughes's
aviation exploits kept him away from the motion picture industry for
several years. When he returned late in 1939, he was much more than
a rich movie producer. He was now a national hero, and he was intent
upon further cementing his legacy in Hollywood. As he had done before,
Hughes continued to insist upon making films independently using his
ever-increasing wealth.

The Caddo Company, Hughes's original production company, was
disbanded in 1933, so he established Howard Hughes Productions,
a department of Hughes Tool, to make motion pictures. Although no
one "expected to relive the lush days when Hughes's Caddo Company
reputedly fired men who suggested ways of saving money," it soon became
evident that time had done little to change Howard Hughes.[1]

Hughes actually registered Hughes Productions as a member of
the MPPDA, a somewhat surprising move given his past actions and
comments. Hughes's decision to enroll, much like the *modus operandi* of
the association, may not have been completely voluntary. Hughes likely
felt obligated to join the MPPDA as the organization had increased its
stranglehold over the industry in the wake of *Scarface* and other attacks
on its hegemony.

Since its inception in 1922, the MPPDA responded to critiques, from
inside and out, by enacting more stringent regulations. The Motion Picture

Production Code of 1930, the cornerstone of the industry's "voluntary" self-censorship, was amended in 1934 to require all films made thereafter to obtain an official seal of approval from the organization which would appear onscreen at the outset of each picture.

The seal would be enforced by the newly established Production Code Administration (PCA) working in conjunction with the Advertising Code Administration (ACA). Through these two subsidiaries, the MPPDA monitored all aspects of a film, from its initial script to the marketing used to promote the completed picture. The code and the accompanying seal were enforced through "substantial and effective penalties" which included a $25,000 fine for every violation.[2]

While producers, distributors, and exhibitors were all subject to the fine, it especially subjugated exhibitors as multiple showings of a single film without a seal would result in multiple violations. This action "put teeth into the Production Code of 1930," and it kept "less responsible colleagues and competitors in line."[3] The MPPDA certainly considered Hughes less responsible, but it would take more than a seal of approval and the threat of a fine to keep him in line.

Upon his return to Hollywood, Hughes reteamed with director Howard Hawks and writer Ben Hecht, both of whom worked on *Scarface*. The duo ultimately came up with a western story ostensibly based on the life of famed outlaw Billy the Kid. Hughes liked the concept, and in July 1940, Jules Furthman was brought in to write the scenario. The independent Hughes signed a contract with Twentieth Century-Fox to distribute the film, which was titled *The Outlaw*.

For the main roles, Hughes was determined to cast unknowns. He had launched the careers of several successful actors, including Jean Harlow and Paul Muni, so he was certain he could repeat his past accomplishments. Hughes chose newcomer Jack Buetel, a twenty-five-year-old native of Dallas, Texas, for the lead role of Billy the Kid.[4] Hughes however knew that the real key to the film's success was the female lead Rio, as the movie would rest primarily on her shoulders. Hughes ultimately found the perfect candidate in a part-time receptionist named Jane Russell, but it was not because of her shoulders.

At 5-feet-7-inches tall, Russell had a bust that measured 37½ inches and hips that measured 35 inches. Her figure captivated Hughes upon their introduction, and along with eight other girls, Russell was tested in a haystack fight scene wearing a scooped blouse. "I shook the hay out of my hair and went home and forgot all about the test," Russell recalled. "Two weeks later I was a full-fledged starlet, with a seven-year contract (with options, of course) starting at $50 a week!"[5] With his latest find in place, Hughes set out to introduce the world to Jane Russell's breasts.

Filming on *The Outlaw* began on November 25, 1940, on the Navajo Nation in northern Arizona. Hughes did not accompany the cast and crew on location, but he did take an active role in all aspects of production. After only two weeks of shooting, Hughes and director Hawks found themselves locked in a heated dispute over expenditures. The conflict, according to a Hughes spokesman, resulted from the fact that Hawks was "going too fast" and not making the picture "lavish enough."[6]

Whereas Hughes wanted to spend upwards of $1,500,000 on the film, the director wanted to spend around $750,000. Hawks had a financial stake in the movie, and he was convinced that Hughes's budget would make a profit virtually impossible.[7] Douglas W. Churchill of *The New York Times* summed up the disagreement best: "The fight is notable on two accounts: it showed that Hughes's generosity has been unaltered by the years, and it is the first time Hawks had ever been accused of production parsimony."[8]

The two could not come to an agreement on a suitable budget moving forward so Hawks was relieved of his duties. It may have been the first time in the history of the motion picture industry that a director was fired for not spending enough money. The cast was subsequently recalled to Hollywood where they learned that Hughes had decided to take over as director, just as he had done on the set of *Hell's Angels*. But instead of going back on location, filming resumed almost immediately at the Samuel Goldwyn Studios where Hughes kept an office.

In contrast to Hughes's only other directing experience, the production went smoothly. A contingent of veteran industry players certainly helped. To compliment his inexperienced leads, Hughes filled out the rest of the cast with notable character actors, like Walter Huston and Thomas Mitchell, who brought stability to the set.

Behind the scenes, Hughes personally benefited from the insight of cinematographer Gregg Toland, one of the industry greats who had just finished working on Orson Welles's *Citizen Kane* (1941). Production manager Cliff Broughton made sure everything on and off set was kept in order, and when Hughes had to excuse himself from the production, often to attend to aviation and military concerns, writer Jules Furthman filled in as director.

With everyone pitching in, principal photography was completed early in February 1941. According to newcomer Russell, the entire process was a learning experience. "I couldn't have been greener," she said years later. "Whenever they asked me to bend over and pick up an apple or something, I went along with the gag."[9]

According to legend, Hughes even went so far as to use his knowledge of engineering to design a special bra to further accentuate the voluptuous actress. Interestingly, Russell both confirmed and denied the story over the years. "There was nothing to that story about Howard Hughes making a bra for me," she stated in her denial. "I don't know how that started, except that Howard was an engineer. It was just a good gimmick."[10]

But in her autobiography, Russell wrote that Hughes wanted a seamless bra, which didn't exist at the time, so he made her one, but it was "uncomfortable and ridiculous." She went on to say, "I *never* wore his bra, and believe me, he could design planes, but a Mr. Playtex he wasn't."[11] As an alternative to Hughes's contraption, she said she covered the seams on her original bra with tissue and pulled the straps to the side to give Hughes the look he desired onscreen. Whether the story of the bra is true or not, Hughes certainly spent a great deal of time, on and off camera, promoting Russell's breasts.[12]

Hughes knew he needed an extensive advertising campaign to publicize his latest film and his return to the motion picture industry. To achieve this goal, Hughes hired Russell Birdwell, Hollywood's highest-paid promoter who had recently spent years working on *Gone with the Wind*. Birdwell, like Hughes, knew Russell was the key to the film's success, and he focused on her in the initial advertising campaign.

The first major story about the film, which appeared in the February 4, 1941, edition of *"Pic"* magazine, described newcomer Russell as a "comely" and "voluptuous" beauty who was about to "blaze a trail to fame and fortune."[13] To supplement the article, images of Russell in a variety of action poses were included. In two of the pictures, including one where Russell was bending over chopping wood, a lot of cleavage was exposed. For 1940s Hollywood under the production code, the images were very risqué. For production manager Cliff Broughton, they were simply unacceptable.

Broughton wrote to Birdwell asking him how the pictures came to be published. Broughton pointed out that they were in "very bad taste," and the pictures certainly did not have the approval of Hughes Productions. Russell, according to Broughton, had no idea that "her breasts were in any way exposed."[14]

Regardless of who was responsible, Broughton noted that the damage had been done. "The fact remains, however, that these pictures have been published," he wrote, "and I am afraid that they may create, in the minds of the public, the wrong impression of Miss Russell who, as you know, has had no experience in this business, or she would never have allowed herself to be photographed in this manner, regardless of who the photographer was."[15]

In his response to Broughton, Birdwell denied responsibility and made it very clear that he was following all the rules the MPPDA had established regarding motion picture advertising. "As you know," Birdwell stated, "we do not release any photographs whatsoever made by anyone in our employ that do not have the seal of the Hays office."[16]

Nevertheless, Birdwell remarked that he was "not in the position to take pictures from a magazine representative and submit them to the Hays office because this would be completely a trespass on the freedom of the press rights."[17] Despite his assurances, it would become clear that Birdwell certainly agreed with and was even complicit in the exploitation centering on Russell's breasts.

The PCA received a copy of the script for *The Outlaw* from Hughes Productions in late December 1940, almost a month after production began. Joseph Breen, the head of the PCA, informed Hughes the film was in violation of the code for several reasons, including the characterization of Billy the Kid as a criminal who is allowed to go unpunished.

Breen also pointed out sequences suggestive of illicit sex between Billy and Rio, such as a "scene of struggle between Billy and Rio in the hayloft" and "the scene of Billy pulling Rio down on the bed and kissing her."[18] Breen had no idea at the time that the scenes involving Rio would be played by the voluptuous Russell in a low cut blouse. Writer Jules Furthman responded on behalf of Hughes, and in a conference with individuals from the PCA, he agreed to correct the major issues pointed out.

A completed version of the film was screened for the PCA on March 28, 1941, and the association got its first view of Jane Russell as Rio. Joseph Breen was horrified: "In my more than ten years of critical examination of motion pictures, I have never seen anything quite so unacceptable as the shots of the breasts of the character of Rio." Breen went on to say, "Throughout almost half the picture the girl's breasts, which are quite large and prominent, are shockingly emphasized and, in almost every instance, are very substantially uncovered."[19]

In an official letter to Hughes denying the film, Breen said that he had two major objections: the "countless shots of Rio, in which her breasts are not fully covered" and the inescapable suggestion that Rio has illicit relationships with both Billy and the character Doc Holliday.[20]

Hughes replied that he "endeavored diligently and sincerely" to produce an acceptable motion picture, so he appealed the decision of the PCA to the MPPDA board of directors, as was his right.[21] At the same time, Hughes and his associates began internal discussions about taking the MPPDA to court to force the issue.

Hughes's confidant Noah Dietrich, who was among other things a board member of Hughes Productions, thought a lawsuit was the best course of action. "It will attract more attention to the picture," Dietrich rationalized, "and, even if Fox refuses to release it, we can do a better job independently, eventually."[22]

Robert Savini of Astor Pictures, a distributor who often worked with Hughes, agreed with Dietrich. Besides the free advertising, Savini argued that a lawsuit would have far-reaching consequences for the industry. "It would eliminate the Hays seal because it is illegal to start with," Savini wrote, "and every independent producer would thank Howard."[23]

Russell Birdwell and attorney Neil McCarthy represented Hughes on May 15, 1941, at the formal appeal to the MPPDA board of directors. The board voted to sustain the decision of the PCA, but in a follow up letter, MPPDA spokesman Carl Milliken informed Hughes that the association's certificate of approval would be issued for *The Outlaw* "upon the condition that the following agreed changes be made in all prints of this picture which are to be publicly submitted."[24] Not surprisingly, all of the required changes dealt with shots of Russell's breasts.

Hughes seemed willing to make the changes, and he was ecstatic over what he viewed as another victory over the censors. "Cannot tell you how glad I am that you have succeeded," Hughes wrote in a telegram to McCarthy.[25] On May 23, 1941, the MPPDA officially granted *The Outlaw* seal of approval number 7440.

Given Hughes's record, Breen felt it necessary to stress to Hughes that the approval was based on Hughes making the required changes in "all prints put into general release." Breen also pointed out that "any and all advertising and publicity matter" must be submitted for approval to the ACA.[26] Hughes initially agreed to make the required cuts, but not surprisingly, he wanted to limit them as much as possible.

As the two sides negotiated, Hughes fought particularly hard to keep a scene where Rio saves Billy, who is suffering from the chills, by getting into bed with the outlaw to warm him up. The PCA demanded that the scene be cut to limit the impression of any sexual connotations, but Hughes argued that trimming that particular scene was not part of the original agreement. Hughes thus felt it should be left alone. The PCA was also concerned about a replacement shot Hughes added that "revealed more of the girl's breast than any other shot in the picture."[27] It appeared Hughes was up to his old tricks.

As discussions with the PCA continued, Hughes submitted the film to New York's Motion Picture Division in July 1941. In a letter denying the film, Irwin Esmond, the new director of the division, instructed Hughes to "eliminate all views where girl's breasts are exploited."[28] Much like his dealings with the PCA, Hughes began a dialogue with the New York censors in hopes of limiting the mandatory changes.

Hughes made some minor alterations to the film, and he got the number of required cuts down from eleven to three. Hughes verbally agreed to make the final cuts, but he actually only made small edits to the scenes in question. Not surprisingly, when the New York censors screened the latest version, it was denied yet again.

Hughes appealed the decision to the state's board of regents, stating that any further changes would "seriously injure the picture, as well as cause considerable additional expense."[29] Director Esmond, in his response, argued that the "eliminations so ordered had not been made" and the "so-called 'changes' made by the petitioner herein did not in any way change the objectionable character of the scenes and dialogue that was ordered eliminated."[30] Esmond stated very clearly that the film would be passed if the cuts were made. The board of regents agreed with Esmond, and Hughes's appeal was denied.

Hughes also submitted *The Outlaw* to other censorship boards across the country, and unlike New York, many passed the film with little or no changes whatsoever. The censors in Kansas City, Missouri, and Virginia passed the film in August and September, respectively, with no eliminations. The censors in the state of Massachusetts passed the film in September with minor changes to the scene where Russell attempts to warm up a freezing Buetel. Censors in the state of Kansas and the city of Chicago also passed the film in 1941.

The states of Pennsylvania and Ohio however proved to be more difficult. Hughes submitted the film to the censors in Pennsylvania in July 1941. The censors denied the film, initially requiring forty-nine revisions, but Hughes wore them down after several months of negotiation. Finally, in January 1942, the Pennsylvania censors agreed to pass the film under the condition that Hughes finally make four cuts that they had been demanding all along. As in New York, Hughes was unwilling to make the final changes to get the film passed.

The Pennsylvania censors believed that they had been "exceptionally lenient" in their dealings with Hughes, and they thought Hughes was "greedy" for his refusal to make the few cuts. The Pennsylvania censors went on to point out that if they were forced to review the film again, "it is quite possible that we would insist on a great many more cuts, particularly breast shots, due to the criticisms which we have been receiving recently from the public at large."[31]

Unfortunately for Hughes, a similar situation was also taking place with the Ohio censors. By June 1942, after months of negotiation, the Ohio censors were still insisting that four scenes and all the shots of "Rio where her breasts are unduly exposed" be eliminated.[32] Unwilling to concede in either instance, Hughes had reached yet another impasse. But his inability to get the film passed in several key markets was not the only thing delaying the general release of *The Outlaw*.

Individuals at Twentieth Century-Fox, the distributor of the film, were also finding it very difficult to work with Hughes. By April 1942, Fox had yet to receive a print of the film, and Hughes had not approved an official advertising campaign. Neil McCarthy, in a letter to Tom Connors, the individual handling the distribution for Fox, assured the company it would get a print very soon. "You know how Howard is," McCarthy wrote. "He is a stickler for perfection and wants the picture in what he considers perfect form before showing it to you."[33]

Connors was not reassured. "The delay in finishing it," he replied in May, "and the delay in delivering it to us has made me afraid of the picture itself."[34] Connors agreed on several occasions to push back the print's delivery date, and Hughes failed to deliver each time. Connors finally notified Hughes that he had not lived up to their agreement, and as a result, the distribution contract was terminated. *The Outlaw* now needed a new distributor.

In spite of the challenges the film still faced, Hughes wanted to roadshow *The Outlaw* in several key markets in an attempt to exploit the picture prior to its general release. Hughes told reporters that the roadshow would coincide with "one of the largest advertising campaigns in the history of motion pictures," and the film would be billed as "the picture that couldn't be stopped."[35] Russell Birdwell suggested the tagline, and in a telegram to Hughes, he conceded "it may lead us into some trouble."[36]

After Detroit was ruled out for the movie's premiere, Hughes settled on San Francisco. The city did not have a censorship board, but Neil McCarthy thought it was necessary to meet with San Francisco Mayor Angelo Rossi to assure him that *The Outlaw* was "not an immoral picture."[37] As McCarthy was reassuring the mayor, Hughes flooded the city with lurid advertisements of Russell.

The most notable was a large billboard that depicted Russell wearing a low cut blouse lying in a haystack with a gun in one hand.[38] As one contemporary described it, the image flaunted "the ripe young figure of Jane Russell with very little on above the waist except an expression of sultry threat."[39] To reinforce the sexual nature of the image, the billboard stated emphatically that "Sex has not been rationed," a reference to World War II conservation efforts which were ongoing. Whether or not the content of the film was immoral remained to be seen, but many citizens of San Francisco certainly believed the advertising was indecent.

The police department was inundated with complaints, and San Francisco Chief of Police Charles W. Dullea felt compelled to take action. Dullea ordered Hughes to take down all the billboards, and although no city official had seen the actual film, Dullea ordered that screenings be delayed until Hughes abided by his ruling. Hughes was reluctant to do so, but he believed the advertising had created such a buzz that he was determined to debut the film in the city at any cost.

Hughes thus removed the billboards, and a new premiere date was scheduled for February 5 at the Geary Theatre. Hughes wanted the film to have a lavish opening, but the government mandated wartime blackout forced him to curtail many of his plans. Hughes nonetheless made sure the premiere received a lot of publicity by inviting over fifty Hollywood syndicate writers and correspondents to cover the event.

In the film, Doc Holliday (Walter Huston) arrives in Lincoln County where his friend Pat Garrett (Thomas Mitchell) has been appointed sheriff. Doc is searching for his stolen horse Red which is in the possession of the outlaw Billy the Kid (Buetel). Doc finds Billy and the two strike up an unlikely friendship. Billy needs a place to stay so Doc invites him back to his house. When Billy arrives, he is violently confronted by Doc's girlfriend Rio (Russell) whose brother was killed by Billy. Billy subdues Rio and appears to force himself on her.

Garrett, resentful of Doc and Billy's new friendship, attempts to arrest Billy for a murder. Billy manages to escape with Doc's help, but Billy is wounded. Doc arranges for Billy to hide out with Rio who is now infatuated with the outlaw. When Billy's wound leads to a terrible fever, Rio starts to undress and remarks, "I'll keep him warm." Doc is jealous when he learns of their emerging relationship. Billy hopes to placate his friend by offering him the choice between Rio and the horse Red. Doc chooses Red which upsets Billy.

Rio is furious at both men, so she helps Garrett track them down. They are arrested and taken prisoner. On their way to jail, the three men are pursued by renegade Indians. Garrett returns their guns, and they manage to elude their pursuers. Doc tries to escape in the aftermath with Red, but Billy pulls his guns on Doc in an attempt to keep the horse. When Billy refuses to fire at his friend, Garrett shoots Doc in a fit of rage. Garrett also tries to kill Billy, but the outlaw outsmarts him and manages to flee. Billy comes across Rio and invites her to join him. She happily agrees.[40]

The reviews were universally negative. Edwin Schallert of the *Los Angeles Times* said the film was "one of the weirdest westerns pictures that ever unreeled before the public."[41] Alexander Fried of the *San Francisco Examiner* blamed the film's failings on Hughes: "His inexperience as a solo director is manifest in the film's slow pace and its laborious emphasis of ludicrously incredible details of romance and melodrama."[42] Claude A. La Belle of the *San Francisco News* commented that the film's release was not delayed long enough. "For our part," La Belle wrote, "he could have kept it locked up for another two years."[43]

*Time* magazine summed up the reaction best: "The audience, politely embarrassed, sat quietly for some time, the critics exchanging incredulous stares as the picture grew steadily cornier. Finally the audience broke down utterly, laughing at serious scenes, groaning at funny ones."[44]

All the reviewers seemingly felt compelled to comment on Russell, Hughes's latest discovery.[45] "Miss Russell's acting talent is undetermined," Schallert wrote of the film's main attraction, "but then that's not exactly what's emphasized in the picture."[46] La Belle noted that Russell was a "sultry beauty" who "has been endowed by nature with a conversation-making torso."[47] *Time* described the "full-breasted" Russell as having a "flaring femininity."[48]

Given the publicity surrounding Russell, many critics conceded that *The Outlaw* would probably do good business, despite the negative reviews. And initial reports seemed to confirm the popularity of the film (or Russell), as the *Los Angeles Times* reported that the film did "enormous business" during its opening week.[49]

Russell Birdwell, in an advertisement designed to look like a news article that ran nationally after the premiere, confirmed that the popularity of the film was due to the appeal of Russell. Once again proclaiming "sex has not yet been rationed," Birdwell described Russell as the "most exciting girl who ever came from the Hollywood incubators." Birdwell went on to argue that great stories, whether they are books, plays, or movies, are all based on sex and action. *The Outlaw* was no exception, but Hughes still had to fight the censors for two years in order to show audiences "the picture that couldn't be stopped."[50]

Birdwell ended the advertisement with a bold statement: "'The Outlaw,' as it is running today, is exactly as Hughes made it. Not one inch of the film has been removed, and any efforts to delete a single piece of the film wherever it may play will be greeted with the toughest court fight that time and patience and resources can wage."[51]

Birdwell's claims aside, many found the film and its advertising offensive, including the National Legion of Decency. Established in 1934, the organization was dedicated to identifying and combating objectionable content in motion pictures.[52] Highly influential, the Legion bound pledge-signers to "remain away from all motion pictures except those which do not offend decency and Christian morals."[53]

The Legion rated films as A-I for morally unobjectionable for general patronage, A-II for morally unobjectionable for adults, B for morally objectionable in part for all, or C for condemned. Just like other censorship organizations, producers often worked with the Legion in an attempt to avoid receiving a C rating.

Hughes never submitted *The Outlaw* to the Legion prior to the premiere in San Francisco, and not surprisingly, the organization condemned the film as soon as they had a chance to screen it. Reverend W. L. O'Connor, one of the reviewers for the Legion, was asked unofficially how the film could be modified to improve its rating. "If any modification were made, the picture would have little or no appeal," he answered. "The only attraction is the objectionable scenes, and I place it in the C because of those objectionable scenes."[54]

The MPPDA was also concerned about the film. The PCA seal of approval was granted in May 1941 on the conditions that all advertising would be submitted for approval and all prints would be exact copies of the one approved. The San Francisco advertising was not sent to the MPPDA prior to its use, and after lengthy discussions between representatives for Hughes and the MPPDA, it was agreed that the matter was a "closed issue" so long as the Hughes organization submitted all future advertising.[55]

As for the movie itself, the MPPDA wanted to make sure the San Francisco print was the approved version. They requested a print from Hughes, and after screening it, they determined it was different from the one being exhibited in San Francisco. Asked to explain why, Hughes said he was "cutting the picture because critics had commented upon its unusual and unnecessary length."[56] While the MPPDA deemed the version submitted as acceptable under the code, they reminded Hughes that all changes required MPPDA approval.

Despite the ensuing controversy, or maybe because of it, the film went on to play in San Francisco for several weeks. Hughes wanted to follow the San Francisco run with an exhibition in Detroit, the city he initially considered for the premiere. Negotiations with the city's censorship board ensued, and as he had done in the past, Hughes was able to wear the censors down. In March 1943, a version acceptable to Hughes was passed in the city. *The New York Times* reported a month later that Hughes purchased the RKO Downtown Theatre in Detroit, at a reported cost of $350,000, to exhibit the film.[57]

As Hughes was preparing the film for its second city, he officially submitted it to the Legion in May. The organization reported that any changes made were insignificant, and the film should thus remain in the condemned classification. Hughes quickly came to realize that he would have a hard time showing the film in Detroit or any other city until the Legion reclassified it. "Aside from its reflection upon [Hughes] as a producer and upon those connected with the picture," Ed Rafferty, president of United Artists, said of the Legion's condemnation, "it will undoubtedly reduce very greatly the amount of money that can be recovered with it."[58]

Distributor Robert Savini said Hughes would have to learn how to work with the Legion and other censors if he wanted to succeed in the business: "You see, Noah, this is the way everybody else does [it] and unless Howard does it this way, he will always have trouble."[59] In his reply, Dietrich reminded Savini that Hughes was not like everybody else. "You should know by this time that he is an individualist," Dietrich wrote, "and you can't expect him to perform according to customs and traditions."[60]

Hughes, true to form, refused to give in to the demands of the Legion. The film was not reclassified, and it was never exhibited in Detroit. After the San Francisco run, *The Outlaw* once again disappeared from the screen, a status that continued into 1944. Many began to question whether it would ever be seen again. "No one has any authority to book 'The Outlaw' any place," Dietrich confided in a letter to Savini, "and I am beginning to question whether or not it will ever be booked any place, just between you and me."[61]

Hughes however had not given up, and in December 1944, he signed a distribution deal with United Artists that covered *The Outlaw*. The contract stated that Hughes had the final say in all matters related to censorship, and no set date or timeframe was given for the film's general release. Although Jane Russell continued to receive a great deal of publicity, much of it spearheaded by Russell Birdwell, the film remained on the shelf for all of 1945.

Besides the Legion of Decency classification, the New York censors' denial of *The Outlaw* remained one of the biggest obstacles to the film's general release. When the state denied the film in May 1942, Neil McCarthy wrote to attorney George Medalie, the former United States attorney for the Southern District of New York, about the possibility of filing a lawsuit in an attempt to get the film passed. "This girl [Russell] has large breasts and improper exposure of her bare breasts is probably subject to criticism," McCarthy wrote to Medalie, "but I feel this picture has been prejudiced."[62] McCarthy wanted to know if Medalie thought a lawsuit would be successful and if he would be willing to represent Hughes.

In his response, Medalie said Hughes had very little chance of winning such a suit. "In cases of this character, where there is a reasonable basis for the determination and where the determination is not arbitrary or capricious," Medalie noted, "the courts will not disturb the findings."[63] Medalie thus advised against filing a lawsuit, and he told McCarthy that he would not conduct it.

Russell Birdwell also advised against using the courts. "If suit in New York against censor board is solely for purposes of publicity," Birdwell stated, "I would like to advise I do not feel we need it for campaign, and I am rather afraid it may react upon us unfavorably in opening spots."[64]

Whether Hughes listened to the advice or simply thought the timing was wrong, he did not file a lawsuit against the New York censors in 1942. In fact, Hughes took no additional action in the state for almost four years.

Hughes eventually filed an application with New York's Motion Picture Division for a license for a revised version of *The Outlaw* in January 1946.

The film was denied, but somewhat surprisingly, the censors demanded only one elimination to a line of dialogue. When Billy tries to return Rio to Doc after she has nursed him back to health, Doc replies, "Cattle do not graze after sheep." The censors found the line indecent, and they ordered its removal. No mention was made of Russell or her anatomy.

Hughes had refused to cut the film further in 1942, but this time he relented. The line was removed, and on February 13, 1946, the film finally was licensed for exhibition in the state of New York. The approval for *The Outlaw*, just like that of *Scarface* over a decade earlier, seemed to come out of nowhere. In fact, *The New York Times* did not report the change in status until two months later in April.

It appeared that Hughes had once again successfully worn down the censors, but as months stretched into years, Hughes made significant alterations to the film in order to get it licensed. When the film was first submitted to the New York censors on July 2, 1941, the film measured 10,969 feet, but the final approved version measured 10,423 feet. In other words, Hughes removed more than 500 feet of film in order to get the film passed.

After the approval by the state of New York, other censorship boards throughout the country began to pass the film with only minor alterations. The city of Atlanta approved the film in February 1946, while the state of Massachusetts passed the film in March. That same month, Hughes was notified that the National Board of Review also passed the film. After years of delays, it seemed *The Outlaw* finally would be exhibited across the country. Unfortunately for Hughes, a new and even bigger controversy was beginning to take shape.

United Artists submitted the film's advertising to the ACA in preparation for the general release of the film, a requirement given the PCA seal of approval granted in 1941. Gordon White, the director of the ACA, stated definitively in a letter to United Artists that all of the one-, three-, and six-sheet posters submitted for the film were unacceptable.

White pointed out that his office had been through a long period of discussion and negotiation with members of the Hughes organization about the images of Russell that would appear on the posters. Although an acceptable image had been agreed upon, Hughes nevertheless used an image of Russell that had not been approved. White felt that Hughes's actions were a "deliberate effort to produce posters in violation of the Advertising Code."[65]

United Artists assured White that they were only acting on Hughes's behalf, and they asked him to take the issue up with Hughes directly. In other words, United Artists was distributing the film, but they certainly were not going to fight Hughes's battles for him. Hughes was informed of the rejection, and he responded by appealing the matter to the president of the Motion Picture Association of America (MPAA), the new name for the MPPDA, which was changed in 1945.[66]

The appeal argued that the advertising material presented "natural proportions of the female figure, fully-clothed and without emphasis, distortion or salacious intent," which certainly was "not detrimental to the prestige and reputation of the motion picture industry as a whole."[67] Many of the advertisements mentioned the battle with the various censorship boards throughout the country, and the appeal justified the use of such language as necessary to explain the film's five-year delay in being released.

The appeal also tried to justify using the phrase "Exactly as it was filmed—Not a Scene Cut." Hughes admitted that various censorship boards had required "certain trimmings," but the appeal attempted to argue that no production was ever completely "filmed" until it had been approved by the PCA. In other words, the film had not been altered since its approval in 1941, thus "'The Outlaw' is 'exactly as filmed' before the PCA at the time it was approved."[68] Although that statement was blatantly false, the film had been altered substantially since 1941, Hughes complained he was being treated differently because he was an independent producer who made very few films when compared to the output of the major studios.[69] Hughes's arguments proved unsuccessful, and the appeal was denied.

Hughes actually went ahead and released *The Outlaw* in several cities throughout the country while the appeal was being heard. The film debuted in Chicago around March 13, and Albert Goldberg of the *Chicago Daily Tribune* noted that it had "survived national censorship unscathed."[70] The film was released in Los Angeles the first week of April, and Philip K. Scheuer of the *Los Angeles Times* thought the "sex passages" went "as far as any since the establishment of censorship, or farther."[71]

*Time* magazine, in its description of the re-release of the film, noted that in Hollywood "'talent' is one of the synonyms for bosom" and everyone knows Russell is "Hollywood's most talented actress."[72] Russell's allure and the controversy surrounding the film helped drive patrons to the theatre, and influential gossip columnist Hedda Hopper reported that *The Outlaw* was doing "phenomenal business."[73]

The re-release of the film coincided with a huge advertising campaign, all of which centered on Russell. One ad, similar to the banned billboard used in San Francisco prior to the film's premiere, had a drawing of Russell lying in a haystack wearing a low cut blouse, which exposed significant cleavage, as she clutched a gun in one hand. The text asked, "How would you like to tussle with Russell?"[74]

Another ad had a drawing of Russell, depicted from above the waist, with even more cleavage. The text read, "What are the two great reasons for Jane Russell's rise to stardom?... She's daring and exciting." Another *double entendre* read simply, "Here They Are!"[75] Some images showed Russell and Buetel locked in a passionate embrace as the two appeared to be consummating their relationship.

Moving beyond the page, for the film's exhibition in Pasadena, California, Hughes hired a skywriting airplane to fly over the city. After spelling out *The Outlaw*, the plane drew two huge circles side by side and placed a dot in the center of each. For many individuals, both in and out of the motion picture industry, Hughes had gone way too far.

It was reported that several publications, including *Photoplay*, refused to run the advertisements. In a letter to Joseph Breen, producer and studio executive Darryl F. Zanuck fumed that the "whole campaign on this picture is a disgrace to the industry and I am on the verge of publicly attacking Howard Hughes with a blast in the newspapers."[76] Archbishop John J. Cantwell of Los Angeles publicly condemned the film and its advertising as "morally offensive to Christian and American womanhood."[77] After repeated complaints and several inquiries into the status of the film, the MPAA felt compelled to act.

The organization wrote a strongly worded letter to Hughes dated April 9, 1946. "Your conduct," the letter began, "in connection with the advertising and exploitation of THE OUTLAW, in the opinion of the Board of Directors of this Association, constitutes grounds for proceedings pursuant to Article XVI of its by-laws for your suspension or expulsion from membership." According to the MPAA, Hughes "openly and repeatedly" violated the tenants of the MPAA by not submitting advertisements for the film, and on the few occasions that he did submit the advertising, he nevertheless used images that had been denied by the organization.[78]

Hughes was summoned to appear before the MPAA board of directors in New York on April 23. *The New York Times* reported that this was the first time that the organization openly threatened to expel a member. In a statement issued jointly with the release of the association's formal letter to Hughes, MPAA president Eric Johnston declared that Hughes "voluntarily subscribed" to the rules of the association and, by using banned advertisements, he "has challenged the association's system of self-regulation."[79] Hughes, as one would expect, was livid.

"I think it is about time people quit trying to tell the American public what it can see, read or listen to," Hughes fumed.[80] One day prior to the mandatory meeting with the MPAA, Hughes issued a more detailed statement which began by stating that *The Outlaw* was playing throughout the country "exactly as it was filmed. Not a scene has been cut." Hughes went on to explain that he wanted the public to know why the film had been delayed, but the MPAA forbid him from even mentioning censorship. "In any event," Hughes said, "the Hays office has no right to tell me that I cannot inform the public of something which is true and a fact." Hughes believed the MPAA was part of a group boycott against him and a violation of the country's antitrust laws. "Therefore," Hughes proclaimed, "I am delivering to the Hays office my resignation, effective immediately."[81]

Hughes also decided it was finally time to take the matter to court, and he initiated a $5,000,000 suit against the MPAA. *Hughes Tool Company v. Motion Picture Association of America*, filed in the United States District Court for the Southern District of New York, laid out a litany of offenses against the organization, all of which centered on its required seal of approval.

> The defendant [the MPAA], by its rigid control over the supply of these pictures, has compelled more than ninety percent of the exhibiting theatres within the United States to accept, book and exhibit only "sealed" pictures and no others, and to refuse to book and exhibit "un-sealed" pictures under economic coercion and the threat of having their supply of "sealed" pictures entirely shut off. In consequence, more than ninety percent of all exhibiting theatres in the United States do refuse to exhibit pictures which do not have the seal of the defendant.[82]

Besides sizable monetary compensation, Hughes sought a ruling which would overturn the MPAA's rejection of *The Outlaw's* advertising material and refrain the organization from rescinding its seal of approval, thus ending an "unlawful system of private censorship."[83]

As the lawsuit was beginning, Hughes continued to exhibit the film in additional locales across the country, with or without the approval of the MPAA. Three years after the film first premiered in San Francisco, it opened to the public again on April 23, 1946, at the United Artists Theatre. The following day, local police raided the theatre, confiscated all prints, and arrested the theatre's manager, Allister Dunn, on misdemeanor charges of exhibiting a movie "offensive to decency."[84] The case made its way through the courts, and May 17, judge Twain Michelsen argued that Dunn's exhibition of the film had not violated the city's code on decency.

Citing everything from case law to the Salem Witch Trials to the work of Leonardo da Vinci, judge Michelsen found nothing immoral in the film and questioned those who did. Michelsen stated that Russell was a "comely" and "attractive specimen of American womanhood," and he wondered why a "mind so vulgar, so lewd and lascivious, so suggestive and obscene" would object to her inclusion in the film simply "because

God made her what she is."[85] A jury agreed with the judge, and Dunn was found not guilty.

A similar situation with a similar outcome took place when the film was shown in Alexandria, Louisiana, at the Joy Theatre. On June 11, the chief of police led a group of officers on a raid of the establishment. The manager of the theatre was arrested and convicted the following day for violating the city's indecency and immorality laws. Although his fine and jail sentence were suspended, city officials threatened harsher action if the film was ever exhibited again.

The theatre company filed suit arguing the city did not have the right to censor the film. The city countered that it was not censorship, but the judge in the case argued that the arrest and fining of the manager constituted "a pretty effective form of censorship of that particular film."[86] Ruling in favor of the theatre, the city was enjoined from taking any further action to interfere with the exhibition of the film, which resumed the following day.

It appeared that Hughes was winning the battle to show *The Outlaw*, but his action against the MPAA had yet to be settled. On June 14, Hughes's string of victories came to an abrupt end when the presiding judge in the case against the industry watchdog ruled against Hughes. "[Hughes Tool] is perfectly willing to accept the benefit of the seal which it says will give it entry into all of the 18,000 theatres in the United States," wrote judge John Bright, "but is not willing to accept the conditions under which it may operate with the seal." The judge stated unequivocally that Hughes was guilty of violating the code on multiple occasions, so he had no right to argue that he was being discriminated against. "In fact," the judge declared, "it seems more an effort on the part of the plaintiff to add this case and its peregrinations through the courts as additional publicity and advertising in promotion of the picture."[87]

In response to the court's decision, Joseph Breen wrote to Hughes on September 6 to inform him that the certificate of approval granted in 1941 "is hereby voided and revoked" for failing to submit and for using unapproved advertising.[88] "The censors may not like it," Hughes replied, "but the public does. If the association is going to try to keep the public from seeing this picture, it appears to me that it is assuming the position of a dictator in the selection of public entertainment."[89]

Stripped of its seal, it was reported the MPAA demanded that *The Outlaw* be withdrawn from member theatres. As one writer accurately observed, "withdrawal of the seal means that the Jane Russell vehicle cannot be shown in some 85% of the nation's theatres, including practically all of the bigger showhouses."[90]

At the same time, the MPAA was forced to reveal that the $25,000 fine for showing a film without a seal had been quietly rescinded months earlier. In other words, theatres could show *The Outlaw*, or any other film devoid of a seal, without immediate financial reprisal. But in reality, the dominance and fear of the Big Five still kept exhibitors from doing so, at least initially.

The bad news for Hughes continued when Benjamin Fielding, New York City's license commissioner, tried to get the state's censorship board to rescind the approval of the film granted in February. Fielding was responsible for overseeing individual theatres in the city, a position which gave him considerable influence over motion pictures within city limits, but the power to truly ban the film rested with the state's Motion Picture Division.

After several months of claims and counterclaims, Ward C. Bowen, the acting director of the state's Motion Picture Division, noted that the advertising in question consisted primarily of billboards displayed in San Francisco in conjunction with the film's premiere in 1943. Since his authority was limited to advertising used within New York, Bowen ruled that the petition to revoke the film's approval was denied. Fielding appealed the ruling to the New York board of regents where Bowen's decision was upheld.

Hughes was winning again, so he turned his attention back to the Legion of Decency. The film had been on the Legion's condemned list since 1943, a status that kept it out of many theatres. Hughes made some of the association's required changes and submitted it for reclassification, but at the same time, he promoted the film in some locales as "the picture condemned by the Catholic Legion of Decency."[91] The Legion was furious and terminated all negotiations with Hughes soon after they had resumed.

Finally recognizing the power of the Legion, Hughes enlisted Martin J. Quigley, a prominent Catholic publisher who helped craft the Motion Picture Production Code, to salvage the situation. Quigley agreed to help, and like many before him, he grew frustrated when Hughes said he would make changes but did not follow through. At one point in the negotiations, Noah Dietrich reminded Quigley and others associated with the Legion that Hughes did not operate with the "same urgency that exists with the regular motion picture production companies."[92]

The statement turned out to be prophetic, as Hughes spent the next two years negotiating with the Legion over minor changes. Hughes contemplated bringing a lawsuit against the Legion, but his advisors cautioned it would be "extremely bad policy."[93] In the end, the two sides finally came to an agreement with Quigley's assistance, and the film was reclassified from C (condemned) to B (morally objectionable in part for all), on October 10, 1949, six years after the film was originally condemned.

The MPAA was now the only organization that stood in the way of the film's national release. Unlike the Legion of Decency, Hughes had no problem taking the industry's internal organization to court. In January 1949, Hughes Tool filed another suit against the MPAA, this time arguing that the association was in violation of antitrust laws.

Director Gordon White of the ACA grew so tired of the battle that he was now willing to approve anything that "I could later justify without completely stultifying my own conscience."[94] Hughes ultimately agreed to curtail some of the more salacious advertising, and two weeks after the Legion reclassification, the PCA reinstated the seal of approval. Hughes's latest lawsuit was eventually withdrawn.

Having seemingly beaten the censors, despite the fact that Hughes made significant changes over the years, Hughes also appeared to have won at the box office. As the film was facing significant challenges in 1946, Hughes solicited comments from exhibitors across the country. The replies were almost universally positive, with comments ranging from "breaking all house records" to "the only picture in the history of the theatre that was ever held over."[95] The *Hollywood Reporter* proclaimed it was "among the first five of the greatest film grossers of all time."[96] Other magazines and newspapers expressed similar sentiments.

But like previous Hughes films, internal company documents show the publicized numbers to be an exaggeration. An analysis of the film's financials, dated March 31, 1950, listed a gross rental of $3,760,567, a figure which was not even among the top five earners of the 1940s.[97] Although the film did not break any records, it did do very well at the box office, despite the fact that it did not have a MPAA seal of approval for a significant period.

The film's success was possible, in large part, because Hughes's actions made exhibitors aware "that they can show pictures lacking a Seal of Approval without fear of being fined."[98] When the $25,000 penalty was initially imposed in 1934, it effectively made voluntary regulation involuntary. Exhibitors faced the most significant financial reprisal, and they had no choice but to further accede to the demands of the Big Five and the MPAA.

When the fine was ultimately rescinded in 1946 over fears it would be used in antitrust suits against the industry, the MPAA did not make it publicly known because it had been such an effective deterrent. Hughes's battle over *The Outlaw* brought the change to light, and exhibitors now knew they could show any movie they wanted. In the words of Ruth A. Inglis, a noted scholar on censorship, this "unquestionably weakened the enforcement mechanism of self-regulation," a key component used by the MPAA and the major corporations to dominate the industry.[99]

When Hughes first challenged the censors over the violent content of *Scarface*, he embarked on a path that would have far-reaching consequences for all of Hollywood. *The Outlaw* brought the journey to fruition. Because of the MPAA and the production code, the motion picture industry produced films that showcased a static and often unrealistic version of American life. Hughes, who was beholden to no one and unwilling to accede to dictates from others, used his position as an independent producer to tackle subjects that American movies were supposed to avoid. In doing so, he took storytelling in a radically different direction. "It is another instance," lamented an officer of the MPAA, "of what Mr. Hughes's conduct has brought upon the industry."[100]

Hughes also became the embattled advocate of free speech. And by directly challenging the MPAA in court, Hughes opened a flood gate that culminated with the United States Supreme Court ruling in 1952 that motion pictures are "included within the free speech and free press guaranty of the First and Fourteenth Amendments."[101] Although the production code limped into the 1960s, Hughes and *The Outlaw* helped bring about an end to movie censorship, paving the way for future generations of filmmakers.[102] Given all that he had accomplished in such a short time, Hughes's impact as an independent producer was substantial. But his biggest challenge to the studio system was yet to come.

# The Finale of the Studio Epoch

"I don't think very much of anything."—
Sam Hurley (Stephen McNally) in *Split Second*

Howard Hughes spent years in the motion picture industry toiling as an independent producer. Despite facing numerous challenges, especially given the control and influence the Big Five exerted over the studio system, Hughes managed to change the way movies were made, and he pushed the boundaries of what was acceptable onscreen. It appeared that Hughes was close to achieving his goal of becoming the world's most famous motion picture producer.

But Hughes always knew that there were limitations to being an independent producer. He only managed to make approximately a dozen movies over the course of twenty years, while a typical studio put out over forty films in a given season. To truly revolutionize the industry, Hughes needed a studio where he could make as many films as he wanted. A studio would also give him a dedicated distribution network and theatres across the country to exhibit his movies. And as a mogul, Hughes could continue his radical approach to filmmaking on an even greater scale.

Stories of Hughes wanting to purchase a studio date to his entrance into the industry, and Hughes admitted that he "almost bought the controlling interest of RKO back in 1933."[1] Internal company documents reveal that he considered acquiring RKO again in 1940, and around the same time, he also looked into Columbia Pictures.

It was ultimately determined that it was "better at present to take a chance on collecting profits from individual pictures than from attempting to invest the amount which would be required in a large production company and trying to operate at a profit."[2] But given his vast resources,

Hughes continued to explore the possibility of buying a studio over the years, with RKO being a likely target.

The Radio-Keith-Orpheum Corporation was one of the Big Five of the studio system. It was established in 1928 when the Radio Corporation of America (RCA) acquired and merged the Keith–Albee–Orpheum Corporation (KAO) theatre chain with the Film Booking Offices of America (FBO), a production and distribution organization. Vertically integrated from the start, the newly established company was initially created to give RCA a guaranteed market for its sound-on-film technology RCA Photophone, one of four such methods competing for dominance as the motion picture industry transitioned to sound.

Corporate executives, which included RCA's David Sarnoff, believed RKO would one day be a giant entertainment conglomerate that combined film, vaudeville shows, radio broadcasts, and television—then in its experimental stage—into a symbiotic package. Unfortunately, the grand designs were never realized as RKO existed in a perpetual state of transition over the next two decades. Unlike the other members of the Big Five, RKO lacked continuity of management and never evolved an overall style unique to the studio.

RKO nevertheless managed to produce classics of nearly every type: the western—*Cimarron* (1931); the horror film—*King Kong* (1933); the musical—*Swing Time* (1936); comedy—*Bringing Up Baby* (1938); the adventure film—*Gunga Din* (1939); the suspense thriller—*Notorious* (1946); *film noir*—*Out of the Past* (1947); and the most extraordinary and influential picture of the entire studio era—*Citizen Kane*. But the company was always the weakest of the Big Five financially, and it languished in bankruptcy receivership for many years. This made it a likely target for acquisition.

Despite reports that Hughes intended "to abandon his motion picture activities 'temporarily'" in the aftermath of *The Outlaw* to focus on his aviation interests, he actually began negotiations in earnest late in 1947 to acquire controlling interest in RKO.[3] Nearly four million RKO shares were outstanding, and the largest single stockholder was investor Floyd Odlum's Atlas Corporation which owned 929,020 shares.

Odlum was a lawyer by training, and after moving into financing, he founded the Atlas Corporation in 1928.[4] Anticipating the stock market crash in 1929, Odlum fortuitously converted Atlas's holdings into cash which he used to acquire companies at bargain prices. He was described at the time as "possibly the only man in the United States who made a great fortune out of the depression."[5]

The diversified Atlas Corporation came to own stock in several entertainment companies, with Odlum serving at one point on the board of Paramount Pictures. Odlum first acquired a sizable stake in RKO in 1935, and he expanded Atlas's holdings until it was the single largest shareholder. After bringing RKO onto firm financial footing in the aftermath of the Great Depression, Odlum grew weary of the challenges facing the industry. He was especially concerned with the government's ongoing antitrust case against the major studios.

Odlum was willing to dispose of his holdings but only if he could find the ideal buyer. "Under today's almost panicky conditions in the production end of the movie industry," Odlum stated, "it is doubtful if any person or group of substance within the industry has the combined money and nerve to meet the faith of the Atlas Corporation in the industry."[6] If there were two things Howard Hughes had it was money and nerve.

Odlum and Hughes were both fierce negotiators, and the two industrial titans spent months bickering over the terms of the deal. Odlum initially dismissed the idea of a sale altogether. "It is true that Howard Hughes has recently had some general and tentative conversations relating to the purchase of RKO stock," he said in a statement released to the press, "but these conversations could hardly be classified as negotiations."[7]

The *Hollywood Report's* banner headline on January 29, 1948, announced that an agreement had been reached, but *Variety* countered with its own headline on April 8 that the negotiations had ended in failure.[8] Gossip columnist Hedda Hopper stated definitively that same day that the "deal is off, finished and closed."[9] Finally, on May 3, fellow gossip columnist Louella Parsons was one of the first to report correctly that "Howard Hughes is the new boss of the RKO Studios."[10]

Hughes paid $8,825,690 cash or $9.50 a share for Atlas's holdings. "There never has been a deal in the history of the motion picture industry that involved a flat financial exchange of such magnitude," proclaimed Hedda Hopper.[11] Hughes acquired approximately twenty-four percent and controlling interest in the Radio–Keith–Orpheum Corporation, which was composed primarily of two subsidiaries: RKO Radio Pictures, a production and distribution organization, and RKO Theatres.[12] With the signing of a check, the independent Hughes was now a studio mogul.

When the deal was finally consummated, Odlum made it clear that he made a conscious decision to sell to Hughes.

The tentative contract that Howard Hughes and I entered into several days ago permitted me to withdraw if within a period of time I should obtain a higher cash offer from others. I have received such an offer but notwithstanding this, I today made the purchase agreement with Howard Hughes firm and final and the shares will change hands within the next day or two. I accepted the Hughes deal in preference to the alternative bid, having in mind Mr. Hughes's indicated plans with respect to the company.[13]

Odlum did not provide any additional information on Hughes's indicated plans, and he also failed to disclose a stipulation in the sales agreement that he hoped would be to his future financial benefit.[14]

When Hughes acquired controlling interest in RKO, the government's antitrust case loomed over Hollywood. Antitrust complaints against the motion picture industry dated back to the early twentieth century and the establishment of the Motion Picture Patents Company (MPPC). The MPPC was forced to disband, but in its wake, the advent of the studio system gave rise to an even more powerful monopoly dominated by the Big Five vertically integrated corporations, including RKO.

While these corporations were involved in all aspects of movie making, their theatre operations were the most profitable, and it was through exhibition that they were able to truly dominate the industry. The Big Five only owned approximately seventeen percent of the nation's theatres, but they owned the largest theatres in the biggest cities which allowed them to take in around seventy percent of the total American box office revenue.

The Big Five solidified their control through a complicated system of regulations and practices that, along with theatre ownership, were at the heart of the antitrust complaints that plagued the industry for years. Block booking was a major component of this system.

Studios knew that movies featuring certain actors and actresses generated greater interest and seemed to guarantee higher box office returns. Capitalizing on this fact, studios forced exhibitors to acquire desirable films featuring popular stars in a large block along with less attractive titles, a practice known as block booking. Block-booking arrangements typically included groups of films anywhere from five to 104 titles, and in many cases, exhibitors were forced to buy films sight unseen, a practice known as blind bidding. The arrangements guaranteed an outlet for all of a studio's films, regardless of quality or even demand.

Another significant aspect of this system was a temporal and spatial separation of the market that used runs, clearances, and zones. A typical film would play the largest theatres for a specific time period (the run) at the highest admission price. The film then would be removed from the market for a duration (the clearance) before moving to a smaller, less expensive theatre. The process was then repeated. All of this was done within a certain geographic region (the zone).

Since the bulk of a film's revenue came from its initial run, due to greater seating capacities and the steady flow of customers who wanted to see a movie when it was first released, the major studios' run-clearance-zone system allowed the Big Five to gain control over an entire region through their ownership of a few large, first-run theatres.

To further solidify control and limit direct competition, the Big Five primarily owned theatres in different parts of the country. Famous Players–Lasky (Paramount) had the largest chain in the country with approximately 1,250 theatres. It dominated the market in the upper Midwest, New England, and the South. Twentieth Century-Fox controlled the area west of the Rockies, while Warner Bros. ruled the mid-Atlantic and the Northeast. Loew's (MGM) focused on the eastern United States, including New York. RKO was the smallest and least regional of all of the Big Five, but it also had significant holdings in New York, the largest market in the country.

While the corporations often owned theatres outright, they also entered into ownership agreements with independent exhibitors. This gave the exhibitor access to the studio's output, but it bound the exhibitor to that particular company. Theatre ownership of any type meant a corporation had a guaranteed market for the movies made by its studio. And in areas with no direct competition, the Big Five exhibited movies made by other members. In an unwritten agreement, they did not subject each other to block booking and blind bidding.

Acting in collusion, the system was designed to benefit all members of the Big Five. Those outside of the system were purposely excluded. Independent exhibitors thus had limited access to the movies made by the Big Five, and independent producers had limited access to the Big Five theatres. Acting on complaints initially made by independent exhibitors, who owned eighty-three percent of the nation's theatres, the Department of Justice initiated antitrust litigation against the major corporations.

*United States* v. *Paramount Pictures, Inc. et al* was filed in 1938 and took its name from the largest defendant. Along with Paramount, the Department of Justice brought suit against all of the Big Five for employing a variety of trade practices which it argued were in violation of the Sherman Antitrust Act. The litigation also included Universal, Columbia, and United Artists, the so-called Little Three that maintained significant production and distribution units but did not own theatres.[15]

The industry responded by proposing new trade agreements, but the government indicated that "divorcement of exhibition from producer–distributor interests offers the only solution of alleged violations of the anti-trust statutes."[16] The case finally went to trial in June 1939, and after a series of delays, a consent decree was signed in 1940. Surprisingly, the government agreed to table the discussion of divorcement for three years, while the Big Five pledged, among other things, to limit block booking to five films, to stop blind bidding, and to get governmental approval before making any additional theatre acquisitions.

Independent theatre owners, whose grievances spurred government action, found the consent decree objectionable from the outset. According to their complaints, block booking five films still allowed bad films to be joined with sought-after ones, the trade shows that replaced blind bidding added additional expense, and the run-clearance-zone system was left virtually intact.

The Justice Department, within a year of signing the decree, again conceded that the antitrust issues facing the industry likely could not be "remedied by measures short of divorcement."[17] An escape clause allowed the government to void the decree, which it did, and a new round of negotiations ensued.

New industry proposals were rejected, and the government let it be known that it finally planned to prosecute the case to conclusion in court. "It is absolutely essential to divorce theatres from producers," declared United States Attorney General Francis Biddle.[18] In October 1945, the two sides were back in New York federal court for the first time since 1940.

A ruling was handed down in June 1946, and while the major corporations were found in restraint of trade, the court ruled that the culprit was their sales policies and not their theatre ownership. "Film Biz Beats Divorcement" proclaimed *Variety* in what appeared to be a victory for the Big Five.[19] A statutory court upheld the ruling, but the Justice Department appealed to the Supreme Court. The Supreme Court agreed to hear the appeal and ultimately handed down its ruling on May 3, 1948.

In a seven-to-one vote with one abstention, the Court ruled that the Big Five, along with the Little Three, had used their dominance over the industry in restraint of trade and in violation of the Sherman Antitrust Act. Practices such as block booking were declared illegal. As for theatre ownership, "it is clear, as far as the five majors are concerned, that the aim of the conspiracy was exclusionary, i.e. it was designed to strengthen their hold on the exhibition field. In other words, the conspiracy had monopoly in exhibition for one of its goals."[20] The Court believed divesture was the likely solution to the problem, but it remanded the decision back to the lower court for further review.

Declaring victory, the Department of Justice believed "the question is no longer whether theatres should be divested, but how many and which ones."[21] Hoping to speed up the process, the Justice Department gave notice that it would enter into a consent decree with any member of the Big Five that wished to opt out of the trial, so long as the corporation agreed to divorce its theatre chain from production and distribution.

Skeptics however considered the ten-year-old fight far from over. With countless resources and the threat of never-ending postponements, the major studios, seemingly united in their opposition, were determined to fight until the bitter end. Unfortunately for the studio moguls, Howard Hughes was in control of RKO.

Hughes purchased one of the Big Five because he wanted "to head a studio where he could have facilities to make as many pictures as he wished without reference to any outside influence. He also wanted a studio with theatres and a releasing organization."[22] But Hughes was already considering the ramifications of the government's antitrust case when he acquired controlling interest in the Radio–Keith–Orpheum Corporation.

In fact, Hughes's purchase agreement with Floyd Odlum's Atlas Corporation stated explicitly "that it is in the interests of [RKO] and its stockholders to segregate the theatre holdings from the combined studio and distribution holdings for several reasons, including the demand on this point expressed by the Department of Justice."[23] The contract went on to say that Hughes would do everything he could as the new controlling owner to enact separation within a year's time.

While the "best interests of RKO and its stockholders" would be cited frequently, Hughes personally had a lot to gain from RKO's separation.[24] RKO had the smallest theatre chain of the Big Five, which meant it was the most reliant on the other members of the oligarchy and independent exhibitors. If divesture was enacted across the industry, the major production companies, devoid of their theatres, would no longer have a guaranteed market for their films. All movies would be treated equally by exhibitors, which in effect would place RKO films (and those of the smaller studios and independent producers) on a stronger, more competitive footing across the country.

Hughes also had a lot to gain from a financial perspective. When Hughes became the largest shareholder in the Radio–Keith–Orpheum Corporation, it gave him controlling interest in all aspects of the corporation, including its subsidiaries RKO Theatres and RKO Radio Pictures. If production and distribution were formally split from the theatre chain, Hughes likely would end up as the largest stockholder in both new companies, depending on how divorcement took place.

If he were forced to sell one of the new companies, he could ask for a significant amount. What's more, Hughes could sell his controlling interest in both companies for even more money. Or Hughes could try to find a way to keep control of both companies while reaping the benefits of industry-wide separation. Hughes's purchase agreement actually outlined one possible sales option if the theatre company was separated from production and distribution, which explained why divorcement was mentioned in the agreement to begin with.

According to the contract, "I [Hughes] give you [Odlum] the optional right to buy from me the securities in the theatre company that I receive as

*Above left:* Howard Hughes moved to Hollywood in 1925 to become "the world's most famous motion picture producer." (*Everett Collection*)

*Above right:* Hughes's first foray into motion picture production was a failed venture with actor Ralph Graves. (*Photoplay*)

Hughes ran his business interests, including his Hollywood operations, out of 7000 Romaine Street in Los Angeles. (*Author's collection*)

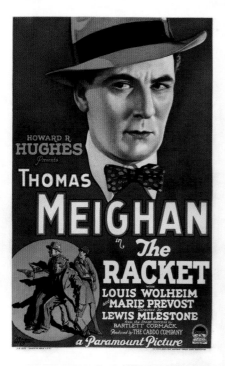

*Above:* The Academy Award-winning *Two Arabian Knights* launched Hughes on a successful career in Hollywood. (*United Artists*)

*Left: The Racket* was the first movie to feature the tagline "Howard R. Hughes Presents."
(*Paramount Pictures*)

*Right:* Marshall Neilan, seated left, directed one of Hughes's early movies and provided the story idea for *Hell's Angels*. (*Artcraft Pictures Corporation*)

*Below:* Hughes took over as director of *Hell's Angels* when two others, including Neilan, left the production. (*Library of Congress*)

*Above left:* Norwegian-born actress Greta Nissen was the original female star of *Hell's Angels* but was recast when the movie was converted to sound. (*doctormacro.com*)

*Above right:* Actress Jean Harlow, Nissen's replacement, was declared the "foremost U. S. embodiment of sex appeal" by *Time* magazine. (*Time*)

*Left:* Hughes proudly advertised *Hell's Angels'* multi-million dollar production cost. (*United Artists*)

*Above:* The extravagant premiere of *Hell's Angels* took place at Grauman's Chinese Theatre in Hollywood on May 27, 1930. (*hollywoodphotographs.com*)

*Right:* The *Los Angeles Times* proclaimed it was "the biggest crowd ever" for a premiere. (*University of Southern California Libraries, California Historical Society*)

*Above left:* Censor Will H. Hays, the "dictator of the cinema," was often at odds with the independent Hughes. (*Library of Congress*)

*Above right:* Hughes was forced to weaken the allusion of an incestuous relationship between the characters played by Paul Muni and Ann Dvorak in *Scarface*. (*Everett Collection*)

*Left:* The release of *Scarface* was delayed for months as Hughes battled censorship boards across the country over the film's violent content. (*SilverScreen/Alamy Stock Photo*)

*Above:* Hughes, left, returned to directing with the western *The Outlaw*.
(*Everett Collection*)

*Right:* The often forgotten male stars of *The Outlaw*, from left to right, Thomas Mitchell, Jack Buetel, and Walter Huston.
(*Photo 12/Alamy Stock Photo*)

*Above:* A variation of the controversial image of Jane Russell used to promote *The Outlaw* in San Francisco for its premiere in 1943. (*Album/Alamy Stock Photo*)

*Left:* An advertisement for *The Outlaw* flaunting Russell and the battle with the censors. (*Author's collection*)

*Above:* The exterior of the RKO Radio Pictures studio at the corner of Melrose Avenue and Gower Street in Hollywood. (*University of Southern California Libraries, California Historical Society*)

*Right:* RKO, like the other "Big Five" vertically integrated corporations, had its own theatre chain. (*Library of Congress*)

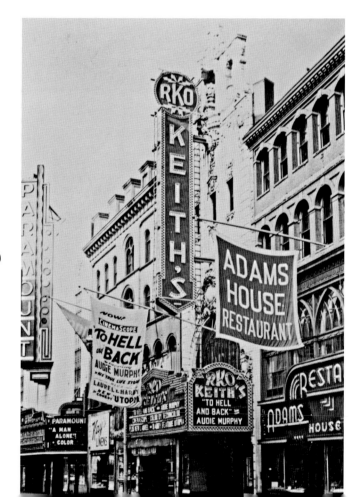

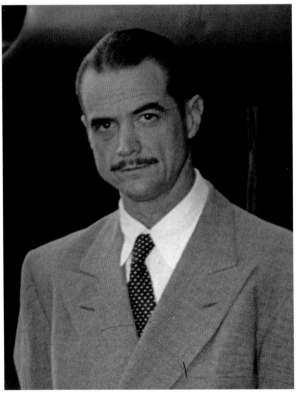

*Above:* Floyd Odlum's Atlas
Corporation controlled
RKO for many years prior
to Hughes's acquisition.
(*International News Photo*)

*Left:* Hughes around
the time he purchased
controlling interest in RKO
in 1948. (*Author's collection*)

*Right:* Businessman Ralph Stolkin led a syndicate that temporarily purchased controlling interest in RKO from Hughes.
(*Keystone Pictures USA/ Alamy Stock Photo*)

*Below:* Hughes rushed *Rachel and the Stranger* into theatres after actor Robert Mitchum was arrested for marijuana possession.
(*Everett Collection*)

The Man Who Bought Her...

The Tall, Dark Stranger Who Sought Her!

DORE SCHARY presents

LORETTA YOUNG · WILLIAM HOLDEN · ROBERT MITCHUM

in

*Rachel* and the *Stranger*

with

GARY GRAY · TOM TULLY

*Left:* Producer David O. Selznick, who jointly owned Robert Mitchum's contract with RKO, initially tried to distance himself from the actor. (*Library of Congress*)

*Below left:* Hughes continued to exploit Mitchum even after he was sentenced to sixty days in jail. (*Walter Oleksy/Alamy Stock Photo*)

*Below right:* Actress Ingrid Bergman and director Roberto Rossellini taking a break during the filming of *Stromboli*. (*Acme Telephoto*)

Gossip columnist Louella Parsons broke the story that Bergman was pregnant with Rossellini's baby while she was still married to her first husband. (*CBS Radio*)

The poster for *Stromboli* sought to exploit the controversy that engulfed the film's leading lady and director. (*Mary Evans/Ronald Grant/Everett Collection*)

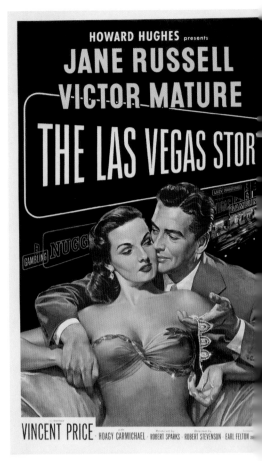

*Above left:* Senator Edwin Johnson denounced Bergman and the film for over an hour on the Senate floor. (*U. S. Senate Historical Office*)

*Above right:* Hughes refused to give Paul Jarrico screenwriting credit for *The Las Vegas Story* because Jarrico was a communist. (*RKO Radio Pictures*)

*Opposite above:* Jarrico, left, waits to testify before the House Un-American Activities Committee in 1951. (*Library of Congress*)

*Opposite below:* Hughes, center, made a rare public appearance before the American Legion to denounce communist infiltration of the motion picture industry. (*University of Southern California Libraries*)

*Above left:* John Wayne was terribly miscast as Genghis Khan in *The Conqueror*, one of the most infamous movies in Hollywood history. (*doctormacro.com*)

*Above right: Jet Pilot*, released in 1957, was the last film to feature Howard Hughes's name above the title. (*Walter Oleksy/Alamy Stock Photo*) a result of such segregation or reorganization with respect to my holdings of stock of RKO (obtained hereunder) for a price to be determined."[25] Odlum would have the right to match any offer Hughes received for the theatre chain within ten days, and if no offers were forthcoming, Odlum could purchase the stock for a price not to exceed $4,500,000.

Hughes's plans for separation (and his deal with Odlum) were not made public at the time of Hughes's acquisition of RKO. A few months after the sale was finalized, in October 1948, it thus came as a complete surprise to many within the industry when Hughes made it known that he planned to accept the government's offer to enter into a consent decree and voluntarily divorce RKO.

As *The New York Times* made clear, Hughes's actions represented "the first break in the solid front which the major motion-picture companies have presented during twenty years of anti-trust litigation by the Government."[26] *Variety* speculated that it "would break the phalanx of the big five defendants."[27] After years of uncertainty, the bedrock on which the studio system was built, theatre ownership, was crumbling.

According to Hughes's proposal, the RKO corporation would be divided into two new, independent companies: a production–distribution company and a theatre company. RKO stockholders would receive a two-for-one split of the corporation's shares. In other words, every share of RKO corporate stock would be converted into a share of the new production–distribution company and a share of the new theatre company. The plan, contingent upon approval of the United States Treasury Department, would be a tax-free reorganization. And it would make Hughes the largest shareholder in both new companies.

The proposal needed approval from the RKO board of directors, and they met on October 30, 1948, for the first time since Hughes acquired controlling interest. The board's initial order of business was to accept the resignation of directors associated with the Atlas Corporation, including Floyd Odlum, and to elect Hughes and Noah Dietrich to the board. The newly reconstituted board then agreed to separate RKO's production and distribution from the theatre operations as outlined in Hughes's proposal.

In a press release, the board stated that the "reorganization is believed by management of RKO to be for the best interests of the company and its stockholders under all of the present circumstances. The management has no doubt that this arrangement will permit the continued successful operation in a highly competitive market both of the RKO theatre and of the production–distribution companies."[28] The Department of Justice subsequently announced its support of the divorcement, and a consent decree was formally entered into in the federal district court in New York.

The significance of Hughes and RKO entering into a consent decree was recognized immediately. "In view of the voluntary action by RKO aiming at separation of its theatres from production and distribution," wrote Edwin Schallert of the *Los Angeles Times*, "it might be concluded that film companies are now viewing such divorcement under anti-trust suits as an impending fact rather than an imminent threat."[29] Thomas F. Brady of *The New York Times* noted that it was an admission that "total divorcement is feasible."[30]

Industry executives were publicly quiet on the subject, but gossip columnist Hedda Hopper believed Hughes "should be congratulated for voluntarily divorcing the RKO theatres from his production studio. All the big studios will eventually have to do it, but Howard made the move without prodding, pushing or being nudged by the government."[31]

While the main requirement of the consent decree was the separation of RKO's production–distribution operations from its theatre chain, several other stipulations were made.

RKO operated ninety-one theatres at the time the consent decree was signed. Eighty-one of the theatres were owned in full, while the other ten were owned jointly with another exhibitor. RKO was the minority owner in an additional 263 theatres. According to the terms of the agreement, the new RKO theatre company was allowed to retain seventy-nine of the eighty-one theatres it already owned, and it could attempt to acquire eight of the ten it jointly owned. RKO could also try to purchase outright twenty-five of the theatres it held a minority interest in, but the remaining 238 had to be sold. Therefore, if RKO was able to acquire all of the theatres allowed under the consent decree, the new theatre company would own 112 theatres.[32]

The other major requirement of the consent decree related to Hughes's controlling interest in the corporation. Hughes owned twenty-four percent of RKO while no other individual stockholder owned as much as one percent. The government agreed to the two-for-one stock split suggested by Hughes and the RKO board, and it even allowed stockholders to retain their holdings in both new companies. The one exception was Hughes.

According to the consent decree, Hughes was required, "by November 8, 1949, to dispose of his stock in either the New Theatre Company or the New Picture Company to a purchaser who is not a defendant or affiliated with or controlled by any defendant, or to deposit such stock with a voting trustee designated by the court."[33] The government demanded that the two new companies be operated independently, and since Hughes was the only shareholder with significant holdings, it believed forcing Hughes to cede control of one would accomplish this goal.

Stockholder approval was the final hurdle to the implementation of the agreement. RKO officials informed shareholders that the corporation had assets valued at $107,692,007. Under the separation, the new theatre company would have a total net worth of $19,620,441, with assets of $50,308,541 and liabilities of $30,688,100. The production and distribution company would be worth $37,704,011, with assets of $57,383,466 and liabilities of $19,679,455.[34]

The theatre company would retain ownership of all affiliated theatres, while the assets of the new picture company would include the studio operations in Hollywood along with domestic and foreign distribution facilities, RKO Pathé (a producer of newsreels and documentaries), and RKO Television (established to produce content exclusively for the medium). The assets also included an "extraordinary distribution" of $10,000,000 of cash, by way of a dividend and reduction of capital, which the theatre operations would make to the production and distribution operations "in order to enable RKO to provide the New Picture Company with adequate initial working capital."[35]

RKO stockholders held a special meeting on March 28 to discuss and vote on the plan. A detailed proxy statement was sent out in advance. More than eighty percent of the total number of shares outstanding and entitled to vote ultimately voiced their approval of divestiture. The dissenting vote was less than one and one-half percent. "I am very pleased," RKO president Ned Depinet said in the aftermath of the vote, "that such a large proportion of the owners of our business has confirmed the judgment of our directors with respect to the proposals which are so important to the future of our operations."[36] With the RKO board, the courts, and the Department of Justice having already accepted the plan, the consent decree was now official.

The decree mandated that the two new companies be separated by November 8, 1949, the same date Hughes was obligated to relinquish control of one of the companies. Hughes indicated from the outset that he planned to operate the production and distribution unit, so he began looking for a buyer for the theatre chain. It was reported that Hughes "placed a $9,000,000 price tag on his theatre interest."[37] The major offers initially came from Malcolm Kinsberg, president of RKO Theatres; a syndicate headed by movie executives George Skouras and Harry Brandt; and another group consisting of theatre operators Stanley Meyer, Matthew Fox, and Cliff Work.

The group headed by Stanley Meyer offered Hughes $6 per share or $5,574,120. This was well below Hughes's reported asking price, but it was a significant offer, so Hughes submitted it to Floyd Odlum as required in their sales agreement. Odlum, believing Hughes was simply trying to negate his purchase option, questioned the validity of the offer and charged Hughes with failing to comply with the terms of their agreement.

Odlum had several grievances. He believed that Hughes did not properly notify him as required, he was never provided with the actual terms of the offer, and he was not given enough time to respond. Odlum also questioned the financial arrangements Hughes reportedly made with the proposed buyers. While Odlum threatened to take Hughes to court to hold him "strictly accountable for all damages we may suffer by reason of any breach," it was reported that Hughes was "sitting tight and not worried in the least bit."[38]

As weeks passed, Hughes refused to commit to any offer, publicly or privately. As one commentator noted, the negotiations had "assumed the aspects of a mystery script as even the principals in the situation admitted they had heard nothing from Hughes up to late yesterday and had no clue as to which way he would move, or when."[39] It was reported that new offers continued to be submitted, and although the exact timeframe for Odlum to counter the initial offer was unclear, "the final deadline by any interpretation of the terms of the original agreement" had clearly passed.[40]

Then, seemingly out of nowhere, Hughes announced that he had "decided not to close any transactions right at this particular time for the sale of my interest in the New RKO Theatre Company."[41] The announcement may have caught potential buyers off guard, but after months of negotiations, Hughes now had a much better idea of how much his theatre stock was worth on the open market. He also freed himself from any obligation to Floyd Odlum.

The deadline to give up control of one of the new companies was nevertheless still approaching, so Hughes filed a formal request for an extension to separate RKO into two companies. RKO president Ned Depinet argued that the "extension is in the interest of all stockholders and should enable the commencement of the operation of separate units under more advantageous circumstances."[42] The Department of Justice, "inclined to be lenient under consent decree procedures in a desire not to impose undue hardships in affecting corporate changeovers," agreed to Hughes's request and pushed the deadline back six months to May 15, 1950.[43]

The decision not to sell and the request for a delay led to speculation of Hughes's motives. Distributor Robert Savini, a Hughes's confidant, asked Noah Dietrich pointedly, "Does Howard want to sell or not?"[44] More offers for Hughes's theatre stock came in, some supposedly as high as $8 per share, but Hughes still refused to sell.

With the latest deadline approaching, Hughes requested and was granted yet another extension. RKO divorcement now had to take place by December 31, 1950, at which time Hughes had to sell his shares in one of the companies or place them into trusteeship. Savini now seemed to understand Hughes's intentions. "I know Howard will make no deal and will hold the theatres as long as he possibly can," Savini said, "it's to his benefit to do so."[45]

After all of the delays, the Radio–Keith–Orpheum Corporation was finally split into two companies, RKO Pictures Corporation and RKO Theatres Corporation, at the end of business on December 31, 1950. Hughes however still refused to sell his controlling interest in either company. Choosing to keep control of RKO Pictures, the production and distribution unit, Hughes's stock in RKO Theatres was placed in a trust overseen by the court-appointed Irving Trust Company, a bank headquartered in New York.

Some critics, including investment counselor David Greene, who reportedly oversaw approximately 300,000 shares or eight percent of RKO stock, questioned "whether Hughes continued to dominate both new companies," in direct violation of the consent decree, by refusing to sell.[46] Speaking on behalf of Hughes, Noah Dietrich countered, "We are complying with the decree in every way."[47] The Justice Department, in an investigation that they described as "routine," looked into the matter "to determine whether the divorcement is a true divorcement."[48] They ultimately found that Hughes was complying with the terms of the consent decree.

But in a related development, the United States Statutory Court ruled that Hughes had to completely divest himself of the theatre stock (or stock in the production–distribution company) within two years. If he did not do so, the Irving Trust had an additional two years to sell it on his behalf. Hughes's attorney argued that "setting a time limit on the sale of Hughes's stock would represent a change in the consent decree," so Hughes took legal action to nullify the ruling.[49] The Supreme Court agreed to hear the case.

In the meantime, David Greene, who was also a member of the New York Stock Exchange, continued to challenge Hughes's supposed control over RKO Theatres. Greene argued that Hughes dictated the naming of the company's board of directors which gave him *de facto* control. Greene also believed that Hughes caused a stockholders' meeting to be delayed for over a year so his handpicked board could not be challenged.

When a stockholders' meeting finally did occur in December 1951, Greene and his supporters argued that the present board did not represent enough corporate stock and the company's financial performance was not keeping pace with its competitors. A "stockholder battle" ensued, with charges and counterclaims levied by both sides.[50] In the end, a compromise was reached which resulted in Greene and one of his associates being named to the RKO Theatres board.

While some still questioned Hughes's role in the management of RKO Theatres, the company's largest shareholder won a resounding victory when the Supreme Court ruled in his favor in February 1951. Overturning the decision of the statutory court, the Supreme Court ruled unanimously that Hughes could not be forced to sell his theatre stock, as the consent decree gave Hughes the right to exercise control over one of the new RKO companies and either sell his shares in the other or place them in a court-appointed trust.

Justice Hugo Black, writing on behalf of the Court, noted that "a reading of the wording would make most persons believe that Hughes was to have a choice of two different alternatives. Hughes would have no choice if the first 'alternative' was to sell the stock and the second 'alternative' was to sell the stock."[51]

Having seemingly found a way to hold onto both companies, while only controlling one, Hughes nevertheless reopened negotiations for sale of his theatre stock. The value of RKO Theatres stock fluctuated around $5 per share on the open market, but Hughes's representatives let it be known that if buyers were "interested in paying at least $7.00 per share we will be pleased to meet with them."[52]

Stockholder and RKO Theatres board member David Greene continued to be dismayed with Hughes's influence over the company, and he proposed having RKO Theatres buy out Hughes's shares. "By having our company repurchase its stock, these very embarrassing conditions could be avoided," he wrote to fellow board member Ben-Fleming Sessel. "There would be no disruption of the morale of the organization, and we would be assured of the continuity of the present management and key personnel who have had many years of training and experience with the company."[53]

Greene was unable to consummate a deal through RKO Theatres, so he teamed up with investors Albert A. List and George Markelson. Finally, after years of negotiations, Hughes sold his shares of the theatre company in November 1953. As *Variety* reported, the "Greene group paid $4.75 per share for Hughes's block of 929,020 shares, or a total of $4,412,845."[54] The stock closed on the New York Stock Exchange at $3.87½ a share on the day of the sale. While Greene was commonly cited as the point person for the acquisition, List actually put up the majority of the funds, approximately $3,400,000, and he was now the largest stockholder of RKO Theatres with 886,353 shares.[55]

Although some outlets questioned why Hughes sold at that time when he had received higher offers in the past, it was learned that Hughes also received approximately 100,000 shares of RKO Pictures stock in the deal. "Had it not been for the possibility of Hughes getting additional stock in the picture company," observed the *Hollywood Reporter*, "there would not have been any sale of his theatre holdings."[56] Thus, by selling the theatre company and increasing his ownership stake in the production and distribution company, Hughes could continue to make motion pictures using the resources of a major studio.

But if he so desired, Hughes always had the option to sell both companies and return to making movies as an independent producer. He had succeeded in the past as an independent, despite the obstacles inherent in the studio system. Now, if divesture was enacted across the industry, which was almost certain given Hughes's actions, independent producers would face fewer challenges and have a greater market for their movies. A lot had changed in a short time, and the benefits of owning a studio, which caused Hughes to purchase RKO, had diminished.

Not surprisingly, as Hughes was negotiating the sale of RKO Theatres, he also entertained offers for his shares of RKO Pictures. Within a few months of separation, Hughes started to receive offers from various parties interested in the production and distribution company. The reported names included San Francisco financier Louis R. Lurie, millionaire ex-convict speculator Serge Rubinstein, and a group fronted by movie executive Sam Dembow Jr. Gossip columnist Louella Parsons, commenting on all the rumors, noted that "the most fantastic was that Eva Peron is buying RKO."[57]

Normally not one to comment on such speculation, Hughes responded to the reports of an impending sale. "Occasionally rumors make their appearance which are damaging to all concerned, and I feel it my duty to reply," Hughes stated publicly. "Therefore let me say: I am not negotiating with any one whomsoever for the sale of my stock in RKO Radio Pictures, Inc. I have no intention of selling my stock. I do not care to entertain or consider any offers for the same."[58]

Despite his public denial, it was believed that the offers simply had not been high enough as Hughes wanted at least $6 per share or approximately $6,000,000 for his controlling interest. His comments were thus an attempt to increase the amount groups were offering. The tactic seemed to work, and on September 19, 1952, the *Hollywood Reporter* announced that the "oft-rumored and more often denied sale of the shares of Howard Hughes in RKO Pictures will, today or tomorrow, be a reality."[59]

A syndicate headed by businessman Ralph Stolkin, which also included A. L. Koolish, Ray Ryan, Edward "Buzz" Burke, and Sherrill Corwin, agreed to pay Hughes $7 per share for his controlling interest of approximately twenty-six percent in RKO Pictures. The stock was selling for $4⅜ on the open market. Hughes held 1,013,420 shares at that time so he was to receive a total of $7,093,940.[60] The contract called for a down payment of $1,250,000, an additional $1,250,000 due in one year, and the final $4,593,940 due in two years. If necessary, Hughes agreed to loan the buyers up to $8,000,000 to facilitate production.

At the time of the sale, Ralph Stolkin was hailed as a "financial wizard who parlayed a $15,000 loan into a mail order business which has netted him millions."[61] Stolkin had limited Hollywood experience as the boss of Screen Associates, a production company whose sole credit was the Dean Martin and Jerry Lewis film *At War with the Army* (1950). A. L. Koolish, "a mail-order man himself," was a "Chicago financier and Mr. Stolkin's father-in-law."[62] Ray Ryan and Edward Burke were said to "have become, during the last three or four years, a pair of the largest oil operators in the country."[63] Sherrill Corwin was a "Southern California theatre exhibitor."[64] Although it was commonly reported that Stolkin and Koolish put up the majority of the funds, the buyers actually were equal partners in the venture.

"The buyers have assured me," Hughes stated in a press release, "that they will pursue a program of top grade production of motion pictures for exhibition in motion picture theatres. Their plans encompass a strong policy of distribution in this country and throughout the world utilizing the full facilities of the entire RKO distribution organization."[65]

Producer Samuel Goldwyn, who had a distribution deal with RKO and was one of the company's most valuable assets, also professed faith in the group. "The new owners of RKO Pictures are a young, aggressive lot," he said, "and I have every reason to believe they will try their best to make a success of their operation in the company."[66]

The Stolkin group issued a statement outlining their intentions: "We expect to continue to produce motion pictures as a major studio operation. We believe a number of substantial economies can be effected, and at the same time, we expect to add to the present staff, the ablest management and talent available."[67] Individuals they reportedly were interested in for the top studio post included Darryl F. Zanuck, who was employed at the time as the production boss at Twentieth Century-Fox, and Louis B. Mayer, who had recently resigned as the top executive at MGM.

At an RKO board meeting in October, all of the members associated with Hughes's tenure, including Hughes and Noah Dietrich, officially resigned to make way for the new regime. Stolkin was elected president of the company, while fellow owners Koolish, Burke, and Corwin were named to the board. The syndicate was now firmly in control, but despite initial reports, very little was actually known about RKO's new owners.

All of that changed on October 16 when the *Wall Street Journal* published the first of a series of articles highlighting the background and financial dealings of several members of the purchasing syndicate. "When Howard Hughes sold out his controlling interest in RKO the other day, it at first seemed questionable whether any new management could possibly be as colorful as he," noted the introduction to the series. "Assurances can now be given, however, that some members of the group which took over from Mr. Hughes are remarkable men in their own right."[68] As the series would make clear, their rise to financial prominence was remarkable, but it was also unsavory and legally suspect.

The first article examined A. L. (Abraham Leonard) Koolish, Ralph Stolkin's father-in-law and a member of the RKO board. Koolish made millions as a mail-order punchboard impresario and insurance salesman. Along the way, he piled up "a bulky record of Better Business Bureau Complaints, three Federal Trade Commission cease-and-desist orders, and one grand jury indictment." In one instance, he was cited for issuing life insurance to a family's dog. It was also reported that Koolish was "deeply interested in philanthropy—that is to say, in running charity drives for profit." When asked by the *Journal* to respond to the charges, Koolish replied "that's going quite a way back," and in his line of work, "a normal number of complaints were expected."[69]

Ray Ryan was the focus of the second article of the series that appeared in the *Journal* on October 17. Although Ryan chose not to sit on the RKO board, his ownership stake was represented directly by his handpicked candidate William Gorman. Ryan made his fortune in oil, but his real passion was gambling. Fellow RKO owner Ralph Stolkin said admiringly, "I would like to have the money that Ray loses." Ryan's gambling activities brought him into contact with a variety of criminal and underworld figures, such as Frank Erickson, the noted bookmaker and racketeer, and Frank Costello, the head of the Luciano crime family and one of the most powerful mafia bosses in American history. Costello even mentioned Ryan by name, "I have known him for a long, long time," when testifying in 1951 before the Kefauver Committee, the Senate investigation into organized crime.[70]

The final article in the series was published on October 20 and dealt with Ralph Stolkin, the public face of the purchasing syndicate. "The rocket rise of Ralph Stolkin to the presidency of RKO Pictures Corp.," the article began, "can only be explained in these terms: Unusual energy; uncommon imagination; unceasing use of the U.S. postal system." Like his father-in-law, Stolkin made a fortune by mailing out thousands of punchboards, which garnered a "fabulous number of complaints" for "failure to fulfill orders." The Federal Trade Commission issued a formal complaint against Stolkin for "misrepresentation and use of lottery methods," while the Postal Service issued its own complaint "charging violation of postal anti-lottery statutes."[71] Stolkin was also accused of operating public charities for personal profit, again like his father-in-law.

The damage from the series was significant and swift. On October 22, two days after the final article was published, RKO board chairman Albert Grant, a seasoned movie executive who was brought in by the new ownership group, forced Stolkin and Koolish, along with Ryan's representative William Gorman, to resign from the board of directors. Stolkin also resigned as president. In an attempt to put a positive spin on the situation, Grant tried to argue that the changes were necessary as "the future good of RKO requires that it be top-staffed with experienced film executives."[72]

It was clear however "that the resignations were the direct result of the series of articles published by the *Wall Street Journal*."[73] The trio admitted as much in a public statement.

> Our only interest in acquiring stock in RKO Pictures Corp. was our belief that this company can be, under able and independent management, brought to the full realization of its great potential. We recognize that a volume of unfavorable publicity directed against us as individuals has or can be damaging to the company. Consistent with our original intention of doing that which is best for the company, and for that reason only, we have submitted our resignations.[74]

Board chairman Grant, again attempting damage control, promised to "fill the vacancies with men of outstanding caliber" as soon as possible.[75]

Owners Edward Burke and Sherrill Corwin were not named in the *Journal* exposé and remained on the board. The status and future role of the other three however was unclear. It was reported that they "have not sold or otherwise disposed of their individual stock holdings in the company and, so far as was known, have no intention of so doing at this time."[76] Board chairman Grant made it clear that the trio were to be treated as minority stockholders with virtually no power over any aspect of company operations or management. Not surprisingly, despite denials, the disgraced owners began negotiations to sell their stake in the company.

The first serious buyer to emerge was Matthew Fox, a former executive at Universal and a pioneer in bringing motion pictures to television. RKO's substantial library, valued by some at a minimum of $10,000,000, was likely his motivation. Fox had previously tried to acquire the RKO Theatres Corporation. Floyd Odlum, the former owner of the Radio–Keith–Orpheum Corporation who also failed to purchase the theatre company after selling out to Hughes, was reportedly interested in reacquiring controlling interest in the production company. Milton Gettinger, Fred Packard, Robert Young, and Eliot Hyman were also named as potential suitors.

Almost all of the negotiations were ultimately called off, it was reported, "because none of those who made overtures had either sufficient cash or credit to swing a deal."[77] A sale nevertheless seemed so likely that Burke and Corwin, the two members of the Stolkin ownership group that still held RKO board positions, continually refused to approve additional board members to replace Stolkin, Koolish, and Gorman until a deal was finalized.

RKO board chairman Albert Grant, who had nominated several candidates, believed such inactivity was causing additional hardship at a precarious moment for the company. "Being legally and factually stymied in this fashion," Grant wrote in a letter to all RKO stockholders, "my continuance as an officer, director or employee of your Corporation would, in my judgment, be a false assurance to the stockholders, employees and others who do business with the Corporation, that the affairs of the Corporation are moving forward with reasonable satisfaction."[78] Grant said he therefore had no choice but to resign as a director and officer of RKO.

RKO's upper management was clearly in turmoil. The company had been operating without a president since Stolkin resigned, while the board consisted of only two members and their future with the company was uncertain. There had been no top executive in charge of production since Hughes sold his controlling interest. Arnold Picker was scheduled to leave his position as a vice president of United Artists to become executive vice president at RKO, but he quit before he even started in response to Grant's resignation. The *Hollywood Reporter* called the latest shakeup "the most dramatic to date," while *The New York Times* described it as another chapter in the "woeful story" of the once great studio.[79]

To make matters even worse, three minority stockholders, in response to the upheaval, filed an application with the New York State Supreme Court for the appointment of a temporary receiver for RKO Pictures. The appointment was sought "in order to protect and preserve this business enterprise from loss, destruction or despoliation, and to prevent it from becoming insolvent."[80]

The case would take months to resolve, and the uncertainty of its outcome stalled the Stolkin group's sale of its controlling interest to Matthew Fox. Hoping to salvage the Fox deal, Stolkin requested concessions from Hughes related to their original sale, including an extension on interest payments.

As time dragged on and a sale to anyone seemed less likely, it was reported that "some members of the Stolkin syndicate favor getting out of the RKO deal to the extent that they are willing to return the controlling stock interest to Hughes and take the loss of a good deal part of their original $1,250,000 payment to Hughes."[81] Negotiations with Hughes on additional concessions intensified, with Hughes reportedly agreeing to a longer pay off period and to allowing any member of the syndicate to sell their stock separately.[82]

Then, the impossible seemed to happen. "What may rank as the financial feat of the year has just been accomplished by Howard Hughes," proclaimed the *Wall Street Journal*, "a demonstration on how to sell a company and keep it too."[83]

While the Stolkin group still retained controlling interest and Hughes technically owned no stock, Hughes was reelected to the RKO board along with several of his handpicked associates, including Noah Dietrich. Stolkin released a statement explaining the action.

> It was toward this end that I contacted Mr. Hughes and asked for his assistance. I felt that he was the one person best qualified to assist in our problem, not only because he has a sizable financial interest in RKO, represented by our commitment to him on the balance of the purchase price, but also because of his familiarity with the fiscal and production problems of the company.[84]

Hughes was also named chairman of the RKO board, a position he never actually held during his tenure of ownership.

With Hughes regaining managerial control of RKO Pictures, the board was fully reconstituted and James R. Grainger, the former executive vice president at Republic Pictures, was named the new RKO president. It appeared the company was returning to normal, at least from an administrative perspective, so the minority shareholders dropped their petition for an appointment of a temporary receiver. New York Supreme Court Justice Henry Clay Greenberg was shocked at what he called "an extraordinary termination of a motion" given all of the charges levied against RKO and its management, but he agreed to the request after making sure no "consideration" was promised for the withdrawal.[85]

Just when it seemed things could not get any stranger for RKO, "the shortest and most bizarre period of studio ownership in film industry history" came to an end.[86] The Stolkin group agreed to forfeit its $1,250,000 down payment and return all of the stock back to Hughes.[87] Stolkin said his group saw no advantage to keeping the stock "if every move we attempted to make would be hampered by other shareholders or outside interests."[88]

The syndicate ultimately lost around $1,750,000 on the deal, inclusive of fees, while Hughes pocketed around $1,350,000, which included the down payment and interest. Only one film, the atomic testing thriller *Split*

*Second* (1953), actually made it before the cameras during the tenure of the Stolkin regime. *Variety* said the story of Hughes's purchase, sale, and reacquisition of RKO was "more fantastic than any film produced in the history of Hollywood."[89]

When Hughes regained ownership of RKO Pictures, the studio system was crumbling around him. In the aftermath of his decision to voluntarily separate RKO's theatres from its production and distribution, Thomas F. Brady of *The New York Times* wrote in 1948 that Hughes's actions had "set a precedent which is expected to affect the entire film industry."[90] Brady was correct, and within a few short months, Barney Balaban, the president of Paramount Pictures, wrote to the company's stockholders to inform them that Paramount "has just entered into a Consent Judgment with the Department of Justice" which "requires the creation of two new companies for the purpose of separating the domestic theatre operation of Paramount from its production-distribution activities."[91]

Paramount was the largest corporation in the industry, and although Loew's, Warner, and Fox tried to fight on, the vertical integration that defined Hollywood during its golden age had come to an end. As film historian Thomas Schatz makes clear, the government's antitrust campaign was "the single defining industry event of the 1940s, striking at the very essence of the Hollywood studio system and bringing about the wholesale transformation of the American movie industry."[92] While many people on both sides played a part in the campaign, "Hughes's decision to break ranks" ultimately brought about, in the words of independent film scholar J. A. Aberdeen, "the finale of the studio epoch."[93]

The end of the studio system, one of the most monumental events in the history of Hollywood, forever changed the ways movies were produced, distributed, and exhibited. Furthermore, according to Michael Conant, an expert in antitrust law, the "most significant impact of the Paramount decrees on motion picture production was the great increase in the number of independent producers."[94] Having spent years battling the studio system from the outside, studio mogul Howard Hughes had finally succeeded in ending the system that had tried to hold him and fellow independent producers back.

# Scandal, Malicious Tongue-Wagging and Dirt

"I may have done wrong. But,
all I want now is a little happiness."—
Karin (Ingrid Bergman) in *Stromboli*

When Howard Hughes acquired controlling interest in the Radio–Keith–Orpheum Corporation in 1948, he immediately set about divorcing RKO's theatre chain from its production and distribution operations. The resulting consent decree brought about an end to the studio system, forever altering the Hollywood landscape, and it left Hughes in control of the newly formed RKO Pictures. Despite his efforts to sell the company, the independent producer was still a mogul in control of one of the largest production studios in the country.

As his actions in the antitrust case demonstrated, Hughes still did not feel compelled to abide by the dictates of the industry, even in his new position. This became even clearer when he finally shifted his focus away from divestiture and resumed the controversial marketing techniques he pioneered with films like *Scarface* and *The Outlaw*. His actions would once again have lasting consequences and forever alter the lives of two of Hollywood's biggest stars.

One of the many jobs of a mogul was to protect the image of the studio and to safeguard the reputation of the company's stars. The top echelon of actors and actresses, whose names appeared at the top of the marquee, had been selling movies since the early days of the industry. A star's popularity often determined the profitability of an entire season of studio releases. Their economic value was in the millions. Recognizing their importance, studios carefully guarded a star's reputation. An arrest, a divorce, or an unwanted pregnancy could have serious ramifications not just for the actor or actress but for the entire studio.

To protect their investment, studio moguls employed highly skilled publicity men whose job was to keep any negative story about a star from ever appearing in the press. Commonly known as "fixers," these individuals covered up any sort of scandal or controversy before the public ever heard about it. Fixers used everyone from reporters to doctors to police officers, almost all of whom were "on the take," to solve stars' problems and hide their secrets.

Howard Strickling, head of publicity at MGM, was a notable example. Along with studio vice president Eddie Manix, Strickling made sure the sordid affairs of the studio's stars never made it into the papers. Actor Clark Gable, whose own indiscretions were hidden from the public for years, spoke about Strickling.

> I used to go over to Howard's house on Sunday mornings for breakfast and it was unusual when he didn't get at least three phone calls while we ate, asking him to keep catastrophes of the night before out of the papers. One star would be picked up drunk in the street, another would have been caught in a raid on a marijuana party, another would have wrapped his car around a tree with someone else's wife in the seat alongside him. The next day I'd always look in the papers to see if anything sneaked through. Nothing ever did. That Howard, he sure is a genius.[1]

Wanting to avoid negative publicity, studios employed fixers like Strickling because scandals and controversies were not good for business. Or so it seemed.

Robert Mitchum was one of RKO's biggest stars when Hughes acquired controlling interest in the studio. Mitchum was born in Bridgeport, Connecticut, in 1917. His father died when he was an infant, and his childhood was filled with trouble. He was expelled from several schools as a youth, and his mother was forced to send him to live with relatives. Mitchum ultimately dropped out of school, and like other drifters of the period, he traveled the country by hitching a ride on railroad boxcars. When he was only fourteen, he was arrested for vagrancy in Savannah, Georgia, and put on a chain gang.

He worked a variety of odd jobs over the years, included digging ditches for the Civilian Conservation Corps and boxing professionally. Mitchum eventually made his way to California where his sister was a stage actress. Shortly thereafter, he married Dorothy Spence, whom he had met a few years earlier. The pair would have three children and be together for fifty-seven years until Mitchum's death in 1997.

Mitchum worked for a time as a machine operator with the Lockheed Aircraft Company, but the monotony caused him to eventually pursue a career in acting. Given his droopy eyes, broad build, and deep voice, he initially was cast as a heavy in Hopalong Cassidy westerns. Mitchum was propelled to stardom and garnered the only Academy Award nomination of his career for his performance as war correspondent Ernie Pyle's lieutenant in *The Story of G. I. Joe* (1945).[2]

According to *Modern Screen*, Mitchum was "the most rugged bit of star stuff to hit Hollywood in ages—a restless, rollicking, talented ex-hobo with the kick of a Missouri mule in both fists and a reckless laugh in his eyes."[3] After a brief stint in the army, he returned to the screen as the personification of the *film noir* hero in movies like *The Locket* (1946) and *Out of the Past*. Mitchum had just finished work on the film *Rachel and the Stranger* (1948) and was in the midst of a seven-year contract owned jointly by RKO and David O. Selznick when his rapidly rising career appeared to come to an abrupt end.

On September 1, 1948, Mitchum and a friend named Robert Ford visited the home of aspiring actress Lila Leeds in a secluded neighborhood in the Hollywood Hills. Leeds had appeared in a few minor, often uncredited roles and was living in the cottage along with dancer Vickie Evans. The group had agreed to meet and, in the vernacular of the day, partake in a marijuana party.

The four were inside smoking when two narcotics officers of the Los Angeles Police Department (LAPD) burst into the home. The LAPD later admitted that both Mitchum and Leeds had been under surveillance for months. Mitchum and his accomplices were arrested on two felony charges that carried a maximum sentence of six years in state prison. Ironically, Mitchum was scheduled to appear at Los Angeles City Hall later that same day to speak about juvenile delinquency as part of National Youth Month.

Mitchum instantly recognized the impact the arrest and the surrounding controversy could have on his career. When the booking officer asked Mitchum his occupation, he replied wryly, "former actor."[4]

The press was alerted to Mitchum's arrest, and reporters swarmed the county jail where he was being held. Never one to hold back, Mitchum spoke freely: "I've got two bosses—David O. Selznick and RKO Studios. Have you ever listened to Selznick or RKO Studio when their (*sic*) peeved? I think I'd just as soon stay in jail."[5] He went on to tell the press that "this is the bitter end" and "I guess I'm washed up."[6] The headline in the *Los Angeles Times* the following morning read "Narcotics Arrest Smashes Film Career, Says Mitchum."[7]

Given the immediate publicity surrounding Mitchum's arrest, which included front-page stories in papers across the country, it was impossible for the incident to be kept away from the public. Since the studios and their fixers normally operated behind the scenes to contain problems before they garnered attention, it was not surprising that a "source close to Howard Hughes" said the owner of RKO "would do nothing to aid the actor... Hughes would pull no political strings or pay for any high-priced legal talent to defend the star against marijuana smoking charges."[8] An individual within the David O. Selznick organization expressed a similar sentiment: "We would, of course, not consider engaging in any so-called wire-pulling nor would we be so foolish as to attempt to use any influence."[9]

Mitchum's arrest and the ensuing legal proceedings were in the headlines for months, which made the scandal "one of the biggest to hit Hollywood in years."[10] The publicity was such that RKO and Selznick were initially worried that the public would rush to judgment and vilify Mitchum. "Both studios feel confident that the American people will not permit Mr. Mitchum's prominence in the motion-picture industry to deprive him of the rights and privileges of every American citizen to receive fair play," they said optimistically in a joint statement. "We request the press, industry and the public to withhold its judgment until all facts are known."[11]

The two organizations had a lot invested in Mitchum's career, including at least $6,000,000 of studio capital tied up in unreleased films featuring the actor. The movies included *Rachel and the Stranger* and *Blood on the Moon* (1948) at RKO and *Red Pony* (1949) at Republic Pictures.

Making matters even worse for the industry in general, law enforcement officials in Los Angeles threatened further action. "This is just the beginning of a Hollywood cleanup," declared the officer who headed up the raid that snagged Mitchum. "We have many other important and prominent Hollywood screen people under surveillance, not only actors and actresses, but others high up in the industry."[12]

It was reported that "film leaders recognized the narcotics exposé might have repercussions that would reflect upon the entire industry."[13] Gossip columnist Hedda Hopper lamented, in flowery prose, that Mitchum's actions "have drawn a torrent of destructive attention upon the entire industry with a free-for-all splurge in 57 varieties of scandal, malicious tongue-wagging and dirt."[14]

Mitchum faced serious charges related to the arrest, and the organizations that owned his contract continued to keep their distance. "Bob must be a sick man," said David O. Selznick. "If he is guilty, let's find the basic reason that led him into it—let's find the root of the evil"[15] Selznick's studio publicly refuted reports that it was contributing to "any alleged fund for his defense."[16] RKO issued its own statement, which read in part, "If he has done it, we hope he will come clean and confess."[17]

Not surprisingly, those close to Mitchum supported him unequivocally. "I am indignant that not only Bob but our whole family should have to suffer," declared Mitchum's wife Dorothy, "simply because he is a motion-picture star, because otherwise I don't think that all this fuss would be made."[18] Mitchum's secretary, Reva Frederick, went so far as to say, "It looks to me like he was framed."[19]

Hughes, despite the posturing of RKO, also supported Mitchum. Wanting to make sure the actor had the best representation possible, Hughes hired noted Hollywood attorney Jerry Giesler, "the man who handles the film capital's troubles from peccadillo to perjury, including pot shots at Pooh-Bahs."[20] Giesler had successfully defended, among others, Errol Flynn on charges of statutory rape and Charlie Chaplin for supposedly taking a woman across state lines for sexual purposes in violation of the White-Slave Traffic Act (1910).[21]

For Mitchum's defense, Giesler immediately sought to question the validity of the arrest. "There are many unexplained facts and peculiar circumstances surrounding the raid in which Mitchum was involved," Giesler said in a statement issued to the press.[22] Giesler also questioned why "this case evidently is to be singled out from the hundreds of identical cases which are not deemed to be of sufficient importance to submit before the grand jury."[23]

Despite Giesler's posturing, Mitchum and his codefendants were indicted by the Los Angeles County grand jury on September 7 on charges of possessing marijuana and criminal conspiracy to violate the state's narcotics laws. Officers involved in the raid testified at the hearing, where they described Mitchum's arrest and the comments he made to authorities and the press while in custody. A police chemist also testified to the potency of the seized marijuana.

Mitchum surrendered to the court the following day. Having already been booked in county jail, Mitchum was released on his previously posted bond of $1,000. The actor was arraigned on September 21, and he officially pleaded not guilty on September 29.

Prior to the plea, Giesler tried to get the indictments thrown out on legal and technical grounds. He argued that the "evidence was insufficient, suggested that smoking marijuana in private did not constitute a public offense, and challenged the constitutionality of the narcotics law."[24] The judge denied Giesler's motion, and a trial date was set for November 22. The date was later pushed to January 10, 1949, when Giesler was seriously injured in an auto accident.

In response to Mitchum's legal proceedings, a "barrage of anti-Hollywood comment began to pile up in the lay and secular press," and many within the industry "feared some permanent harm may be done."[25] The independent

Hughes however saw an opportunity, which once again put him at odds with the conventions that traditionally governed the industry.

Instead of invoking the morals clause in Mitchum's contract, which would allow RKO to distance itself from the incident by suspending or even terminating the actor, Hughes decided to capitalize on the publicity surrounding one of his studio's biggest stars. Hughes had RKO "rush [*Rachel and the Stranger*] into release immediately on as wide a basis as possible," even going so far as to displace films that had already been booked.[26] As a result, *Rachel and the Stranger* appeared onscreen the same week Mitchum was formally arraigned on felony charges.

In the film, Big Davey (William Holden) is a pioneer who lives in the backwoods of Ohio in the mid-nineteenth century. His wife has passed away, and believing his son needs a female influence, he purchases an indentured servant named Rachel (Loretta Young). The two marry, but Big Davey treats her as a housemaid and not a wife. Jim Fairways (Mitchum), a family friend, arrives at the homestead. Recognizing the marriage is a sham, Jim falls in love with Rachel. Jim and Big Davey quarrel, but everyone is brought together to repel an Indian invasion. After Jim leaves to pursue the Indians, Big Davey finally embraces Rachel as his wife.

The decision to rush *Rachel and the Stranger* into theatres was criticized by many within the industry. The Associated Theatre Owners of Indiana, in their weekly bulletin, took especially sharp aim at Hughes and RKO. "This is not to heap coals on the head of Robert Mitchum," they wrote. "The greater transgressors are those who rush in to grab off a few dollars as a result of the publicity attached to the affair. We advise every independent exhibitor who is conscious of his own local public relations to pass up these pictures, at least until the current publicity is long forgotten."[27] It was reported that even some executives at RKO thought it was best to delay the film "hoping for the press furor [to] die down."[28] Motion Picture Association of America (MPAA) president Eric Johnston was forced to respond to the scandal by making public relations a key topic of discussion at a week's long meeting that including all the organization's members.

Despite some backlash, *Rachel and the Stranger* received generally positive reviews. *The New York Times* said it had the "necessary complements of fine story spinning, subdued and natural characterizations and excellent moviemaking."[29] The *Chicago Tribune* wrote that it "offers an excellent cast, an interesting early American background, and some pleasing old ballads."[30] The reviewer for the *Los Angeles Times* noted that Mitchum "provides an impressive portrait of a happy-go-lucky wanderer who turns into a backwoods Cupid."[31]

More importantly, the film performed well at the box office. *Variety* reported that exhibitors were "almost falling over themselves in efforts to book it."[32] According to internal company documents, *Rachel and the Stranger* earned a profit of $395,000, which made it one of RKO's biggest hits of 1948.[33]

As Mitchum's trial date approached, Hughes continued to publicly support the actor in defiance of industry norms. "In a surprise move," Hughes announced that Mitchum would star in a new movie, entitled *The Big Steal* (1949), and filming would begin immediately.[34] Hughes said RKO had "kept Mitchum out of work for five months. That's long enough."[35] When asked what would happen to the production if Mitchum was convicted, Hughes replied, "We will cross that bridge when we come to it."[36] Although he did not admit it, Hughes hoped the idea of shutting down production and putting 100 people out of work would entice the presiding judge in the case to offer Mitchum probation instead of a jail term.

When the trial finally began on January 10, 1949, "the courtroom and corridors were jammed with the bobby soxers and the smiling Mitchum scrawled autografs (*sic*) as he advanced to the bench."[37] In a series of legal maneuvers, some of which had been negotiated in advance, Giesler got the two counts, conspiracy and possession, severed. The court agreed to begin with the conspiracy charge, and the defense waived a jury trial.

The prosecution planned to call around a dozen witnesses, but in a risky legal gamble, Giesler waived a defense and had the case submitted on the grand jury testimony alone. The transcripts were read into the record, and a little over an hour after the hearing began, judge Clement D. Nye found Mitchum, along with Leeds and Ford, guilty of conspiracy.[38] A sentencing date was scheduled, and when Mitchum left the courtroom, "he was literally mobbed by the hundreds of persons who were unable to get into the courtroom."[39]

At his sentencing in February, Mitchum was ordered to serve sixty days in jail followed by two years of probation. It was agreed that the more serious charge of possessing marijuana would be dropped upon completion of the term. Judge Nye said he handled the case "the same as I would any other case of similar nature," but he nevertheless admonished Mitchum for having "overlooked the responsibilities that go with such prominence and failed to set an example of good citizenship."[40] As he was being led out of the courtroom in handcuffs, Mitchum spoke with reporters. "This has been a sad lesson," said the actor. "It's the last time anything like this will happen to me."[41]

Mitchum was back in court two days later as Giesler, at the behest of Hughes, sought a postponement of the jail sentence so Mitchum could finish filming *The Big Steal* which was about halfway through production. "I'm not speaking for Mr. Mitchum as an individual, but rather for the more than 100 people who face a layoff on the studio lot because of his enforced absence," Giesler pleaded.[42]

Judge Nye was not persuaded. "If I tried to aid every innocent person who suffers with every convicted person I would have to empty the jail," he said in reply. "The studio officials should have realized that there was a hazard about Mr. Mitchum's appearance from the time he was arrested last September."[43] The motion was denied, and Hughes was forced to postpone filming until Mitchum was released.

Instead of letting the story quietly disappear as Mitchum served his time, Hughes continued to exploit the scandal as a way to further promote his star. Hughes made sure the press was on hand and given access to Mitchum throughout his confinement. Papers across the country featured photographs of prisoner number 234 in prison garb doing menial tasks such as mopping the floor. "I've been pretty happy in the tank here," Mitchum told reporters.[44] When asked what he did with his spare time, Mitchum replied sarcastically that he and the other prisoners "just talk over our lives of crime."[45]

When Mitchum was transferred to a work farm about a week into his sentence, he continued to make headlines. He was photographed milking cows and making cement blocks. He proudly reported that he was losing weight "in the proper places" and had a ".800 batting average on the softball team."[46] "Never felt better in my life," Mitchum proclaimed. "That farm's just like a weekend in Palm Springs. Great place to get into shape."[47] Mitchum ultimately had to be transferred from the farm back to the county jail because, in the words of chief jailer Charles Fitzgerald, "too many people came to see him there."[48]

Critics thought the promotional campaign had gone too far. "It is a little difficult to determine at this distance whether Robert Mitchum is serving a jail term in California," lamented the *Minneapolis Tribune*, "or is dancing a publicity schottische with his studio press agent."[49] Many were especially worried about the impact on children. "Mitchum's film company gave him a tremendous amount of publicity," complained Spruille Braden, chairman of the New York Anti-Crime Committee. "It is discouraging to the citizenry and a bad example to our youth."[50] A letter to the *Los Angeles Times* wondered, "With the cries of 'juvenile delinquency' filling our ears, how are we expected to combat that problem, when a star like Mitchum, who portrays the role of a virile, brave he-man in pictures, and whom many of our youngsters are apt to pattern their actions after, is protected by the movie colony?"[51]

Hughes however was happy with the exposure, and he made sure it was well known that "Mitchum's career would be resumed without a hitch as soon as his 60-day jail term ends."[52] Following Hughes's lead, RKO and the

Selznick organization, Mitchum's official employers, changed their public stance and finally embraced the actor. An RKO spokesman acknowledged that Mitchum had a morals clause in his contract but conceded that there was no chance "it would be brought to bear in an effort to end the star's four-year agreement with the studio."[53] Selznick went ever further and hailed Mitchum as a "superb artist and an intelligent man" who will "go on to even greater success than he enjoyed prior to this unfortunate situation."[54]

Mitchum was released from jail on March 30, 1949, having served fifty days of his sixty-day sentence.[55] Less than a week later, he was back on the set of *The Big Steal*. His ordeal had finally come to an end, and despite his prediction on the night of the arrest, Mitchum was still an actor. In fact, he was an even bigger star upon his release from jail, having been transformed from a popular actor to "a cult icon, the screen's new godfather of cool."[56]

Hughes defied conventions, yet again, and he was proven correct, yet again. Hughes was even successful in getting organizations that were critical of his actions in the past to concede they were virtually powerless to stop him. The MPAA said the "matter of censure or similar action is one between the actor and his studio," while the Legion of Decency noted that they were "interested solely in the finished product of the studios and not in the private lives of the men who make pictures."[57]

This attitude was put to the test a little over a year later when Hughes found himself involved in an even bigger scandal which centered on the RKO film *Stromboli* (1950), directed by Italian auteur Roberto Rossellini.[58] Rossellini had made a name for himself in the Italian neorealist cinema with films like *Open City* (1945) and *Paisà* (1946). Italian neorealism told stories set among the poor and working class that used a documentary style and featured non-professional actors filmed on location. Rossellini often used only a loose outline when filming, as scenes were written as conditions and inspiration dictated.

Having worked almost exclusively in Europe, Rossellini's relationship with Hollywood was complicated. "I am not one to say Hollywood is terrible," he was quoted in *Time*. "It is like a sausage factory that turns out fine sausages."[59] Rossellini had come to the meat grinder in January 1949 in search of financing for his latest film, which was tentatively titled *After a Storm* (or *Against the Storm*) at the time. He was also there to woo his latest muse, actress Ingrid Bergman.

Born in Sweden in 1915, Bergman studied acting at the state-sponsored Royal Dramatic Theatre School, the same institute Greta Garbo had attended years earlier. Discovered by the head of a Swedish movie studio, she acted in a dozen Swedish films before catching the eye of producer David O. Selznick. "The minute I looked at her, I knew I had something,"

Selznick recalled years later. "She had an extraordinary quality of purity and nobility, and a definite star personality that is very rare."[60]

Bergman made her American film debut in 1939. During a five year period—1942 to 1946—she emerged as the biggest female star in the world, with hits like *Casablanca* (1942), *For Whom the Bell Tolls* (1943), *Gaslight* (1944), *Spellbound* (1945), *Saratoga Trunk* (1945), *The Bells of St. Mary's* (1945), and *Notorious* (1946). Her performance in *Gaslight* earned her an Academy Award for Best Actress in a Leading Role.

Beyond her obvious talent, her fame was due in part to a carefully crafted persona and reputation. A publicity man who worked for Selznick listed a few of the rules: "There were dozens of 'don'ts': Don't show her legs, don't show her smoking, don't show her drinking. Don't ever use slang in connection with her name. Don't refer to her as anything except 'Miss Bergman,' even in office memos."[61] Bergman came to be known publicly as a natural beauty (she didn't pluck her eyebrows!) who was humble and pure. And more than simply an actress, she was also a seemingly devoted wife and mother. She met her husband Dr. Petter Lindström in Sweden, and the couple had a young daughter named Pia.

"I'm afraid I'm responsible for the public's image of her as Saint Ingrid," Selznick admitted. "I hired a press agent who was an expert at shielding stars from the press, and we released only stories that emphasized her sterling character. We deliberately built her up as a normal, healthy, non-neurotic career woman, devoid of scandal and with an idyllic home life."[62] Bergman herself noted that she was "regarded as the wholesome, well-mannered girl, the actress without make-up, the Hollywood exception. People didn't expect me to have emotions like other women."[63]

Bergman's reputation was so powerful it obscured the fact that she often portrayed less than virtuous characters onscreen. Bergman was promiscuous in several films, such as *Dr. Jekyll and Mr. Hyde* (1941) and *Notorious*, while her character was having or had an affair in others, including *Casablanca* and *For Whom the Bell Tolls*. While one critic commented that it was "hard to accept this proper lady as the willful courtesan she's supposed to be" in *Saratoga Trunk*, the public had no trouble believing because they saw the role as a devotion to her craft rather than an indication of her personality off screen.[64] If life imitated art, it was more obvious when she played a nun in *The Bells of St. Mary's* or a saint in *Joan of Arc* (1948).

After her initial seven-year contract with Selznick expired, she decided to pursue opportunities independently with her husband serving as her manager. A series of financially disappointing movies followed, including *Joan of Arc*. Bergman longed to play the French icon, and after a successful stint on Broadway, she brought the story to the big screen. Bergman helped finance the production, and while it was one of the top-grossing films of the year, its huge budget made it unprofitable.

Bergman felt lost, professionally and personally. "I had success. I had security," she confided. "But it wasn't enough. I was exploding inside."[65] She was drained physically and emotionally, but her artistic drive was renewed when she saw Roberto Rossellini's gritty and honest work. She reached out to the director, and the two agreed to collaborate on their next picture.

While Rossellini was in Hollywood, he and Bergman initially approached producer Samuel Goldwyn about funding their project. Goldwyn was interested but insisted that Rossellini use a detailed shooting script so the producer could track the film's schedule and finances. Rossellini replied that he did not use scripts. "Since I shoot in real interiors or in exteriors that haven't been touched-up beforehand," he wrote in a French magazine in 1955, "I can only improvise my stagings in function of the setting I find myself in."[66]

Goldwyn was incredulous but with Bergman, not Rossellini. "Everyone in town is offering her scripts. Why does she want to get into a story without a script?" Goldwyn wondered. "There's got to be something else going on. They're either having an affair or about to have one."[67] Goldwyn refused to finance the movie, so the pair scrambled to find a different backer.

Subsequent studios and producers reacted as Goldwyn did to Rossellini, so the duo finally turned to RKO and Howard Hughes. Bergman had worked with RKO in the past, the company having most recently distributed *The Bells of St. Mary's* and *Joan of Arc*, and she had met Hughes a year earlier. Bergman later confided that she did not like Hughes as he made her feel uncomfortable, but she was running out of options.

A meeting was set up between the star, the director, and the mogul. "How much money do you need?" Hughes asked Bergman completely ignoring Rossellini. Bergman tried to talk about the film's story, but Hughes cut her off. "No... I don't care what sort of story it is. Are you beautiful in it? Are you going to have wonderful clothes?"[68] Bergman informed Hughes that the film would be more realistic and austere. Hughes was disappointed, but he agreed to finance and distribute the film with the understanding that Bergman would make a follow-up film at RKO. She agreed.

Rossellini had his money, but he was not impressed with Hughes. "Hughes had a tone of great contempt, great superiority," he was reported as complaining. "He was the sort who says: 'I don't give a damn about the film he wants to make! To make you see who I am, I'll make the contract and assume the distribution, and he can make any kind of film he wants.'"[69]

Rossellini could take comfort in the fact that the final contract with RKO was rather generous for the director and star. Rossellini would receive twenty percent of net profits, while Bergman would receive forty percent along with a salary of $175,000. While the final contract did not require a second picture for Bergman, it did specify that two prints of the movie would be made. Rossellini had control over the film that would be shown in Italy, but Hughes had final edit on the English version which would be exhibited in the rest of the world.

The film was to be shot on the island of Stromboli, some forty miles off the northeast coast of Sicily, and the location would ultimately be used for the film's title. Built by a series of volcanic eruptions, Stromboli is one of the liveliest volcanoes on Earth, having been active for the last 2,000 years. The island's continual eruptions led to rampant speculation over the years. Upon passing Stromboli in the twelfth century, "returning crusaders professed distinctly to have heard the lamentations of tortured souls in purgatory, to which this was said to be the entrance."[70]

The island is around five square miles, but only a few acres are inhabitable. When Rossellini and Bergman arrived, accompanied by a crew of sixty-five, approximately 500 people inhabited the isolated and desolate location. "All this talk about authenticity is swell," observed Harold Lewis who had been sent to the island by Hughes to oversee the film for RKO, "but you sure can overdo it."[71]

Rossellini had enlisted two fishermen from Salerno to play the male leads with the rest of the supporting cast filled out by locals on the island, most of whom had never even seen a movie. To get the amateurs to react and speak at the appropriate time, Rossellini would pull on a string he tied to their toes. The director was in his element working on location and without a script, but for the professionally trained Hollywood actress, the conditions were brutal.

"You can have these realistic pictures," Bergman shouted to Rossellini at one point of utter frustration. "To hell with them! These people don't even know what dialogue is, they don't know where to stand; they don't even *care* what they're doing. I can't bear to work another day with you!"[72]

Bergman never fully adjusted to living and working on the island. She nevertheless managed to persevere because she and Rossellini had fallen in love. The romance between Hollywood's sweetheart and the Italian director, who was known to be a playboy, would have been controversial by itself, but the fact that the two were married to others and had young children made it especially scandalous.

Gossip columnist Cholly Knickerbocker was the first to speculate publicly on the affair: "Rumors of a romance between Ingrid Bergman, Sweden's greatest gift to Hollywood since Greta Garbo, and Roberto Rossellini, Italy's foremost director, have been rampant ever since Ingrid flew to Rome to star in a new Rossellini picture. But the rumors were only repeated in discreet whispers, since both Miss Bergman and Signor Rossellini are married."[73] *Life* magazine followed by printing a photograph of the two holding hands.

When pressed by the media, Rossellini said, "I do not choose to answer. I neither confirm nor deny. I have nothing to say as yet. She is an excellent actress and it is pleasure to work with her."[74]

If Bergman was still under the protection and watchful eye of producer David O. Selznick, a fixer likely would have squashed any rumors before they had a chance to appear in the press. But Bergman was now on her own, and as it would soon become clear, Howard Hughes certainly was not going to protect her.

Joseph Breen however felt compelled to act. As head of the Production Code Administration (PCA), it was his job to safeguard the reputation of the entire motion picture industry. Recognizing the looming controversy and the impact it could have, he wrote a letter to Bergman.

> In recent days, the American newspapers have carried, rather widely, a story to the effect that you are about to divorce your husband, forsake your child, and marry Roberto Rossellini. It goes without saying that these reports are the cause of great consternation among large numbers of our people who have come to look upon you as the *first* lady of the screen—both individually and artistically... Such stories will not only not react favorably to your picture, but may very well *destroy your career as a motion picture artist*.[75]

Hollywood producers and corporate executives, like Breen looking out more for the industry than Bergman, expressed similar concerns.

As the rumors intensified, filming on the island continued. Rossellini initially indicated to Hughes and RKO that filming would take ten weeks. When RKO executives reviewed the early footage shipped back to the studio in Hollywood, they realized ten weeks was overly optimistic. "I wonder how anybody can spend the whole day getting so little," RKO studio manager Sid Rogell commented after looking at dailies.[76] Hughes did not mind spending endless amounts of time and money when he was directing a picture, but he was not about to let someone else waste resources, especially on a film that was never intended to be epic or glamorous.

Hughes grew so frustrated that he threatened to cut off funds and abandon the production. "Now RKO tries in every possible way to kill [Rossellini]," Bergman wrote to her confidant and press agent Joseph Steele. She went on to lament "all these stories [about the affair] and the outrageous way the Rome office of RKO behaves have broken RR's spirit."[77] Bergman and Rossellini nonetheless managed to carry on despite the increased supervision of Hughes and RKO.

Rossellini even managed to adapt when the volcano erupted on June 7 spewing lava down the uninhabited side of the island. "The volcano was very good to me," Rossellini said years later. "The finale was supposed to be like that, though it was difficult to see how it could be made. But it started erupting quite happily. I always have confidence that these things will work out."[78]

Bergman, a consummate professional even when surrounded by amateurs, also learned to adapt to the director's style. "Sometimes he had a bit of trouble explaining what he wanted, but after that it was a communication by thought process," she wrote in her autobiography. "I could read his eyes. Even when he couldn't explain in words what he wanted, I felt *what* he wanted."[79]

But tragedy almost struck when Bergman, who did not have a double onset, was instructed to scale the volcano in one of the final scenes to be shot on the island. The conditions were difficult as the ground was hot from lava and toxic fumes permeated the air. Bergman was making her way up the volcano when she lost her footing and slid several hundred feet down a rocky incline. Her arms and legs were left bruised and bleeding. "It was one of the most dangerous shots I ever saw," said a technician working on the film.[80] Bergman was naturally proud of her work. "I would like to see another actress work on the edge of a volcano with sulphur fumes choking her almost to death and the wind trying to blow her into the crater," she boasted. "Well, I did it."[81]

Finally, after 102 days of filming and scrutiny, production on the island concluded on August 2. A few days of filming on the mainland followed. Having spent months battling press scrutiny, Rossellini and Bergman now had to face Howard Hughes.

The pair were contractually obligated to return to Hollywood for postproduction, but wanting to remain in Europe, Rossellini "kidnapped" some of the negatives and refused to deliver them until Hughes relented and allowed them to stay.[82] After Rossellini dubbed and edited the film for its exhibition in Italy, the director sent his cut to Hughes so it could be used as the basis for the English version which would be shown in the rest of the world.

The contract gave Hughes final edit on the English version, and he made significant changes in an attempt to turn a slow European film into a manageable Hollywood movie. Around thirty-five minutes were removed, a prologue was added to the beginning, voiceover narration was employed to help explain what was going on, and the ending was altered.

A horrified Rossellini believed Hughes had butchered the film so he filed suit to stop the English version from being exhibited anywhere. Rossellini lost in court, and he lamented that he was "living proof of the brutality that dominates Hollywood."[83]

In the film, Karin (Bergman) is a Czech refugee stranded in a displaced persons camp in the aftermath of World War II. Antonio (Mario Vitale), an ex-Italian soldier and former prisoner of war, attempts to romance Karin despite their language and cultural differences. Desperate to leave the camp, she marries Antonio and accompanies him to his home on the island of Stromboli.

Karin is shocked to learn that the island is bleak and almost devoid of life, human or otherwise. Karin tells Antonio that she wants to leave, but he tells her that she has to stay because she is his wife. The island's inhabitants shun Karin because she is different. The only exception is the lighthouse keeper (Mario Sponza). Antonio comes to believe the two are having an affair, so he beats Karin and confines her to their home.

When Karin learns she is pregnant, the island's volcano erupts in fury. She escapes from her house, and not wanting her child to be born in such a place, she tries to cross the volcano to catch a boat off the island. Overcome by the volcano's heat and fumes, Karin collapses. She awakes the next morning to find the volcano peaceful and beautiful. Seeing God in its serenity, Karin decides to return to Antonio and their life together.[84]

As the film was being prepared for its American release, Bergman and Rossellini remained at the center of intense scrutiny. The couple finally confirmed that the rumors of a romance were true, but conflicting reports said Bergman had nonetheless decided to return to her husband. In reality, both Bergman and Rossellini had informed their respective spouses that they planned to seek a divorce.

The couple also learned that they were expecting a child. A romance was one thing, but the consummation of an illicit affair would be an even greater publicity disaster, so they tried to hide the news. "Ingrid declares she will bring suit against the Italian papers which said she was going to have a baby," gossip columnist Hedda Hopper wrote in her influential column. "I don't blame her; there is not a word of truth in it."[85] One person Bergman did confide in was Joseph Steele, and she assured him that "no storm will be strong enough to wash us away."[86]

Although Steele was a seasoned publicity man, he was first and foremost Bergman's friend. He worried from the outset about the impact the romance with Rossellini would have on Bergman's career, but he knew she was not content with her husband. If she was happy with Rossellini, he was happy. Steele likely thought that when the time was right he could spin the romance into something out of a fairy tale. But a child born out of wedlock while she was still married to someone else was harder to control. Steele knew the public outcry would likely ruin Bergman's career.

Making matters worse, Bergman was also facing serious financial troubles. Her salary for the film went to her husband to take care of their daughter, and the IRS had a lien on her income for unpaid taxes.[87] Set to receive forty percent of the net profits on *Stromboli*, Bergman had a lot riding on the film. Steele desperately wanted to help, and he believed the only solution was to rush the film into theatres prior to the birth of the child "before anybody starts banning it."[88] The only person who could do this was Howard Hughes, so Steele decided to meet directly with the owner of RKO.

Steele told Hughes about the pregnancy imploring him to keep it a secret: "If this gets out there'll be hell to pay. I'm doing it only for Ingrid, but if she knew about it, she'd never forgive me."[89] He pleaded with Hughes to rush the film into theatres in hopes of saving it not just for Bergman but also for RKO. Hughes agreed, and Steele felt confident he had done the right thing for Bergman.

The next day, Steele woke up to a headline that appeared in over 1,000 papers worldwide. It proclaimed "Ingrid Bergman Baby Due in Three Months at Rome."[90] Steele's attempt to control the story backfired in a way he never could have imagined.

Gossip columnist Louella Parsons broke the news. "The story created a sensation," she later recalled. "The greatest ever, I believe, in relation to a story about a movie personality." Parsons refused to disclose how she learned of the pregnancy, but she gave a clue in her autobiography. "I was given a message from a man of great importance not only in Hollywood, but throughout the United States," she wrote. "He had connections in many parts of the world—including Italy—whose sources of information could not be questioned."[91] Although some have speculated the source may have been newspaper tycoon William Randolph Hearst, Steele believed that Hughes disclosed the information he had provided only twenty-four hours earlier in an attempt to further publicize the film.[92]

Hughes's subsequent actions certainly seem to indicate that he was complicit in divulging the secret. Instead of trying to avoid the controversy surrounding Bergman's pregnancy, Hughes timed the release of *Stromboli* to coincide with the birth, just as he had done with Mitchum's arraignment and *Rachel and the Stranger*.

Going even further, *Stromboli*'s marketing campaign, which was "prepared by Hughes himself," was a thinly veiled allusion to the affair at the center of the production.[93] Using the tagline "Raging Island… Raging Passions!" and the backdrop of an exploding volcano, posters and advertisements showed Bergman, with a look of ecstasy upon her face, locked in a heated embrace with her co-star Mario Vitale. "This is it!" was written in large letters, along with the keywords Stromboli, Bergman, and Rossellini.

Gordon White, head of the Advertising Code Administration (ACA), noted that the "circumstances under which these ads have appeared have caused people both in and out of our industry to see trouble with them." He went on to say that the complaints "made no reference to the advertising as such, but have objected bitterly to the very idea of cashing in on the scandal by heavy advertising."[94]

White told Hughes the posters and other advertisements were in bad taste and recommended they not be used. "My advice was not taken," White reported to MPAA president Johnston, "as it turned out, this is the very thing Mr. Hughes picked for heavy use, and the other ads were thrown out."[95]

But since the film and the advertisement used to promote it were not technically in violation of the code, there was nothing the ACA or the MPAA could do to stop them. Hughes's refusal to work with the censors, voluntarily or not, had taken its toll. "I would be less than human, I suppose," White lamented, "if I were not affected at all by the unrelenting pressure which Mr. Hughes brings to bear on us whenever he chooses to take a personal interest in an advertising campaign."[96] It appeared Hughes had found a new way to beat the censors.

Hughes ordered 800 prints of the film in anticipation of its nationwide release on February 15, 1950. (Renato Roberto Giusto Giuseppe Rossellini, son of Ingrid Bergman and Roberto Rossellini, was born on February 2.) A typical print run for RKO was anywhere from 300 to 500, so Hughes was clearly expecting high demand for the film. The *Hollywood Reporter* noted that it could reach "a maximum of 1,500 prints, an all-time company and industry record."[97]

But as the opening neared, a backlash against the film and its participants arose. "You can't disassociate the film from its principles," said reverend C. E. Byrne, bishop of the Galveston Diocese of the Catholic Church. "[Bergman and Rossellini] have been guilty of the most contemptible and outrageous conduct in centuries."[98]

Exhibitors and civic groups across the country called for a ban on the film. "It is time the exhibitors of the nation refused to play pictures starring persons who bring discredit to them and the motion picture business," proclaimed J. P. Finneran, an exhibitor with theatres in six Indiana cities. "That will make immorality and misconduct unprofitable for Hollywood and force them to deal with the public."[99]

Some censorship boards "decided it wasn't objectionable, but banned the picture anyhow because it starred Miss Bergman."[100] Hughes responded by successfully bringing suit against exhibitors and boards for censoring the film for reasons not contained in the film itself.

The uproar surrounding the film reached the hallowed halls of the United States Congress. Senator Edwin Johnson of Colorado, a leader in the Swedish–American community, spent more than an hour on the Senate floor denouncing Bergman and the film. He was especially infuriated with the way Hughes marketed the film and his legal action against those who refused to exhibit it.

> Their disgusting publicity campaign for it permitted no revolting bedroom scene to escape, and stressed passion in its worst sense. RKO had word that the anticipated birth should take place about February 15, so that was the day RKO selected to run the film in their theatres. The nauseating commercial opportunism displayed by this corporation and their partner, the vile and unspeakable Rossellini, sets an all-time low in shameless exploitation and disregard for good public morals. When they deliberately exhibited the moral turpitude of the leading lady to pack their theatres, how can they contend that since the weak, pointless, and ugly film itself was not definitely immoral, no question of morality was involved?[101]

Hoping to ban "a powerful influence for evil" like Bergman, Johnson called unsuccessfully for a bill that would require all entertainment industry members to be licensed to work.[102]

The film was released as scheduled on February 15 in those areas of the country where it had not been banned. *Variety* claimed that the "amount of newspaper space and radio time garnered by the film is undoubtedly the greatest that any picture has ever received."[103] Even Bergman conceded that the publicity surrounding the film could be a good thing. "The scandal probably has helped, I think," she said, "there can't be a man, woman, or child who won't be curious to see *what* happened in Stromboli, even if the picture is bad."[104] And the critics certainly thought it was bad.

Bosley Crowther of *The New York Times* lamented that "it comes as a startling anticlimax to discover that this widely heralded film is incredibly feeble, inarticulate, uninspiring and painfully banal."[105] The *New York Herald Tribune* said there was "no depth to Ingrid Bergman's performance, no vitality to Roberto Rossellini's direction."[106] *Time*, which called the film "a bleak, draggy little picture," argued that "would-be moralists who are trying to punish [Bergman] and Director Rossellini for their private transgressions by banning *Stromboli* might serve their own ends better by having the picture shown as widely as possible."[107]

Despite the negative reviews, the controversy surrounding the film initially did draw patrons to the theatre. *Variety* sent correspondents across the country, and they reported it "smashed [an] opening day record" in Chicago, was the "best pix RKO has played" in San Francisco, and there was a "line half a block long" in Miami.[108] But after a week, the novelty apparently diminished, and attendance plummeted. *Stromboli* turned out to be a financial disappointment, losing approximately $200,000 on an $847,000 budget.[109] Rossellini blamed Hughes for butchering the film, and in an ironic choice of words, he "repudiated the paternity" of the English version.[110]

After transitioning from an independent producer to a studio mogul, Hughes continued his unorthodox approach to filmmaking. Studios in the past tried to avoid controversy, and they carefully guarded the reputation of their biggest stars. But Hughes had seemingly sought controversy his entire career, and as a mogul, he was the first to actively embrace scandal as a way to promote his motion pictures. The results were mixed.

Robert Mitchum's arrest and conviction for conspiring to possess marijuana helped make *Rachel and the Stranger* a hit, and it solidified Mitchum's status as the biggest star at RKO. His career was not "washed up for good" as Mitchum speculated the night of his arrest.[111]

Ingrid Bergman was not so lucky. The affair and pregnancy at the center of *Stromboli* did not help the movie financially. Bergman's career was left in shatters, and she was absent from Hollywood for six years "while American film moguls blackballed her."[112]

Bergman starred in several European productions for Rossellini and one for French director Jean Renoir before returning to prominence with the Twentieth Century-Fox film *Anastasia* (1956). Her performance garnered rave reviews, and she was awarded an Academy Award for Best Actress, the second of Bergman's career. Audiences in the United States finally seemed to have forgiven her after years of exile, but the scandal followed Bergman for the rest of her life.[113] Her reputation never recovered.

Looking beyond the initial test cases, Hughes had unleashed a force greater than he could have ever imagined. As one studio executive said in the aftermath of the Bergman affair, "I can tell you it hit Hollywood with the greatest impact I've ever witnessed. That's all anybody is talking about."[114] And that was the point.

People, in and out of the industry, in America and around the world, were talking about the film. The publicity was unparalleled, and while the MPAA responded by trying to ban material that exploited the misconduct of screen personalities, the embrace of scandal would eventually become industry wide. "The public's fascination with such disgraceful—sometimes tragic—activity among Hollywood's famous is boundless," notes James Robert Parish, author of *The Hollywood Book of Scandals*.[115] Fixers would thus give way to a new breed of publicity people who sought to spin and capitalize on transgressions rather than hide them. Hughes had changed the industry yet again, and his tenure at RKO was not over.

# In Absolute Charge

"You're beautiful in your wrath."—
Temujin (John Wayne) in *The Conqueror*

Howard Hughes had a long track record as an independent producer prior to purchasing controlling interest in RKO in 1948. That history clearly indicated that Hughes was a hands-on filmmaker interested in all aspects of moviemaking, from story conceptualization and production to marketing and exhibition. It also showed that Hughes was willing to do whatever he thought was best for his movies, regardless of industry norms or the opinion of others, in and out of Hollywood.

It therefore should not have been a surprise that Hughes was intricately involved in studio operations as a mogul. His role in theatre divorcement and the exploitation of scandals were two obvious examples, but his time at RKO was filled with other equally important moments that had a profound impact on the history of the motion picture industry. As Noah Dietrich rightly surmised when Hughes first acquired RKO, "it was like turning a boy loose in a candystore and expecting him not to touch the merchandise."[1]

When rumors of Hughes's desire to acquire RKO first emerged, studio employees, mindful of his reputation, were "jittery for weeks pending the outcome of negotiations."[2] RKO president N. Peter Rathvon issued a statement in the aftermath of Hughes's purchase to alleviate their concerns. "Mr. Hughes has no hungry army of relatives looking for your jobs or substitutes waiting to step into the RKO management," Rathvon assured employees. "I have had numerous conversations with Mr. Hughes, and we seem to be in agreement in all matters of policy, and there is no reason to assume that it will be otherwise in the future."[3]

Dore Schary, RKO's vice president in charge of production, also felt compelled to comment. "We have a big schedule planned," he said without mentioning Hughes, "and we must bend our energies to making as many good pictures as we possibly can."[4] Schary was responsible for all studio operations as RKO's production chief, and he had operated with significant power and autonomy since taking the reins in 1947. But as his vague comments seemed to indicate, he was also apprehensive given Hughes's history of micromanagement.

Although Schary was "assured there would be no interference in production plans he had set up," Hughes cancelled a quartet of films a mere eight weeks after assuming control of RKO.[5] One of the films was *Battleground* (1949), a story centering on the Battle of the Bulge that Schary had taken a special interest in and was personally producing. Schary's worst fears were realized, and he quit in protest. He was the first but not the last casualty of the new regime.[6]

President Rathvon once again tried to reassure anxious employees and industry observers. "RKO basically is in good shape," he commented tentatively in the aftermath of Schary's resignation. "Our problems are the same as those which face the film industry as a whole."[7] But a little over a week later, Hollywood was rocked by the news that RKO was cutting studio personnel by seventy-five percent as "part of the complete realignment of the company's policy and production program."[8] An estimated 600 employees out of a normal roster of 2,500 would remain.

As Thomas Brady of *The New York Times* reminded his readers, "the Hughes policy has come as something of a surprise during the last two weeks because, when Hughes acquired control of RKO in May, N. Peter Rathvon, president of the company, issued a strong policy statement denying the prospect of wholesale changes in personnel."[9] President Rathvon was not consulted on the layoffs, and feeling publicly betrayed, he too quit in protest. Hughes chose executive vice president Ned Depinet to succeed him, while a three-man executive committee was appointed to temporarily oversee studio operations in place of Schary.

Regardless of the new assignments, it was clear that Hughes was in complete control of RKO, even if he did not have an official title. Finally, in July 1949, Hughes assumed the newly created post of managing director production, "in absolute charge of all phases of studio operation."[10] It was reported that the board of directors made the decision "recognizing Hughes's experience of more than a score of years in motion-picture work."[11] The *Hollywood Reporter* proclaimed it was "a smashing vote of confidence in the RKO controlling owner's production policies of the past several months."[12]

Under Hughes's leadership, the studio was "operating under bedrock efficiency" and producing very few films of its own.[13] RKO did manage to release thirty new films in 1948 and thirty-six in 1949, but this was due primarily to a combination of independent productions and ones completed in-house prior to Hughes's arrival. More importantly, the studio was operating in the red under Hughes, with a loss of $5,288,750 in 1948 and $3,721,415 in 1949.[14]

RKO executives nevertheless praised Hughes's initial contributions. Executive producer Sid Rogell, the nominal number two at the studio behind Hughes, stated emphatically that "under the leadership of Howard Hughes, every possible bit of waste and duplication of effort has been eliminated," which resulted in the annual reduction of $1,500,000 in overhead.[15] It was reported that studio operations were about to increase dramatically, and president Depinet said Hughes was instrumental "in finalizing our new program, which I consider the greatest array of entertainment this company has ever presented."[16]

Hughes further solidified his control of RKO in 1950. Hughes and Noah Dietrich were appointed to the RKO board of directors shortly after Hughes acquired controlling interest, and in March 1950, Hughes was able to appoint two replacements to the seven-man board. This gave him four of seven seats or majority representation. Shortly thereafter, Dietrich was named chairman of the board. The board then appointed Hughes, Dietrich, and Depinet to the company's newly established executive committee.

Producers at the studio had been reporting to executive producer Sid Rogell, but it was clear that his role was diminishing so he quit. Instead of naming a replacement, Hughes chose to "handle production operations himself without any intermediate executive."[17] RKO producers responded by noting their "complete satisfaction" with Hughes's management, and their "earnest desire to cooperate with Mr. Hughes in every way."[18] Despite the professed faith in Hughes's management, RKO continued to rely on independent productions and co-productions made with other studios.

*Variety*, speaking on behalf of the industry, was perplexed by the "inexplicable failure of RKO to release new product," as less than half of the thirty-two films distributed by RKO in 1950 were outright RKO productions.[19] It was commonly reported that the studio was losing $100,000 a week under Hughes, which was confirmed when the studio's annual financial statement listed a net loss of $5,832,187 for 1950.[20] The studio proved to be such a financial drain that the Radio–Keith–Orpheum Corporation also lost money in 1950, the first time under Hughes's ownership that the profits from the theatre chain did not outpace the picture company's losses.

With theatre divorcement officially taking place at the end of business on December 31, 1950, RKO Radio Pictures, the production and distribution subsidiary of the Radio–Keith–Orpheum Corporation, became the principal subsidiary of the newly established RKO Pictures Corporation. Without a corporate theatre chain, the studio no longer had a guaranteed market for its products at a time when the quality and appeal of RKO movies was in decline, as evident by the fact that not a single film produced by RKO in 1950 managed to earn a profit of $100,000, a first in the studio's history.

RKO executives nevertheless claimed to be undeterred. "We have had a theatre company for 20 years," noted president Depinet, "but I have always held that RKO can operate successfully with or without a theatre company."[21]

Hoping to assuage concerns, RKO heralded the schedule for the upcoming year. "Besides blueprinting an operational format designed to insure (*sic*) the company functioning profitably as a production–distribution organization from here on in," wrote the *Hollywood Reporter*, "Hughes and his associates have lined up in the 1951 program what insiders say will be the company's best in many years."[22]

The results however were no different than any other year under Hughes, with forty-one new but mediocre films distributed by the company. RKO Pictures Corporation actually managed to post a meager profit of $334,627 for 1951, the first profit under Hughes, but it was the result of the recovery of $3,000,000 which had been frozen abroad.[23] Without the overseas assets, the studio would have reported another significant loss.

After years of mediocrity, 1952 proved to be especially noteworthy for Hughes and RKO. Unfortunately, it was the result of Hughes finding himself at the center of another controversy that engulfed the entire industry. And it all had to do with *The Las Vegas Story* (1952), a rare film produced in-house by the studio.

To celebrate the movie's opening in February, Hughes staged "one of the most lavish premieres of recent times."[24] Sixty-six Hollywood reporters and columnists were flown to the title city at the studio's expense, and they were each given fifty silver dollars to use toward gambling. Prior to the screening, which took place at two theatres, Las Vegas's lights were extinguished, "for the first time in its long and gaudy history," to mark the commencement of activities, which included a fireworks display, a parade, and a promenade of celebrities.[25]

One critic in attendance liked the festivities but hated the movie, so he suggested that RKO "should have filmed the premiere and thrown away the picture."[26]

In the film, Lloyd Rollins (Vincent Price) and his wife Linda (Jane Russell) decide to spend a few days in Las Vegas, where Linda once lived. Lloyd is desperate for cash for his failing business so he pawns Linda's expensive necklace for gambling money. Linda runs into her former lover Dave (Victor Mature), a sheriff's lieutenant who still has feelings for Linda.

When the necklace is stolen and Linda's former boss is murdered, both Lloyd and Linda are suspects. Dave discovers that an insurance investigator is to blame, and after a thrilling chase, he is apprehended. The insurance investigator reveals that Lloyd has been stealing from his company, so Lloyd is also arrested. Linda ultimately decides to stay in Vegas with Dave.

The film and its lavish premiere were not controversial. The problem had to do with a missing credit. The movie and all related advertising listed a "screenplay by Earl Felton and Harry Essex," despite the fact that the Screen Writers Guild arbitration committee determined months earlier that Paul Jarrico should be credited as the first screenwriter followed by Felton and Essex.[27] Jarrico's name however was nowhere to be found.

According to the Guild's contract with producers, the Minimum Basic Agreement of 1951, the decision of the Guild arbitration committee "shall be final, and the Producer will accept and follow the designation of screen credits contained in such decision."[28] RKO was a party to the agreement, and the studio was informed in September 1951 that the Guild had determined Jarrico was the principal screenwriter for *The Las Vegas Story* and should be credited accordingly. But Hughes refused to abide by the ruling because Jarrico was a communist.

As the Cold War between the United States and the Soviet Union intensified in the aftermath of World War II, the House Committee on Un-American Activities (commonly known as the House Un-American Activities Committee or HUAC) intensified its efforts to investigate "the diffusion within the United States of subversive and un-American propaganda that is instigated from foreign countries or of a domestic origin and attacks the principle of the form of government as guaranteed by our Constitution."[29] The main tactic of the committee was identifying and publicly exposing communists within the United States. If an individual was unwilling to cooperate with the committee, which often meant admitting one's communist ties and naming other known affiliates, contempt charges and jail were likely outcomes.

The left-leaning reputation of the motion picture industry, especially among screenwriters, made Hollywood a likely target. In 1947, HUAC held nine days of hearings on the industry, during which friendly and unfriendly witnesses testified before the committee. Ten individuals ultimately refused to answer questions about their alleged involvement with the Communist Party, and they were held in contempt.[30] In an attempt to safeguard the industry, forty-eight key Hollywood personnel, including Dore Schary of RKO, issued a statement saying they would "discharge or suspend without compensation" those held in contempt, and moving forward, they "will not knowingly employ a Communist."[31] The Hollywood Blacklist had begun.

HUAC temporarily halted its investigation after the initial hearings, but many within and outside the industry, most notably the American Legion, took it upon themselves to try and rid the industry of communists. HUAC investigations resumed in 1951, and on April 13, screenwriter Paul Jarrico was subpoenaed.

Jarrico was a "true-blue Red," as he later admitted proudly, and a member of the Hollywood section of the Communist Party.[32] The day before he was subpoenaed fellow screenwriter Richard Collins appeared before the committee. Collins admitted to being a former member of the Communist Party, and as a friendly witness, he ultimately named twenty-six colleagues who had also been members, including Jarrico.[33]

Jarrico claimed Collins perjured himself while testifying, but when asked directly if he was or had ever been a member of the Communist Party, Jarrico exercised his Fifth Amendment rights. "I refuse to answer that question on the ground that it might tend to incriminate me," Jarrico told the committee, "as I shall refuse to answer any questions regarding my political affiliations or activities."[34] Five subsequent witnesses testified to Jarrico's long association with communism.

Jarrico had been employed at RKO as a screenwriter since January 1951, and one of the screenplays he worked on was *The Las Vegas Story*. When Hughes learned of Jarrico's communist ties, he issued immediate orders for his termination. "I didn't know what he was doing or what picture he was working on," Hughes later testified in court.[35] "I wanted every piece of paper he had laid a hand to thrown in the wastebasket and burned up. I issued such violent instructions in the Jarrico matter that his work be discarded, and even sanctioned a loss of money in taking the time to rewrite it, that I cannot believe my subordinates would have dared disobey."[36] Hughes even admitted to firing Jarrico before he testified before HUAC.

When advertising for *The Las Vegas Story* appeared in advance of the film's release without Jarrico's screenwriting credit, which the Screen Writers Guild had already ruled was required, the Guild attempted to contact RKO to inform them they were in violation of the Guild's Minimum Basic Agreement. Not wanting to appear to be overtly supporting a communist, "the Guild made its position clear that it was not involved in the merits of RKO's position with Jarrico but was insistent that RKO be held responsible for the breach of its obligation to the Guild."[37] Representatives of the Guild, including president Mary McCall, met with individuals from RKO on several occasions but were unable to reach an agreement.

Hoping to force the issue, Hughes filed suit against Jarrico in March 1952 arguing that the screenwriter violated the morals clause in his contract by his association with communism and by refusing to answer questions before HUAC. "His said conduct and statements," read the complaint, "tended to and did degrade him and bring him and the plaintiff and the motion picture industry into public disgrace, obloquy, ill will, and ridicule, and offended public morals and decency."[38] Hughes sought a ruling affirming his right to deny Jarrico "any screen credit whatsoever" in association with the film.[39]

In his counterclaim, which sought $350,000 in damages, Jarrico stated that his contract with RKO assured him screenwriting credit and any disputes were to be handled under the Guild's Minimum Basic Agreement. Jarrico also argued that he did not violate the morals clause in his contract "in the ordinary sense of said words" because the clause "has special meaning in that industry different from its ordinary meaning." To make his point, Jarrico referenced Hughes's handling of Robert Mitchum's arrest in 1948, as the "conviction of prominent motion picture stars employed by plaintiff for offenses involving moral turpitude and including among other offenses, the use of marijuana, and imprisonment as a result of such conviction" did not result in the invoking of the morals clause.[40]

Hughes, not content to simply attack Jarrico, also directly challenged the Screen Writers Guild. It was speculated within the industry that the Guild was contemplating a strike against RKO, so Hughes wrote a strongly worded letter to the Guild which was leaked to the press.

> Various rumors have reached me, the last of which was that you intended to make this an all-out fight—that your president, Mary McCall, and your board of directors intended to uphold Paul Jarrico to the last ditch… My determination that I will not yield to Jarrico or anyone else guilty of this conduct is based on principle, belief and conscience. These are factors that are not subject to arbitration… You gentlemen are professional writers and I am not. I am sure that in any letter-writing contest with the Screen Writers Guild I can only finish second best. Therefore I hope this will not be a teeing-off point for a series of letters and name calling back and forth as so frequently occurs in Hollywood. All I want is a simple answer to a simple question: Are you going to strike or aren't you?[41]

The Guild replied that they would not call a strike simply to appease Hughes, and they would continue to defend Jarrico, "however regnant [his political beliefs] might be to you or us."[42]

Hughes's handling of the Jarrico case, "the first legal action brought by any motion picture studio against any of the men or women who were subpoenaed by the House Un-American Activities Committee," was applauded by people in and out of Hollywood.[43] "Howard Hughes, who heads up RKO, is one of the great Americans of our day," proclaimed W. R. Wilkerson, publisher of the *Hollywood Reporter*. "He hates commies, their sympathizers and what they seek, and will leave nothing unturned in his effort to defeat them at that purpose in any of the vast enterprises he operates."[44] John D. Home, department commander of the American Legion in California, wrote to Hughes to commend him "for your fearless action and particularly on the stand that you took that the matter should be fought out in the courts and not settled."[45]

Politicians on both sides of the aisle were especially enthusiastic in their praise. Republican Congressman Donald Jackson described Hughes's actions as "the healthiest indications to come out of that great industry in many months," and they would be met with "wide-spread approval throughout the country and here in Washington."[46] Democrat John Stephens Wood, the chairman of HUAC, was "highly gratified Howard Hughes has taken this position."[47] Republican Senator Richard Nixon praised Hughes for taking action "which deserved the attention and approval of every man and woman who believes the forces of subversion must be wiped out."[48]

Hughes was also showered with awards. The Council of the City of Los Angeles and the Los Angeles County Board of Supervisors both adopted resolutions honoring Hughes. The Veterans of Foreign Wars, in presenting Hughes with the association's first Loyalty Award, cited Hughes as "the American who has done the most inspiring and courageous work to promote loyalty to the American way of life."[49] And the American Legion Press Association gave Hughes its President's Merit Award for "his sturdy support of the principles of Americanism, marked by his refusal to countenance Communist infiltration of the motion picture industry, and his leadership in active opposition to such subversive influence."[50]

Hughes was never one to shy away from publicity, but it was rare for him to make public appearances. But on April 1, 1952, Hughes attended a meeting at the American Legion Hollywood Post #43. Speaking extemporaneously, he railed against communism.

> But I can say one thing, in spite of all the movement to whitewash the industry, to say that there was no Red influence in Hollywood; to sweep this matter under the carpet and hide it and pretend it doesn't exist, in spite of that, there is a substantial number of people in the motion picture industry who follow the Communist party line. And if there were not a substantial number—if there were only one, that would be too many.[51]

Hughes concluded his remarks by lashing out at Jarrico for taking the Fifth Amendment, an act Hughes labeled a "crime" which he would not tolerate.[52]

A few days later, Hughes shocked the industry and horrified the employees of RKO when he announced that he was curtailing production, which was already at a minimum, and placing 100 employees on administrative leave. Branding the employees "innocent victims of the Communist problem in Hollywood," Hughes said the action was necessary "to make RKO one studio where the work of Communist sympathizers will not be used."[53]

To demonstrate how bad communist infiltration had gotten within the industry, Hughes said the studio examined 150 scripts as potential vehicles for two stars. Eleven were considered suitable, but all eleven had to be disqualified because someone working on the script or story had ties to communism. "I do not mean to imply that it is impossible to make pictures under these circumstances," Hughes maintained, "but it certainly is not easy."[54]

As Hughes was seemingly winning the war of public opinion, the Screen Writers Guild continued to argue that they were the final authority in the battle over screen credit. "I consider that all contracts are jeopardized," wrote Guild president Mary McCall, "when one contract is breached, and when the facts relating to one contract are obscured by ignorance, blurred by irrelevancies, and buried under prejudice."[55]

The Guild tried to get Hughes to agree to arbitration, and when he refused, they filed a petition in Superior Court. Judge Roy Herndon denied the request arguing that the "language of the arbitration provision was intended to exclude powers of arbitration over matters of this kind."[56] The Guild appealed, but the District Court of Appeals declined to review the case.

Many within the Guild were worried about the impact the controversy was having on the organization's reputation. Hoping to salvage the situation by highlighting their patriotism, the Guild met in May 1952 and overwhelmingly adopted a resolution that reiterated "its historic stand against Communism, and Communists within and without the Guild."[57] Paul Jarrico was one of the few who voted against it.

The Guild also debated whether it should continue to support the Jarrico case. While many members stated they did "not wish to press a legal right against a moral right," a simple majority nevertheless decided in a close vote to continue its support as proponents feared not doing so could weaken the Guild's bargaining power in the future.[58]

Despite the Guild's posturing, they were never a real force in the legal battle continuing to take place between Hughes and Jarrico. The main issue for the court was whether Hughes had the right to invoke the morals clause in Jarrico's contract because of his communist affiliations and his refusal to answer questions posed by a government body.

Jarrico's attorneys in pre-trial motions tried to get Hughes to answer questions about his handling of the morals clause in Robert Mitchum's contract in light of his arrest and conviction, but Hughes refused. The presiding judge ultimately ruled that Hughes could not be forced to answer such questions as they had "no bearing on the suit," a clear victory for Hughes.[59]

The case finally made it to court in November 1952. Jarrico was the first to take the stand, and he tried to explain why he had refused to answer questions before HUAC. "When I was asked if I would be willing to help uncover subversive activity I replied 'Yes, but one man's subversion is another man's patriotism,'" Jarrico testified, "'and I considered this un-American committee to be subversive of constitutional rights.'"[60]

Subsequent witnesses for RKO provided polling data that showed that the majority of Americans believe those who refused to answer such questions were in fact communists. RKO executives also testified that the film was likely to lose money due to Jarrico's actions.

On November 20, the fourth day of testimony, Hughes took the stand for a little over two-and-a-half hours. He admitted to firing Jarrico when he learned of his communist affiliation, and he testified that the decision to remove Jarrico's name from the credits "was given by myself after the camera work on the picture had been completed."[61] In his cross examination, defense attorney Edward Mosk asked Hughes if he was simply using this suit as an excuse to close RKO which was losing $100,000 a week. "That is a ridiculous assumption," Hughes replied tersely. "I didn't want to invest any more money in pictures until we had machinery to determine who was a Communist sympathizer and who was not."[62]

As for the morals clause, Mosk implied that Hughes's past conduct as a producer of films like *The Outlaw* could be considered a violation of such standards, a claim which caused Hughes to laugh.[63]

Additional witnesses for both sides testified after Hughes with mixed results. American Legion officials spoke of the public boycotting films associated with communists, but attorney Mosk got one official to admit that he could not recall the names of any supposed communists except Jarrico and "a man named Lawson."[64] A publicist working on Hughes's behalf described the publicity surrounding Jarrico and *The Las Vegas Story*, which Mosk countered was initiated by Hughes's "high powered publicity machine."[65] An official for the Screen Writers Guild addressed the importance of onscreen credits for writers, but the judge refused to allow her to discuss customs surrounding how those credits were determined. Jarrico also returned to the stand to describe the support he had received in and out of the industry.

Judge Orlando H. Rhodes handed down his ruling on November 26.

The Court considers... that one who, under circumstances as did the defendant in this case, asserts the privilege of the Fifth Amendment is believed to be, by the American people either, first, a Communist, or that he has been a Communist, or that he is a Communist sympathizer, or any combination of the three. In view of the judicial notice which the Court takes, that a Communist or one who had been a Communist, is an object of disgrace and ill-will of the American people, the Court finds that the defendant in this matter is, in the belief of the American people, an object of ill-will... The Court holds and finds that the plaintiff producer [Hughes] is entitled to assert the provisions of Paragraph 3 of the employment agreement, and needs not accord the defendant [Jarrico] credit in the production under consideration.[66]

The ruling was a resounding victory on all counts for Hughes, as the judge also decided against Jarrico's counterclaim for damages. "I hope this court decision will encourage the rest of the motion picture industry, and indeed all industry, to weed out these men and women from their ranks," Hughes replied in triumph.[67]

Attorney Mosk opined after the case that "this decision will live to haunt the motion picture industry," and in many ways he was correct.[68] While steps had already been taken to shield the industry from the threat of communism, real or imagined, the ruling gave legal justification to such actions, which continued in earnest for years.

As for the Screen Writers Guild, they caved to pressure and agreed to allow studios and producers to remove any blacklisted writer's name from the credits of a film.[69] Having fought for years to get control over screen credits, it took almost two decades for the Guild to get it back. Jarrico subsequently was blacklisted, but as he admitted years later, "the great significance of that suit was not that I lost, but that the guild buckled."[70]

After months of front-page headlines and a lengthy legal battle, Hughes was vindicated in his dispute with Jarrico and the Screen Writers Guild. But the toll on RKO was immense. Production levels were so low Hughes reached out to Twentieth Century-Fox about possibly purchasing films to fill out the studio's schedule.

A total of thirty-two new movies ultimately were released in 1952, the majority of which were independent productions, with eleven reissues supplementing the program. It was reported that the studio lost over

$10,000,000 for the year.[71] The continuing financial decline of RKO was nonetheless overshadowed by Hughes's controversial sale of the studio to the Stolkin syndicate in September.

The sale of RKO was one of many issues cited in a lawsuit filed against Hughes by three RKO stockholders, Eli Castleman, Marion Castleman, and Louis Feuerman, in November 1952. In a sweeping indictment, the stockholders alleged the sale was in violation of Hughes's fiduciary duties and the curtailing of production was evidence of the wanton neglect of the studio.

They also argued that Hughes forced RKO to employ Jane Russell who was under contract to Hughes Tool. "It is the consensus of the motion picture critics that the acting ability and talent of Jane Russell are of a minor nature and the payment of $100,000 for her services for a feature picture constituted a waste of corporate funds," read the complaint. "Such hiring would not have taken place nor payment made except for the economic coercion and domination by Mr. Hughes of the R.K.O. enterprise."[72]

The suit sought an accounting of Hughes's "stewardship of the parent company and its subsidiary, and for an accounting of all damages caused by his management, neglect and reckless disregard of his duties" as managing director.[73] The trio ultimately filed separate suits in New York, Los Angeles, and Las Vegas, all possible points of jurisdiction, seeking a temporary receiver for the company and the return of up to "$7,000,000 which they allege Hughes took from RKO."[74]

When Hughes regained control of RKO in February 1953 following the Stolkin debacle, he assumed the formal title of chairman of the RKO board for the first time. Like every other year under Hughes's tenure, grand assertions were made for the upcoming season. It was reported that Hughes was planning to "redouble his energies, insiders say, to pull the company of the red."[75] RKO announced yet again it was slashing expenses as a way to save money.

Newly-appointed president James R. Grainger made it clear that the company was looking to the future. "Every effort is being made by your management," he declared, "to improve operations by effecting substantial economies in distribution and by exercising caution in planning future productions pending some degree of standardization in the new processes and clarification of the public's attitude toward these new media."[76]

The minority suit nevertheless remained an issue throughout the year. The request for a temporary receiver was dropped when Grainger became president and the board of directors was reconstituted in the wake of the Stolkin forfeiture, but the suit was amended to include the charge that Hughes made over $1,000,000 on the failed sale while the company lost over $2,000,000.

A similar accusation was made by a different stockholder, Milton Friedman, who filed another derivative suit against Hughes in April 1953. Arguing that Hughes used "inside information" for "personal and private gain," Friedman wanted the profits from the sale turned back over to the company.[77] Friedman, like the others, filed multiple suits. "This is the fifth time in recent months," noted one paper, "that the multi-millionaire movie man and industrialist has been named in similar actions."[78]

Adding to Hughes's legal trouble, yet another derivative suit was filed in New York by stockholders Jacob Sacks and Louis Schiff. The duo charged that Hughes ran the corporation and its studio subsidiary as if "they were wholly owned by him, and the directors of both are obedient to him, and carry out his policies."[79]

They specifically focused on Hughes's proclivity to place beautiful, young women on the RKO payroll for large sums without ever using them in a movie. "Talent was employed at the whim and caprice of Hughes," the complaint charged, "and solely for the purposes of furthering his personal interests without regard to the interests of RKO and Radio Pictures."[80] A few of the women named were Italian Gina Lollobrigida, Merle Oberon, and French ballerina Zizi Jeanmaire. The suit demanded the court appoint a receiver for RKO.

In response to the latest accusations, individuals associated with RKO filed 148 pages of affidavits defending the company's operations under Hughes. President Grainger cited the significant cost saving initiatives which resulted in reductions of hundreds of thousands of dollars annually. Treasurer William Clark reported that total business for the first half of 1953 was $23,000,000, which was higher in comparison with the previous year. Comptroller Garrett Van Wagner declared the company had a net worth of $22,900,000 with $4,000,000 in cash on hand. C. J. Tevlin, studio operations vice president, denied that Hughes alone made decisions and labeled similarly false accusations that young actresses were hired simply at Hughes's behest. He also stated emphatically that Hughes "spends long hours on the job."[81] Individual producers, including Roy Disney, and even Floyd Odlum, who still owned stock in the company, argued that receivership would be very damaging for RKO.[82]

The year 1953 came to a close with Hughes embroiled in legal proceedings. "Probably no litigation in recent motion picture history has created as much confusion," stated *Variety*.[83] Thomas Pryor of *The New York Times* said "it is a matter of record that the company and Mr. Hughes are more actively involved in fighting stockholder lawsuits than in making motion pictures."[84] At an industry luncheon, actor and director Dick Powell, who had recently finished a movie for the studio, quipped, "R.K.O.'s contract list is down to three actors and 127 lawyers."[85]

The numbers for the year justified the critiques, as the studio distributed a mere twenty-four new films in 1953, only a third of which were RKO productions. Both numbers were new lows for the company and the Hughes regime. In just the first nine months of the year, RKO reported a net loss of $3,700,000, bringing the total for the years 1949 to 1953 to over $20,000,000.[86]

While the mountain of litigation and the sea of red dominated the headlines throughout the year, a single story in the industry trade paper *Variety* was seemingly overlooked. On August 12, 1953, it was reported that Hughes was "angling to bring his holdings up to a minimum of 90% via a tender to buy out minority holders at a price of $6 per share, according to reports from usually accurate N.Y. and Hollywood financial sources."[87] No other articles were written on the subject during 1953, but *Variety's* reporting proved to be correct.

On February 7, 1954, Hughes wrote a letter addressed to the RKO Pictures Corporation: "I hereby offer to purchase from RKO Pictures Corporation all of its assets as of the date of transfer to me, including any and all claims or causes of action of every kind or character against, or which might be asserted against, any person or persons, including me. I agree to pay for such assets the sum of $23,489,478 in cash upon transfer of assets to me."[88] At the time of Hughes's offer, there were 3,914,913 shares of stock outstanding, of which Hughes already owned 1,262,120, so he was effectively offering $6 per share. The stock was trading at the time on the open market at $2.87 per share.

Asked why he was offering more than double the stock's apparent value, Hughes replied, "This will give them a clear profit. Nobody can say he lost any dough."[89] Hughes may have wanted to seem altruistic, but in reality, he was getting a lot for his money. The main asset of the RKO Pictures Corporation was RKO Radio Pictures, the production and distribution subsidiary. Hughes would also assume ownership of real estate, a film library, and the contracts of stars.

The acquisition would also effectively squash all shareholder lawsuits against Hughes and the company. Speaking of the Castleman case, the *Wall Street Journal* explained why.

> This suit, like all suits brought by stockholders against company managements, is technically a suit on behalf of or for the benefit of the corporation itself. Thus legally it must be regarded as an asset. But if Mr. Hughes acquires all the assets of the corporation he can request the court to dismiss the suit since he would be the only stockholder and the suit would benefit only himself.[90]

Regardless of his motivations, the acquisition would make Hughes the first individual to solely own a major Hollywood studio, allowing him "to run the firm as he sees fit" and "without interference of stockholder suits."[91] And as a private company, Hughes would not have to report annual financial information.

Hughes's offer also had ramifications for the corporation itself. Shareholders were given the option to trade in their stock for $6 per share. Hughes already owned thirty-two percent of the corporation, and under the proposal, he planned to keep his shares. But if other stockholders cashed in, thus decreasing the number of shares outstanding, Hughes's ownership stake would increase proportionately. If Hughes ended up owning over ninety percent of the corporation, he would be considered its sole owner under corporate law.

Hughes could then capitalize on the corporation's history of losing money, again as explained by the *Wall Street Journal*: "Under U.S. tax laws a company that loses money in one year can use that loss to reduce its taxable income in any of the five succeeding years. A money-losing concern [RKO] can thus be merged with a money-making company [Hughes Tool], with the loss-carryover of the former being used to offset the profit of the latter."[92] Furthermore, while the corporation itself technically would be a mere shell with no assets, it would have at least $7,572,720 in cash, the amount of the sales price that covered Hughes's shares that would not be redeemed.

Given all that it entailed, the offer elicited praise and superlatives from industry insiders. The *Hollywood Reporter* heralded it as "one of the most astounding moves in the entire annals of the motion picture business," while *Variety* proclaimed it was "one of the most spectacular stock offers in recent industrial history."[93] *Film Bulletin* said the offer was the "happiest, most gratifying stroke of financial engineering in years."[94] *Boxoffice* hailed it as an "unusually shrewd move, one without parallel in the annals of American business—possibly because never before has there been a tycoon with the fortitude, wherewithal and rugged individualism that Hughes possesses in the outsize quantities that have established him as a colorful and enigmatic figure among the world's industrialists, past and present."[95]

The offer had to be ratified by the RKO Pictures Corporation board of directors, and if they approved, it went before stockholders. On February 15, RKO president Grainger wrote to Hughes to inform him that the board had met and agreed "to accept unconditionally" the offer as outlined in Hughes's letter.[96] A meeting of stockholders then took place in Dover, Delaware (RKO was a Delaware corporation), on March 18. Approximately 8,000 stockholders were represented at the meeting, and seventy-seven percent exclusive of stock owned by Hughes voted "in favor of acceptance of the offer."[97]

The sale became official on March 31, 1954, when "all of the assets, rights and properties, of any kind whatsoever" of RKO Pictures Corporation were transferred to Hughes.[98] The assets included, but was not limited to, RKO Radio Pictures (the production and distribution studio), RKO Pathé, and RKO Television Corporation.

With the consummation of the transaction, "Howard Hughes, in one of the largest industrial purchases by a single person in American financial history, yesterday became the first individual ever to be sole owner of a major production company."[99] Equally impressive, "Hughes acted alone in the deal and used his personal funds out of a fortune estimated as high as $500 million."[100]

While most of the reporting focused on Hughes's ownership of the production studio, Hughes also received "all claims, demands and causes of action which the Corporation now has or may have against any person or persons, including Howard R. Hughes."[101] Hughes now effectively owned the derivative lawsuits filed against him by angry stockholders.

The Castleman suit in Las Vegas, the first to make it to trial, was actually dismissed just prior to the completion of the sale. In his ruling, the presiding judge stated that "Jane Russell is not a waste of corporate assets" and losses during Hughes's tenure were the result of "mistakes of judgment" rather than willful mismanagement.[102] The other stockholder suits were dismissed after the sale, as were new suits which sought to deny the sale.

Hughes now owned RKO Radio Pictures and other assets, but the status of RKO Pictures Corporation still needed to be resolved. In a letter to stockholders, president Grainger reminded them that "holdings of your Company now consist only of the cash purchase price of $23,489,478, equivalent to $6 per share of stock outstanding."[103] Stockholders who wished to redeem their stock for $6 in cash per share had until May 17, 1954, but they were under no obligation to do so.

Despite the large majority that agreed to the sale, shares "were being turned in for redemption slowly" and "below expectations."[104] Hughes still hoped to reduce the number of shares outstanding so he could reach the ninety percent threshold, so he agreed to extend the deadline to June 30. Only 932,918 of the possible 2,652,793 shares were ultimately turned in, so the deadline was extended yet again to July 31.

The price of RKO Pictures Corporation stock had increased dramatically since Hughes made his initial offer, and it was even selling above $6 at times. Some investors may have misunderstood the nature of Hughes's offer, assuming incorrectly that Hughes could only acquire the assets if he managed to acquire the corporation, or they believed that the corporate shell was worth more than $6 per share to Hughes or another potential buyer.

And another potential buyer had emerged. Multiple sources reported that the "recent heavy buyer of the stock on the Exchange had been Atlas Corp., of which Floyd B. Odlum is president."[105] Odlum's history with RKO went back years, and after selling controlling interest to Hughes in 1948, his presence continued to be felt.

After failing to acquire RKO Theatres after the original corporation was separated, he purchased a small but significant block of stock in RKO Pictures Corporation in the first half of 1951. It was also reported that Odlum considered reacquiring controlling interest from the Stolkin syndicate before they turned the stock back over to Hughes. Odlum was now interested in the RKO corporate shell because it was "already capitalized, already formed corporately, and listed on the stock exchange."[106] Odlum gradually increased his holdings until he owned 884,900 shares.

As the *Los Angeles Times* reported, "two of the legendary figures in the financial world, Howard Hughes and Floyd Odlum, appeared today to be jockeying for possession of RKO Pictures Corp."[107] Odlum increased his holdings even further to 1,250,000 shares, compared to the 1,262,120 owned by Hughes. Odlum also managed to turn the tables on Hughes by persuading the corporation to offer to buy out Hughes's holdings at $6 per share, the exact same offer Hughes had made to other stockholders. The offer for both sides was extended to September 30, and when neither side budged, it was pushed to December 31.

When the final deadline expired, a total of 952,987 shares had been turned in by stockholders other than Hughes and Odlum. But the two principal owners refused to sell their shares to the other. A variety of rumors circulated, and finally in September 1955, "discussions and negotiations stretching over more than a year seemingly came to sudden fruition late yesterday when it was announced that RKO Pictures Corp. would be merged with Atlas Corp."[108]

Under the terms of the merger, Hughes and others would receive Atlas stock for their RKO shares. Some minority shareholders expressed concerns over the value placed on the RKO stock, which came out to be approximately $7.87½ per share, but the addition of a conversion feature for the new shares of Atlas common stock "melted away" any opposition.[109] After decades of operation, the RKO Pictures Corporation effectively ceased to exist.

Hughes however continued to solely-own RKO Radio Pictures, the production and distribution studio. In the aftermath of the acquisition, publisher W. R. Wilkerson noted in his front-page editorial of the *Hollywood Reporter* that "the entire history of Hughes's business operations has been marked by a resentment and contempt for stockholders... He didn't want

RKO stockholders, and since he acquired control of the company his one thought has been its sole ownership. Now he has it. What now?"[110]

The answer was more of the same for the beleaguered studio. A mere fifteen new films were released in 1954, and after a wave of layoffs, it was reported that the once great studio was "stepping out of all production during the foreseeable future."[111] As one reporter put it simply, "the outlook is bleak."[112] The *Hollywood Reporter's* Wilkerson, a long supporter of Hughes, said "the place is a morgue."[113] The studio only started one picture of its own during the year, and it proved to be one of the most infamous films in Hollywood history.

*The Conqueror* (1956) began production in May 1954, with the outdoor filming taking place primarily around St. George, Utah. As a local newspaper reporter supposedly said, "'The Conqueror' is the biggest thing that's happened to Utah since Brigham Young!"[114] When the film was finally released two years later, it was marketing as having cost $6,000,000, "the latest—and undoubtedly the most costly—example of [Hughes's] lavishness."[115] The film starred John Wayne as the Mongol chief Temujin. He fights Tartar armies on the battlefield and palace intrigue at home, as he seeks the affection of a captive Tartar princess (Susan Hayward). He ultimately triumphs over all three and is heralded as Genghis Khan, the perfect warrior.

The film did good business, taking in an estimated $4,500,000 in the United States and Canada. This made it the eleventh highest grossing film of 1956, but it was unable to recoup its sizable budget.

Critically, the film was ravaged. The reviewer for the *Chicago Daily Times* said he was "sickened over the colossal waste represented by this plotless, pointless, utterly boring 12th century tale of conquest by rape and murder."[116] *The New York Times* commented that John Wayne's "appearance in wispy mustaches and Mongol make-up is a mite startling," while "the childish dialogue and rudimentary romance" was likely to elicit "unintentional laughs."[117] Over time, *The Conqueror* was recognized as one of the worst movies ever made, due in large part to the dialogue and the miscasting of John Wayne as the Mongolian Genghis Khan.[118]

But the film is infamous because ninety-one of the 220 members of the cast and crew ultimately contracted cancer by 1980, with over half dying of the disease. This included director Dick Powell who died of stomach cancer on January 2, 1963; Susan Hayward who contracted lung, then brain, cancer and died on March 14, 1975; and John Wayne who died of stomach cancer on June 11, 1979. Many believe that the cancer was a result of exposure to radioactive fallout while filming in St. George.[119]

The Nevada Test Site at Yucca Flat, Nevada, only 137 miles from St. George, was the principal location for the testing of American nuclear weapons during the Cold War. Thirty-one nuclear devices were detonated at the site from 1951 to 1953, and winds commonly carried fallout over a large area, including St. George.

No testing took place during the filming of *The Conqueror*, but the effects lingered. "Fallout was very abundant more than a year after Harry," said former Atomic Energy Commission researcher Dr. Robert C. Pendleton in reference to a particularly dirty bomb that was tested in May 1953. "Some of the isotopes, such as strontium 90 and cesium 137, would not have diminished much."[120]

Speaking directly of *The Conqueror*, Dr. Pendleton, who was also the one-time director of radiological health at the University of Utah, stated:

> With these numbers, this case could qualify as an epidemic. The connection between fallout radiation and cancer in individual cases has been practically impossible to prove conclusively. But in a group this size you'd expect only 30-some cancers to develop. With 91, I think the tie-in to their exposure on the set of *The Conqueror* would hold up even in a court of law.[121]

While no definitive connection will ever be made between the filming of *The Conqueror* and the death of so many of its participants, the reputation and notoriety of the movie are firmly established.

The year 1955 began, like every other under Hughes's ownership, with completely unrealistic declarations. "We are seeing the development of the greatest boom days that have ever prevailed for films," proclaimed president Grainger, "and we expect to take full advantage of the current bullish conditions by producing a fine quality of picture with genuine entertainment value."[122] While it appeared that nothing would change in the foreseeable future for RKO, in reality, Hughes was looking to relieve himself of the troublesome studio once and for all.

Floyd Odlum's Atlas Corporation made an offer in May 1954, but the sale never materialized. Then, after eight weeks of negotiations, Hughes sold the studio to General Teleradio, a subsidiary of the General Tire and Rubber Company, in July 1955. The purchase price was $25,000,000 in cash. Howard Hughes tenure as a studio mogul had come to an end.

General Tire and Radio began as a rubber company that expanded into a variety of other fields. The entertainment subsidiary, which was operated by Thomas O'Neil, the son of the company's founder, owned four television stations, five radio stations, and three radio networks. O'Neil initially expressed interest in acquiring RKO's movie catalog, but Hughes was only interested in selling all of the studio operations.

O'Neil said Hughes refused to sell just the film library as Hughes was "opposed to the break-up of RKO Radio Pictures because it would cause widespread distress and unemployment, and would accentuate the film shortage." With absolutely no hint of irony, O'Neil went on to say that "a great deal of credit is due to [Hughes] for that humanitarian stand."[123]

A few months after purchasing RKO from Hughes, O'Neil made 740 feature length films available for television, "the first time the entire product of a major Hollywood studio has been sold for TV use."[124] While the studio's catalog was the impetus for their acquisition of the studio, the new ownership sought to revive production at RKO. O'Neil made his intentions known in an article he wrote for *Film Bulletin* in August 1955.

> I am no Cecil B. DeMille, but of this I am sure: the world market for motion pictures is steadily increasing. Our expansion in that field is, we feel, a far more compelling job than releasing backlog films for television. I think we shall have all the money we need for making pictures. I hope it won't be too long before those pictures earn something for us and for exhibitors. If we can attract important producers now releasing through other companies, we shall be delighted. We have bought RKO as a going concern, and when I say going I mean GOING![125]

But years of cuts, layoffs, and shuttered production under Hughes made it virtually impossible to operate the studio profitably.

O'Neil eventually sold off all of the studio components, and by 1957, the "fade of RKO as a major entity in the film business became a reality."[126] While other studios of the golden age of Hollywood have gone through mergers and acquisitions over the years, RKO is the only member of the Big Five that no longer exists.[127]

Years earlier, when Hughes first purchased controlling interest in RKO in 1948, *Variety* said the acquisition, "one of the most important in motion picture history, is expected to have far-reaching ramifications."[128] No one however could have imagined how consequential Hughes's ownership would actually be.

As independent as ever, Hughes ran the studio as he saw fit. This resulted in the hunt for communists, massive layoffs, lawsuits, and the shuttering of production. For many, both then and now, that is Hughes's legacy as a mogul. As one RKO veteran summed it up, "Working for Hughes was like taking the ball in a football game and running four feet only to find that the coach was tackling you from behind."[129] But the significance of Hughes's actions should not be overlooked.

Film historian Peter Lev says the Hollywood blacklist "ruined lives, silenced voices, and tarnished survivors, and it contributed to the decline of a democratic and cosmopolitan strain in American popular culture."[130] While the blacklist is commonly critiqued today, Hughes was once commended for being the person to take "the first positive stand against Communism in the film industry."[131] His role in this seminal moment in film history, be it good or bad, cannot be overlooked.

The same goes for RKO. Author Richard Jewell states emphatically that Hughes "will be remembered as the only man who single-handedly destroyed a major motion picture company," which might be true, but the distinction of being "the first individual to gain sole ownership of a major film company" nonetheless remains.[132]

In the end, Howard Hughes's reign as a studio mogul was groundbreaking and revolutionary. Like his tenure as an independent motion picture producer, Hughes's actions had profound and lasting implications for all of Hollywood, paving the way for the motion picture industry that exists today.

# Epilogue:
# The Tabloid Train Wreck
# Yet to Come

The sale of RKO "ended a weird chapter in Hughes's career," but the former mogul was not completely finished with the studio.[1] In January 1956, Hughes reacquired the rights to two films he had taken a special interest in at RKO: *The Conqueror* and *Jet Pilot* (1957). Hughes bought back both movies in a distribution and licensing deal that was basically a loan to the company in the amount of $8,000,000. The money was intended to help Thomas O'Neil fund additional production at RKO. Although Hughes now owned the films, RKO retained distribution rights and was responsible for all costs associated with releasing the movies.

Hughes was involved with both productions, but *Jet Pilot* had been his passion project for years. Hughes wanted the film to be an aerial epic along the lines of *Hell's Angels* for the modern jet age. Preproduction on the film started when Hughes acquired RKO in 1948, and filming began the following year with John Wayne and Janet Leigh under the direction of Josef von Sternberg.

Much like *Hell's Angels*, Hughes tinkered excessively with all aspects of the film delaying its release. It was listed on RKO's schedule every year beginning in 1949, but it was never completed and therefore never publicly exhibited during Hughes's ownership.

When *Jet Pilot* finally premiered in late 1957, it had taken so long to get to the screen that RKO no longer existed.[2] The airplanes featured in the film, which were state of the art when production began, were now outdated. Commentators also noted that John Wayne looked significantly younger onscreen in *Jet Pilot* than he did in real life or other movies released around the same time.

Bosley Crowther of *The New York Times*, summing up the film's critical response, called it "a dud" with a "weak script, poor direction and indifferent performances."[3] Not surprisingly, the film was a box office disappointment. *Jet Pilot* nevertheless holds the distinction of being the last film to feature the name Howard Hughes above the title.

As the years went by, Hughes still held the contract on several actors and actresses. He kept his office at the Samuel Goldwyn Studios for a brief time, and his varied business interests continued to be run out of 7000 Romaine Street. At one point, it was believed that Hughes was the largest shareholder in Twentieth Century-Fox, although his stake was nowhere near a controlling interest.

Reports continuously circulated that Hughes planned to reemerge as an independent producer or even a mogul. Some outlets described such stories as "the kind of rumor that set everyone from stage grips to front office magnates agog with uneasy speculation," while others hoped his return would "galvanize and stimulate the kind of enthusiasm and glamour of the good old days throughout the business."[4] But the rumors were just that. As the 1950s came to a close, Hughes was essentially done with Hollywood.

From one fiefdom to another, Hughes eventually settled in Las Vegas where he established a new empire. He ultimately purchased the Desert Inn, Sands Hotel, Frontier Hotel, Landmark Hotel, Castaways Hotel and Casino, Silver Slipper Casino, Alamo Airways Airport, North Las Vegas Airport, and the KLAS television station. His acquisitions made him the single largest employer in the state of Nevada.

From the penthouse of the Desert Inn, windows blocked from the sun and isolated from direct human contact, Hughes conducted his gambling and real estate operations with the same unpredictability and disdain for tradition that he had exhibited as a producer and studio mogul. All the while, his fortune and notoriety continued to increase.

And this leads us back to our original problem: the failure to understand and appreciate the impact Hughes had on the motion picture industry. During most of his lifetime, Hughes was known as a Renaissance man whose interests took him to the top of many fields. His exploits in Hollywood were chief among his credentials.

But in the last two decades of his life, Hughes descended into self-imposed exile and apparent madness. As he moved from hotel to hotel and country to country to stay ahead of the press and process servers, Hughes became a cautionary tale. Las Vegas businessman and newspaper editor Hank Greenspun summed it up best: "The richest man in the world and he's dying of starvation."[5]

The dashing young man who arrived in Los Angeles in 1925 determined to be the world's most famous motion picture producer no longer existed. The press became so enamored with Hughes's eccentricities in his final years that his contributions to the motion picture industry were reduced and distorted to fit the narrative of a rich playboy to whom "film producing has been a hobby rather than an occupation."[6]

Filmmaking might not have been Hughes's occupation, but it was certainly much more than just a hobby.

When the extent of Hughes's decline and neglect became apparent upon his death in April 1976, the storyline took on mythic proportions. Hughes's Hollywood achievements were replaced with bizarre stories foreshadowing his impending demise. Instead of challenging this narrative, scholars and biographers, both then and now, simply repeated and expanded upon the legend.

A marathon screening session that supposedly took place at the height of Hughes's Hollywood tenure is the perfect example. It is written about in almost every biography of Hughes, and it was recreated in Martin Scorsese's Academy Award-winning biopic *The Aviator* (2004) starring Leonardo DiCaprio as Hughes. The description that appears on the website for the magazine *Wired* is a typical example.

> Hughes didn't just enjoy making movies. He enjoyed watching them. A lot. He kept a private screening room at Hollywood's Samuel Goldwyn Studios through the 1950s. During one marathon session that would put today's Netflix bingers to shame, he camped out in that darkened room on Santa Monica Blvd. for more than four months—without leaving. Sprawled in a chair, often nude, he remained transfixed for days at a time, sipping milk and nibbling chocolate bars. He didn't even take bathroom breaks between reels. Instead, like an asylum inmate, he relieved himself in glass bottles and containers. When he finally emerged from that cinematic cocoon in the spring of 1948, he looked gaunt, pale, and withered, a harbinger of the tabloid train wreck yet to come.[7]

*Wired* is supposedly dedicated to showing how technology affects culture, but instead of examining Hughes's impact on the greatest mass medium of our times, the article focuses on bottles of urine.

And whether the story is true is not important. The fact that it is repeated so often and is now emblematic of Hughes's tenure in Hollywood is what matters. The independent producer who pioneered the multi-million dollar blockbuster and fought censors over onscreen violence and sex had been erased from history. The mogul who ended the studio system, promoted scandal, fought communists, and was the first person to ever completely own a major Hollywood studio had been replaced by a caricature. Hughes had moved from the front page to the gossip column.

But Hughes was much more than the legend that persists to this today. Going beyond the folklore and back to the historical record, the true story of Hughes as an independent producer and studio mogul can be told. After decades of myth and misinformation, Hughes's contribution to the motion picture industry and his influence on American popular culture is now understood and appreciated. Having separated fact from fiction, Hughes emerges as the most important producer during the golden age of cinema. Finally, it is clear that Howard Hughes, for good or bad, for right or wrong, was instrumental in the creation of modern Hollywood.

Every time you see a blockbuster with an astronomical production budget, now in excess of hundreds of millions of dollars, think of *Hell's Angels*. If a movie is filled with violence and sex, as virtually all of them are nowadays, remember *Scarface* and *The Outlaw*. As you are deciding which multiplex to attend, many of them offering the same variety of movies, consider the demise of the studio system. When you are bombarded with the latest celebrity scandal, a new one seems to happen every day, keep in mind the test cases of Robert Mitchum and Ingrid Bergman.

And remember, it all began with Howard Hughes, the world's most famous motion picture producer.

# Endnotes

Introduction

1  Don Dwiggins, *Howard Hughes: The True Story* (Santa Monica, CA: Werner Book Corporation, 1972), 4.
2  *Summa* is Latin for "highest." Hughes apparently did not like the name as it was chosen without his consent or approval. The company was ultimately renamed the Howard Hughes Corporation in 1994, a version of which, a real estate development firm, still exists.

Chapter 1

1  Charles J. V. Murphy, "The Problem of Howard Hughes," *Fortune*, January 1959, 160.
2  Harvard College, *Harvard College Class of 1897, Fourth Report* (Boston: Rockwell & Church Press, 1912), 218-219.
3  *Ibid.*, 219.
4  Daniel Yergin, *The Prize: The Epic Quest for Oil, Money & Power* (New York: Free Press, 2008), 71.
5  J. B. Conroy, "Copy that Stages the Product," *Judicious Advertising*, February 1919, 31. The article, based on an interview with Big Howard, discusses how Toolco developed its advertising campaign for the revolutionary drill bit.
6  Howard R. Hughes, United States Patent No. 930,758, United States Patent and Trademark Office, August 10, 1909.
7  Hughes Tool Company, Inter-Company Transactions-History of, Howard Hughes Collection, Film Department, University of Nevada Las Vegas (hereafter referred to as HHC-Film).
8  "The Tool Behind Our Oil Supply," *Manufacturers Record*, April 19, 1957, 43.
9  Letter from R. C. Kuldell to the National City Company, March 26, 1931, Hughes Tool Company, HHC-Film. Kuldell was an executive at Toolco.
10  As quoted in Peter Harry Brown and Pat H. Broeske, *Howard Hughes: The Untold Story* (New York: Dutton, 2004), 10.
11  "Hughes Tool: A Gusher of Money," *Fortune*, January 1959, 172.

12  Florabel Muir, "Howard Hughes—Rich Boy Who Made Good," *New York Daily News*, September 19, 1948, 76. There is some debate surrounding the date Hughes was actually born. A baptismal record supposedly lists the date as September 24, 1905, but Hughes and members of his family always cited December 24 as his birthday.

13  *Ibid.*, 76.

14  Stephen White, "The Howard Hughes Story," *Look*, February 9, 1954, 25.

15  Data Re-Cost of Hughes Tool Company Stock, 1940, Hughes Tool Company, HHC-Film. This document was prepared in response to an inquiry from the Internal Revenue Service and detailed, among other things, the number and book value of Hughes Tool Company stock upon the death of Hughes's parents.

16  Muir, "Rich Boy Who Made Good," 76.

17  This number is clearly lower than the listed stock value at the time of Big Howard's death, which was likely a result of creative accounting. See Data Re-Cost of Hughes Tool Company Stock, 1940.

18  John C. Moffitt, "A Texan with Ideas of His Own Risks His Millions in Movies but Finds Originality Pays," *Kansas City Star*, August 3, 1930, 1C.

19  "Gusher of Money," 82; Murphy, "Problem of Howard Hughes," 79.

20  Rush Loving Jr., "The View from Inside Hughes Tool," *Fortune*, December 1973, 109.

21  *Ibid.*, 107.

22  Hughes deeded the Hughes Aircraft Company to the non-profit Howard Hughes Medical Institute in 1953, an action many observers say was designed to avoid paying income taxes. Hughes Tool no longer owned the Hughes Aircraft Company, but Howard Hughes was the sole trustee of the institute and the president and director of the aircraft company. This gave him almost complete authority over the resources of both. Furthermore, Hughes Tool retained the real estate and other fixed assets of the aircraft company.

23  The only other American to be classified as a billionaire at the time was J. Paul Getty, founder of the Getty Oil Company. Although their exact net worth could not be determined because most of their wealth was privately held, both liberal and conservative estimates showed Hughes as the richest, with a fortune estimated between $985,500,000 and $1,373,000,000. See Arthur M. Louis, "The Richest of All," *Fortune*, May 1968, 157.

24  Jerome Beatty, "A Boy Who Began at the Top," *American Magazine*, April 1932, 35.

25  Noah Dietrich, *Howard: The Amazing Mr. Hughes* (Greenwich, CT: Fawcett Publications, 1972), 73.

26  Arelo Sederberg, "Howard Hughes: 1905–1976," *EPI-HAB Salutes Howard Hughes*, 1977, 19.

27  Stephen W. Stathis, *Congressional Gold Medals, 1776-2009* (Washington D.C.: Congressional Research Service, 2009), 25, accessed March 7, 2018, Google Books.

28  "Rich Young Texan with a Poet's Face Gets Hero's Welcome on World Flight," *Life*, July 25, 1938, 9.

29  Moffitt, "Texan with Ideas," 1C.

30  Walter Wanger, "Mr. Wanger on the Stand: The Prominent Producer Has His Say About American and Foreign Films," *The New York Times*, May 15, 1938, X4.

31  Alfred Dupont Chandler Jr., *The Visible Hand: The Managerial Revolution in American Business* (Cambridge: Belknap Press, 1977. Reprint, Cambridge: Belknap Press, 1980), 363. Chandler said such barriers were a natural evolution of successful businesses.

32 Telegram from R. A. Rowland to Neil S. McCarthy, December 11, 1926, McCarthy Caddo Gen 1926-27, HHC-Film.

33 Telegram from Neil S. McCarthy to Richard A. Rowland, December 15, 1926, McCarthy Caddo Gen 1926-27, HHC-Film. First National was ultimately acquired by Warner Bros. in 1929 and dissolved shortly thereafter.

34 The studio was Paramount Pictures. Hughes often made business inquiries in an attempt to glean information about his competitors and his own companies. Sometimes his inquiries were serious, and other times they were simply an attempt to gain information. It is impossible to determine Hughes's intentions in reaching out to Paramount, but it certainly made good business sense for any producer to know the terms of such an alliance. See Telegram from Neil S. McCarthy to Jesse L. Lasky, March 7, 1927, McCarthy Caddo Gen 1926-27, HHC-Film.

35 White, "Howard Hughes Story," 26. Even the author of the article admits the story is likely apocryphal.

36 Beatty, "Began at the Top," 78.

37 Muir, "Rich Boy Who Made Good," 77.

38 "Angle Shots: Around Hollywood Studios," *The Motion Picture Director*, September 1925, 36.

39 Letter from Jacob Wilk to Neil McCarthy, November 28, 1927, Caddo General 1926 thru 1927, HHC-Film.

40 Beatty, "Began at the Top," 78.

41 Muir, "Rich Boy Who Made Good," 77.

42 Multicolor, a forerunner of Cinecolor, used a subtractive coloring process that required two film negatives to be fed simultaneously into a standard camera. It was established in 1928, and hoping to capitalize on the future of color film, Hughes invested heavily in the company in 1930. The process never took off, and the company closed in 1932.

43 See Contract between Howard Hughes and Marshall Neilan, 1926, McCarthy Neilan, HHC-Film.

44 The original contract for *Everybody's Acting* was between Hughes and Neilan. Caddo was reorganized shortly thereafter, and the company assumed control of the film on Hughes's behalf. This may explain why the film technically is not listed as a Caddo production. See Contract between Howard Hughes and Marshall Neilan, 1926.

45 Epes W. Sargent, "Everybody's Acting," *Moving Picture World*, November 27, 1926, 232.

46 Mary Astor, *A Life in Film* (New York: Delacorte, 1967), 69.

47 Moffitt, "Texan with Ideas," 1C.

48 Mordaunt Hall, "An Intelligent Pictorial Comedy," *The New York Times*, October 24, 1927, X7.

49 "'Knights' Producer Appointed," *Los Angeles Times*, October 16, 1927, C13.

50 The first Academy Awards celebrated movies that were made in 1927 and 1928. It was the only time directing was split into two categories: comedy and dramatic.

51 Conversation between Messrs. Hughes and White, Howard Hughes Collection, Lied Library Special Collections, University of Nevada Las Vegas (hereafter HHC-Lied). The interview session in 1954 with White was quite extraordinary. Hughes rarely granted personal interviews at that point and was infrequently seen in public. Whether there was a formal agreement in place about the parameters of White's series is uncertain, but it is clear that the author realized his access came with a price. In the final series of three

articles, entitled "The Howard Hughes Story," White removed all mentions of Milestone as Hughes insisted.

52  Beatty, "Began at the Top," 72.

53  Moffitt, "Texan with Ideas," 1C.

54  "The Racket," *Variety*, July 11, 1928, 13.

55  Quoted in Advertisement, *Motion Picture News*, August 18, 1928, 500.

56  Henry F. Pringle, "Movie Magician," *Colliers*, March 19, 1932, 32. *Two Arabian Knights* carried the tagline "Howard Hughes and John W. Considine Jr. presents." Considine was the supervisor on the film. *The Racket* was thus the first to carry the line "Howard R. Hughes presents."

57  Joe Blair, "Meighan With U.A. Rumor," *Exhibitors Daily Review*, October 5, 1926, 4; "Baltimore Has Good Week With Poor Weather," *Motion Picture News*, December 29, 1928, 146.

58  Dietrich, *Amazing Mr. Hughes*, 47.

59  "'Hell's Angels' Completed," *American Cinematographer*, January 1930, 30.

60  Lincoln Quarberg, "Biography of Howard Hughes," Lincoln Quarberg Papers. Special Collections, Margaret Herrick Library, Academy of Motion Picture Arts and Sciences (hereafter Academy). This same quote also appears almost verbatim in Bogart Rogers, "4 Million Dollars and 4 Men's Lives," *Photoplay*, April 1930, 31.

61  For financial figures on all the films, see After Print Costs, McCarthy Mot Pic Prod Dist Am 1934-35 #2, HHC-Film.

## Chapter 2

1  Production contract between the Caddo Company and United Artists Corporation, August 1, 1927, McCarthy United Artists Contracts, HHC-Film.

2  Letter from Neil S. McCarthy to Joseph W. Engle, October 21, 1927, McCarthy Caddo Gen 1926-27, HHC-Film.

3  Mourdant Hall, "Exceptional Performance Given by Talented Young Norwegian Actress," *The New York Times*, June 28, 1925, X2.

4  Letter from Whitman Bennett to Neil S. McCarthy, November 7, 1927, McCarthy Caddo Gen 1926-27, HHC-Film.

5  Letter from Whitman Bennett to Neil S. McCarthy, November 8, 1927, McCarthy Caddo Gen 1926-27, HHC-Film.

6  Letter from Whitman Bennett to Neil S. McCarthy, November 9, 1927, McCarthy Caddo Gen 1926-27, HHC-Film.

7  Letter from Whitman Bennett to Noah Dietrich, November 11, 1927, McCarthy Caddo Gen 1926-27, HHC-Film.

8  Production contract between the Caddo Company and United Artists Corporation, August 1, 1927.

9  Letter from Whitman Bennett to Neil S. McCarthy, November 25, 1927, McCarthy Caddo Gen 1926-27, HHC-Film.

10  "'Hell's Angels' Completed," *American Cinematographer*, January 1930, 30.

11  Richard Maltby, *Hollywood Cinema*, 2d ed. (Oxford: Blackwell Publishing, 2003), 131.

12  See Jay Edwards, "Hustling for the 'Movie Fan,'" *Motion Picture Classic*, July 1917, 22; Richard W. Saunders, "Finance and Pictures," *New York Times*, November 7, 1926, X7. Saunders was the controller at the Famous Players–Lasky Corporation.

13  "High Movie Costs Halt Production," *The New York Times*, October 27, 1923, 15.

14  *Ibid.*, 15.

15  Johnson Heywood, "How 'Movie' Industry Got on Sound Financial Basis," *Forbes*, March 1, 1927, 13.

16  "Movies as Investments," *Barrons*, April 14, 1924, 10.

17  The continuity script was an important aspect of this new system. Replacing the more generic scenario script, continuity scripts were a detailed record of the film containing descriptions of scenes, shooting dates, footage estimates, and budgetary data.

18  Heywood, "Sound Financial Basis," 14.

19  Jerome Beatty, "A Boy Who Began at the Top," *American Magazine*, April 1932, 78.

20  Special Memo from Lincoln Quarberg to Herbert Cruikshank, undated, Lincoln Quarberg Papers, Hell's Angels Publicity, Academy.

21  Lincoln Quarberg, "'Safety First' is Slogan for 'Hell's Angels,'" Lincoln Quarberg Papers, Hell's Angels Publicity, Academy.

22  Contract between the Caddo Company and Al Johnson, undated, Jolson Accident, HHC-Film. The file name clearly was a misprint and should read Johnson, not Jolson.

23  Comments of Frank B. Tomick, January 3, 1928, Jolson Accident, HHC-Film.

24  Ridgeway Callow, "Oral History with Ridgeway Callow," interviewed by Rudy Behlmer, September 12, 1976, Film History Program, The American Film Institute (hereafter AFI).

25  "Job for Pilot, but Risk Great," *Los Angeles Times*, March 4, 1929, A10.

26  Wilson was also involved in an accident earlier that summer when his plane's propeller fell off in midair over Hollywood. Wilson safely parachuted to the ground, and the propeller landed on Hollywood Boulevard just missing a pedestrian. The plane crashed into a home owned by Joseph Schenck, the president of United Artists, the film's distributor.

27  Lincoln Quarberg, "The True Story of the Filming of 'Hell's Angels,'" United Artist Press Book, Hell's Angels-Publicity, Lincoln Quarberg Collection, Academy.

28  Bogart Rogers, "4 Million Dollars and 4 Men's Lives," *Photoplay*, April 1930, 118. The article's title refers to four deaths, as opposed to the three discussed. The fourth fatality was cameraman E. Burton Steene. He specialized in aerial work and devoted many hours to the film. Family and friends advised him he was working too hard, but the large salary he received kept him on the film. The stress ultimately caught up with him, and he had a fatal heart attack during the production.

29  Callow, "Oral History."

30  Marquis Busby, "'Hell's Angels' to Take Flight," *Los Angeles Times*, February 3, 1929, C22; Rogers, "4 Million Dollars," 118.

31  Callow, "Oral History."

32  Rogers, "4 Million Dollars," 119.

33  Letter from Neil S. McCarthy to Dr. A. P. Gianinni (*sic*), April 7, 1928, Caddo General 1928 thru 1930, HHC-Film.

34  Letter from Harold Abbets to Howard Hughes, December 14, 1928, United Artist Release Hell's Angels, HHC-Film.

35  See Caddo Company Production Cost Report, "Hell's Angels," December 29, 1928, Production Costs, HHC-Film.

36  Silent films were not actually silent. Live music, most commonly a piano, was played during the film. The music initially was improvised, but as feature films became more dominant, the studios began sending prearranged musical scores to the theatres.

37  Lee De Forest was not the first to patent sound-on-film technology, but he was the first to use it successfully for commercial applications.

38  Sound for *Don Juan* was achieved using the vitaphone system which was actually sound-on-disc as opposed to sound-on-film technology. In this system, the audio was recorded onto a phonographic disc. Synchronization was achieved through a turntable that was connected by a mechanical interlock to a specially designed film projector. Sound-on-disc technology was inferior to sound-on-film, causing the industry to settle on the latter.

39  Al Jolson sang a few songs and spoke several lines of dialogue in *The Jazz Singer*.

40  For Warner Bros. profits, see Mark H. Glancy, "Warner Bros. Film Grosses, 1921-51: The William Schaefer Ledger," *Historical Journal of Film, Radio and Television* 15, issue 1 (March 1995): 55-73.

41  John C. Moffitt, "A Texan with Ideas of His Own Risks His Millions in Movies but Finds Originality Pays," *Kansas City Star*, August 3, 1930, 1C.

42  See Caddo Company Production Cost Report, "Hell's Angels," December 28, 1929, Production Costs, HHC-Film.

43  Joseph Moncure March, "Letters to the Editor: About *Hell's Angels*," *Look*, March 23, 1954, 14. March wrote to the magazine in response to Stephen White's three-part series on Hughes which gave Hughes complete credit for writing, producing, and directing the film. This is the same series in which Hughes demanded White remove all mentions of director Lewis Milestone for his contributions to *Two Arabian Knights*.

44  Ironically, Nissen's replacement in *Hell's Angels* spoke with an American accent and not an English one as the character should have required.

45  Nissen was cast in her first major role after her dismissal from *Hell's Angels* in the film *Women of All Nations* (1931) because she had an accent. But in an attempt to further her career, she took English lessons and worked tirelessly to get rid of her Norwegian accent.

46  Kevin Brownlow, "Flashback: Howard Hughes's Maiden Flight," *American Film*, November 1981, 36. The introduction turned out to be one of the great Hollywood finds, so it is not surprising that many people have been given credit for the "discovery" of Jean Harlow, including her agent Arthur Landau, actor James Hall, and Joseph Engel, a manager at the Caddo Company.

47  March, "About *Hell's Angels*," 14.

48  Callow, "Oral History."

49  March, "About *Hell's Angels*," 14.

50  Harlow would later call it the "corniest line in movie history." See Jesse L. Lasky, Jr., *What Happened to Hollywood?* (New York: Funk & Wagnalls, 1975), 95.

51  "New Season," *Time*, August 19, 1935, 26. Harlow graced the magazine's cover that week.

52  See Caddo Company Production Cost Report, "Hell's Angels," December 28, 1929.

53  See Caddo Company Production Cost Report, "Hell's Angels," October 25, 1930, Production Costs, HHC-Film.

54  Beatty, "Boy Who Began at Top," 80.

55  "Hall Weary of Hero-ing," *Los Angeles Times*, October 20, 1929, B14. Fellow star Ben Lyon was also quoted as making a similar joke. See "Current Films," *Los Angeles Times*, March 3, 1929, C15.

56  Rogers, "4 Million Dollars," 30.

57  Lincoln Quarberg, "Suggestions on Exploitation of 'Hell's Angels,'" Lincoln Quarberg Papers, Hell's Angels-Publicity, Academy.

58  *Ibid.*

59  "Dedication: Grauman's Chinese Theatre, Hollywood, 1927, Opening Night Booklet," Grauman File, Academy.

60  Hell's Angels Advertisement, *Los Angeles Times*, May 15, 1930, A19.

61  Hell's Angels Advertisement, *Los Angeles Times*, May 21, 1930, A9.

62  "Hollywood Puts on Gala Dress for Premiere," *Los Angeles Times*, May 27, 1930, A11.

63  Myra Nye, "Society of Cinemaland," *Los Angeles Times*, June 1, 1930, B6.

64  Edwin Schallert, "Great Thrills in Air Feature," *Los Angeles Times*, May 29, 1930, A9.

65  Hell's Angels United Artists Press-Book, Hell's Angels Publicity, Lincoln Quarberg Papers, Academy.

66  Sid Grauman, "Something New," *Variety*, August 6, 1930, 35.

67  Roadshow was a term used to describe the release of a film in major cities, in the biggest theatres, before it was released to other cities across the country. Prestige films typically received this treatment.

68  The synopsis of the film is based on the 131 minute uncut version. This was the version exhibited at the Grauman's Chinese premiere and is currently available on DVD.

69  Prunella Hall, "Air Epic Thrills at Tremont," *Boston Post*, September 25, 1930, 10.

70  "Hell's Angels," *Time*, June 9, 1930, 50.

71  "Hell's Angels," *Variety*, June 4, 1930, 25.

72  Mordaunt Hall, "The Screen: Sky Battles," *The New York Times*, August 16, 1930, 13. Hall's biggest critique was Harlow's acting.

73  Harleigh Schultz, "'Hell's Angels' Magnificent Air Spectacle," *Boston Evening American*, September 25, 1930, 16.

74  Maj. C. C. Moseley, "War Ace Gets Thrill From Air Combat Film," *Los Angeles Times*, June 1, 1930, B9. The paper's staff critic, Edwin Schaller, also reviewed the film. He said it was a "magnificent picture." See Schallert, "Great Thrills," A9.

75  Letter from Joseph M. Schenck to Neil S. McCarthy, June 22, 1931, United Artists Schenck, Joseph, HHC-Film.

76  *Ibid.*

77  "'Hell's Angels' Completed," 30. This is the first of many times Hughes cites the figure of $4,000,000. The only other film with a comparable cost up to that point was *Ben-Hur* (1925). It reportedly cost $3,900,000, but the majority of its cost was due to acquiring the story rights.

78  Rogers, "4 Million Dollars," 31. The same itemized figures appear in several articles on the film.

79  Maltby, *Hollywood Cinema*, 113.

80  See Caddo Company Production Cost Report, "Hell's Angels," October 25, 1930.

81  See After Print Costs, McCarthy Mot Pic Prod Dist Am 1934-35 #2, HHC-Film.

82  See Letter from Noah Dietrich to Walter J. Braunschweiger, August 11, 1931, McCarthy Bank of America Loan, HHC-Film. Braunschweiger was the manager of the Bank of America.

83  Rogers, "4 Million Dollars," 30.

84  Henry F. Pringle, "Movie Magician," *Colliers*, March 19, 1932, 32.

85  Beatty, "Boy Who Began at Top," 80.

86  Stephen White, "The Howard Hughes Story: Part II," *Look*, February 23, 1954, 74. For the $4,000,000 figure, see "The Mechanical Man," *Time*, July 19, 1948, 40. Hughes was on the cover of the magazine that week.

87  "Report Creator of HELL'S ANGELS, SCARFACE, FRONT PAGE, Discoverer of Harlow, Russell, Muni, George Raft Forming Indie Co.," *Hollywood Close-Up*, November 10, 1960, 3.

88  Letter from Al Lichtman to H. Wayne Pierson, February 18, 1931, Exhibit 11, HHC-Film.

89  Hughes seemed to be somewhat cognizant of the financial climate afflicting most Americans for he noted on at least one occasion, albeit inaccurately, that the "tremendous cost of 'Hell's Angels' was not the result of waste or inefficiency." See Quarberg, "True Story of the Filming of 'Hell's Angels.'"

90  Rental Reduction Notice for Wayne Palace, Philadelphia, PA, Rental Reductions, HHC-Film.

91  Rental Reduction Notice for the Valley, Dayton, OH, Rental Reductions, HHC-Film.

92  See Letter from Noah Dietrich to Walter J. Braunschweiger, August 11, 1931. This total did not include $1,255,000 in receipts from the roadshowing of the film. Sid Grauman was in charge of the roadshows, and he received twenty percent of the total profits from such exhibitions. The cost of roadshowing the film was quite expensive, and it is impossible to tell how much profit actually was received.

93  See After Print Costs.

94  See Letter from R. M. Savini to Roy Sherwood, June 1, 1949, folder #58, HHC-Film.

95  Letter from Noah Dietrich to R. M. Savini, January 19, 1944, folder #42, HHC-Film.

96  See Noah Dietrich, *Howard: The Amazing Mr. Hughes* (Greenwich, CT: Fawcett Publications, 1972), 126.

97  Lincoln Quarberg, "Biography of Howard Hughes," Lincoln Quarberg Papers, Academy.

98  Rogers, "4 Million Dollars," 30.

99  Beatty, "Boy Who Began at Top," 80.

100  Lloyd Shearer, "Howard Hughes: Hollywood Outlaw," *Pageant*, August 1946, 17.

101  White, "Howard Hughes Story: Part II," 74-75. This was the specific article Joseph Moncure March was responding to in his letter to the magazine's editor.

102  "An Angel to 'Angels,'" *The New York Times*, May 11, 1930, 122.

103  Pringle, "Movie Magician," 32.

104  "Ten," *Time*, August 10, 1931, 30. It should be noted that Lewis Milestone was also on the list for *All Quiet on the Western Front* (1930) and *The Front Page* (1931), a film produced by Hughes.

105  Rogers, "4 Million Dollars," 30-31.

106  "Biographical Cycle," *Variety*, February 13, 1934, 3.

107  *Gone with the Wind* reportedly cost $4,085,790.

108  Letter from David O. Selznick to John Wharton, December 16, 1935, as quoted in Rudy Behlmer, ed., *Memo from David O. Selznick: The Creation of Gone with the Wind and Other Motion-Picture Classics—as Revealed in the Producer's Private Letters, Telegrams, Memorandums, and Autobiographical Remarks* (New York: Modern Library, 2000), 106.

109  Tino Balio, *Grand Design: Hollywood as a Modern Business Enterprise 1930–1939*, History of the American Cinema, ed. Charles Harpole, no. 5 (New York: Charles Scribner's Sons, 1993; reprint, Berkeley: University of California Press, 1995), 179.

110  Rogers, "4 Million Dollars," 120.

1  Jerome Beatty, "A Boy Who Began at the Top," *American Magazine*, April 1932, 78, 80.

2  *Ibid.*, 80.

3  The films included *The Age for Love* (1931), *Cock of the Air* (1932), and *Sky Devils* (1932). *The Age for Love* and *Cock of the Air*, both starring Billie Dove, cost a combined total of $1,052,755 and only returned a producer's revenue of $312,281. *Sky Devils* cost $702,876 and returned $406,132. See After Print Costs, McCarthy Mot Pic Prod Dist Am 1934-35 #2, HHC-Film.

4  The other two nominations were for Best Director (Lewis Milestone) and Best Actor (Adolphe Menjou).

5  See After Print Costs.

6  M. L. C. Funkhouser, "The Pro and Con of Police Censorship: The Police Viewpoint," *Photoplay*, March 1915, 66. Funkhouser was the head of the Chicago censorship board from 1912 to 1918.

7  The first attempt at federal oversight was the Smith-Hughes Bill of 1915. (The bill took its name in part from Georgia Congressman Dudley Hughes and had nothing to do with Howard Hughes.) It was never passed, and other such attempts over the next four decades were also unsuccessful. See Samantha Barbas, "How the Movies Became Speech," *Rutgers Law Review* 64, no. 3 (2012): 665-745.

8  Motion Picture Producers and Distributors of America, "By-Laws," March 10, 1922; reprinted in Raymond Moley, *The Hays Office* (New York: Bobbs-Merrill, 1945), 226-227.

9  "Will Hays, Movie King," *Los Angeles Times*, July 23, 1922, II4; "High Priest of Screen Industry Lifts Banner," *Los Angeles Times*, July 25, 1922, II1; "Better Motion Pictures, Industry's New Pledge," *Los Angeles Times*, July 27, 1922, II1.

10  Will H. Hays, "Supervision from Within," *The Story of the Films: As Told by Leaders of the Industry to the Students of the Graduate School of Business Administration George F. Baker Foundation Harvard University*, ed. Joseph P. Kennedy (Chicago: A. W. Shaw, 1927), 48.

11  Association of Motion Picture Producers, *A Code to Maintain Social and Community Values in the Production of Silent, Synchronized and Talking Motion Pictures* (Hollywood: Motion Picture Producers and Distributors of America, 1930), 4.

12  *Ibid.*, 4.

13  *Ibid.*, 4.

14  "End the Reign of Gangdom," *Chicago Daily Tribune*, June 20, 1930, 12.

15  Letter from Jason Joy to Howard Hughes, May 1, 1931, MPAA Production Code Administration Files, Scarface (UA-Hughes, 1932 #1), Academy.

16  Hecht won his first of two Best Original Screenplay Academy Awards for *Underworld*. The second win was for *The Scoundrel* (1935). Hecht was nominated another four times.

17  Many years later, Burnett claimed in an interview that he wrote the entire screenplay for Hughes, but the final draft was not to everyone's liking so Hecht was brought in to tighten it up. The film's final credits and copyright, along with newspaper reports, do not substantiate Burnett's claim. See Ken Mate and Pat McGilligan, "Burnett," *Film Comment* 19, no. 1 (February 1983): 61.

18  Pasley, for reasons unknown, was not given any formal credit for his participation.

19 The first sound film Howard Hawks directed was the aerial drama *The Dawn Patrol* (1930). Hughes actually filed suit against the makers of the film, including Hawks, claiming a large portion was taken directly from *Hell's Angels*. Hughes's attempt for an injunction to restrain showing the film was ultimately denied. In a sworn affidavit for the case, Hawks said Hughes told him personally that he did not blame the director for the disagreement. See Affidavit of Howard W. Hawks, August 2, 1930, Hell's Angels Defendants Rebuttals, HHC-Film.

20 Letter from Dr. Carleton Simon to Will H. Hays, June 1, 1931, MPAA Production Code Administration Files, Scarface (UA-Hughes, 1932 #1), Academy.

21 Colonel Joy's Resume, June 17, 1931, MPAA Production Code Administration Files, Scarface (UA-Hughes, 1932 #1), Academy.

22 Lee Shippey, "Lee Side o' L.A.," *Los Angeles Times*, August 14, 1931, A4.

23 Letter from Jason Joy to E. B. Derr, June 4, 1931, MPAA Production Code Administration Files, Scarface (UA-Hughes, 1932 #1), Academy.

24 Letter from E. B. Derr to Jason Joy, May 26, 1931, MPAA Production Code Administration Files, Scarface (UA-Hughes, 1932 #1), Academy.

25 Memorandum by Will H. Hays, May 27, 1931, MPAA Production Code Administration Files, Scarface (UA-Hughes, 1932 #1), Academy.

26 Letter from Jason Joy to Lamar Trotti, June 29, 1931, MPAA Production Code Administration Files, Scarface (UA-Hughes, 1932 #1), Academy.

27 Colonel Joy's Resume, June 16, 1931, MPAA Production Code Administration Files, Scarface (UA-Hughes, 1932 #1), Academy.

28 Letter from Jason Joy to Lamar Trotti, June 29, 1931.

29 Colonel Joy's Resume, July 11, 1931, MPAA Production Code Administration Files, Scarface (UA-Hughes, 1932 #1), Academy.

30 A serious accident did take place during the filming of the scene based on the infamous St. Valentine's Day Massacre. To replicate men being lined up and shot, dynamite caps were placed at intervals against a wall to give the effect of bullets striking it. One of the dynamite caps exploded prematurely sending bits of metal splinters and stone into the face of five men. Although most of the injuries were minor, Gaylord Lloyd, a spectator on the lot, got shrapnel lodged in his retina that ultimately caused him to lose sight in one eye.

31 According to the contract, the producer (Hughes) agreed to make "reasonable effort to replace or rearrange that portion of said photoplays so condemned" by censor boards if "practical and desirable." The opinion of the producer "to be final in said matter." See Distribution Contract between the Caddo Company and United Artists Corporation for "Scarface," "Sky Devils," and "Age for Love," September 25, 1931, McCarthy United Artists Contracts/Front Page/Scarface..., HHC-Film.

32 Telegram from Jason Joy to Jack Wilson, June 3, 1931, MPAA Production Code Administration Files, Scarface (UA-Hughes, 1932 #1), Academy.

33 Colonel Joy's Resume, September 8, 1931, MPAA Production Code Administration Files, Scarface (UA-Hughes, 1932 #1), Academy.

34 Inter-office Memo from Jason Joy to Will Hays, November 3, 1931, MPAA Production Code Administration Files, Scarface (UA-Hughes, 1932 #1), Academy.

35 The third ending was shot without two key participants. Director Howard Hawks agreed to do the second ending, but he thought the latest request was absurd so he refused to take part. Star Paul Muni was unavailable when it came time to shoot the third ending, so a stand in was used for the scene where Camonte is taken to the gallows.

36  The synopsis is based on the third ending of the film. As noted, the original ending had Camonte shooting it out with the police after Cesca died. When he runs out of ammunition, Camonte continues to brave the onslaught of bullets until he is finally gunned down. The second ending had Camonte flee without a gun upon the death of Cesca. Cornered by the police, Camonte turns into a coward and pleads for his life. When the police go to arrest him, Camonte attempts to escape and is shot. He dies in the gutter. The DVD of the film includes the second and third endings.

37  Letter from Jason Joy to Will H. Hays, September 30, 1931, MPAA Production Code Administration Files, Scarface (UA-Hughes, 1932 #1), Academy.

38  Inter-office Memo from Jason Joy to Will Hays, November 3, 1931.

39  Letter from Jason Joy to Will H. Hays, September 30, 1931.

40  Colonel Joy's Resume, September 22, 1931, MPAA Production Code Administration Files, Scarface (UA-Hughes, 1932 #1), Academy; Letter from Jason Joy to Will H. Hays, September 30, 1931. It was Harold Lloyd's brother Gaylord who was injured in the accident on set.

41  Telegram from Lamar Trotti to Jason Joy, October 7, 1931, MPAA Production Code Administration Files, Scarface (UA-Hughes, 1932 #1), Academy.

42  Lincoln Quarberg thought it was better to wait until the censors officially approved the film before seeking President Hoover's approval. After the film ran into trouble, the idea of reaching out to Hoover was abandoned.

43  The MPPDA, in one of its most visible functions, acted as an intermediary between producers and outside censors who often demanded cuts beyond those suggested by the industry's association.

44  Telegram from Jason Joy to Lamar Trotti, October 13, 1931, MPAA Production Code Administration Files, Scarface (UA-Hughes, 1932 #1), Academy.

45  Memorandum from Will Hays, November 4, 1931, MPAA Production Code Administration Files, Scarface (UA-Hughes, 1932 #1), Academy. The executives were Nicholas Schenck, president of MGM; Robert Cochrane, vice president of Universal; and Hiram Brown, president of RKO.

46  Memorandum from Will Hays, November 4, 1931, MPAA Production Code Administration Files, Scarface (UA-Hughes, 1932 #1), Academy. This is a different memorandum from the one above also dated November 4, 1931.

47  Colonel Joy's Resume, November 16, 1931, MPAA Production Code Administration Files, Scarface (UA-Hughes, 1932 #1), Academy.

48  Screenwriter W. R. Burnett claimed that one of the main reasons Hughes bought the rights to Armitage Trail's book *Scarface* was for the title. See Mate, "Burnett," 61.

49  The film would eventually be released in some areas, primarily those without censorship, as *Scarface* and *Scarface: The Shame of a Nation* in those areas with censorship.

50  Letter from Lincoln Quarberg to Hal Horne, October 23, 1931, Lincoln Quarberg Papers, Correspondence 1931, Academy.

51  *Ibid.*

52  Telegram from Howard Hughes to Lincoln Quarberg, January 21, 1932, Lincoln Quarberg Papers, Correspondence 1932, Academy. Publix was the theatre chain for Paramount.

53  "Shame of a Nation," January 6, 1932, Department of Education, New York State Archives (hereafter NY Archives).

54  Letter from James Wingate to Harry D. Buckley, January 29, 1932, Department of Education, NY Archives. The letter has "not mailed" written across the top, but the sentiments expressed were nonetheless true.

55 Letter from Lincoln Quarberg to Howard Hughes, January 30, 1932, Lincoln Quarberg Papers, Correspondence 1932, Academy.

56 Letter from Hal Horne to Lincoln Quarberg, January 30, 1932, Lincoln Quarberg Papers, Correspondence 1932, Academy.

57 *Ibid.* After years of evading the law, Capone was finally convicted in October 1931 of income tax evasion and sentenced to eleven years in federal prison. He initially was confined to Cook County Jail before being transferred to the federal penitentiary in Atlanta. He was moved to Alcatraz in August 1934. He finished his sentence at Terminal Island in California before being paroled in 1939.

58 See Robert Donaldson, "Shall the Movies Take Orders from the Underworld?" *Movie Classics*, May 1932, 43.

59 Quoted in Donaldson, "Orders from the Underworld," 62.

60 Memorandum from James Wingate to Harry Buckley, March 4, 1932, Department of Education, NY Archives.

61 Letter from Joseph Schenck to Will Hays, February 26, 1932, MPAA Production Code Administration Files, Scarface (UA-Hughes, 1932 #2), Academy.

62 Memorandum in RE: "Scarface," March 4, 1932, MPAA Production Code Administration Files, Scarface (UA-Hughes, 1932 #2), Academy. The memorandum describes the three different versions of the film.

63 Letter from Joseph Schenck to Will Hays, February 26, 1932.

64 Memorandum in RE: "Scarface," March 4, 1932.

65 The only reference to a potential premiere was a report on January 24, 1932, in the *Los Angeles Times* that stated the film would be released in California sometime in March. The article was rather speculative. See Philip K. Scheuer, "A Town Called Hollywood," *Los Angeles Times*, January 24, 1932, B9.

66 Edwin Schallert, "Gang Feature Experimental," *Los Angeles Times*, March 3, 1932, A11.

67 Memorandum from Jason Joy to Will Hays, March 5, 1932, MPAA Production Code Administration Files, Scarface (UA-Hughes, 1932 #2), Academy.

68 Dictated copy of telegram from Howard Hughes to Joseph Schenck, undated, MPAA Production Code Administration Files, Scarface (UA-Hughes, 1932 #2), Academy. The original telegram was likely dated March 8, 1932.

69 RE: "Scarface" from Will Hays, March 10, 1932, MPAA Production Code Administration Files, Scarface (UA-Hughes, 1932 #2), Academy. The memorandum includes Hays's dictation of Hughes's comments made over the telephone, along with Hays's reply to Hughes and additional commentary Hays made for other members of the MPPDA.

70 *Ibid.*

71 *Ibid.*

72 Schallert was not sure what version B was or what happened to it.

73 Edwin Schallert, "Much Scarred 'Scarface,'" *Los Angeles Times*, March 9, 1932, 7.

74 Chapin Hall, "In the Realm of Shadow Stories: Hughes Turns a Deaf Ear to Hays in Releasing 'Scarface,' a Gangster Film Beside Which Others Pale," *The New York Times*, March 13, 1932, X4.

75 Memorandum by James Fisher, March 18, 1932, MPAA Production Code Administration Files, Scarface (UA-Hughes, 1932 #2), Academy.

76 The National Board of Review was originally called the New York Board of Motion Picture Censorship, but the name was changed to avoid any direct association with the term censorship.

77  The National Board of Review of Motion Pictures, Inc., "The National Board of Review of Motion Pictures, Inc.," Censorship New York State, HHC-Film.

78  James Shelley Hamilton, "Scarface," *National Board of Review Magazine,* March 1932, as quoted in Stanley Kauffmann, ed., *American Film Criticism: From the Beginnings to Citizen Kane* (New York: Liveright, 1972), 260-261.

79  Scarface Advertisement, *Los Angeles Times,* April 18, 1932, 11.

80  Scarface Advertisement, *Los Angeles Times,* April 19, 1932, A9.

81  Scarface Advertisement, *Los Angeles Times,* April 20, 1932, A2.

82  Philip K. Scheuer, "'Scarface' Gangland Epic," *Los Angeles Times,* April 23, 1932, A7.

83  Letter from the MPPDA to Joseph Schenck, April 27, 1932, MPAA Production Code Administration Files, Scarface (UA-Hughes, 1932 #2), Academy. The letter does not have an author, but it was most likely written by Will Hays.

84  Letter from James Wingate to Harry D. Buckley, April 20, 1932, Department of Education, NY Archives.

85  "Hughes to do Battle," *Los Angeles Times,* March 13, 1932, B25.

86  "The New Pictures," *Time,* April 18, 1932, 17.

87  The National Civil Liberties Bureau was dissolved and reorganized as the American Civil Liberties Union in 1920. Ernst would go on to successfully defend James Joyce's banned novel *Ulysses* (1922) against obscenity charges in 1933.

88  Letter from the MPPDA to Joseph Schenck, April 27, 1932.

89  Telegram from Al Lichtman to Howard Hughes, April 23, 1932, Burger, HHC-Film.

90  Telegram from Howard Hughes to Al Lichtman, April 23, 1932, Lincoln Quarberg Correspondence 1932, HHC-Film.

91  *Ibid.*

92  "Here's Latest Static on Affairs Cinematic," *Los Angeles Times,* April 26, 1932, A1.

93  "Projection Jottings," *The New York Times,* May 1, 1932, X5.

94  "Here's Latest Static," A1.

95  Ronald Wagoner, Untitled Article, April 25, 1932, found in Lincoln Quarberg Scarface Publicity, HHC-Film.

96  Letter from Fred W. Beetson to Frank (illegible), May 2, 1932, MPAA Production Code Administration Files, Scarface (UA-Hughes, 1932 #2), Academy.

97  Letter from Al Lichtman to Howard Hughes, April 30, 1932, Burger, HHC-Film. Lichtman believed that Lincoln Quarberg, Caddo's publicity director, was using the press to publicize the controversy in an attempt to promote the film. Unbeknownst to Lichtman, Quarberg said months earlier that he wanted the film banned for that exact reason. Many individuals at the MPPDA also blamed Quarberg for the controversy. Everyone nonetheless agreed that Hughes was actively involved, and as Quarberg's boss, Hughes shared equal guilt.

98  Report of Examiner, "Shame of a Nation," May 6, 1932, Department of Education, NY Archives.

99  Harry D. Buckley, "Shame of a Nation," May 9, 1932, Department of Education, NY Archives.

100 Chapin Hall, "Pictures and Players in Hollywood," *The New York Times,* May 22, 1932, X3.

101 Norbert Lusk, "'Scarface' Finally Escapes New York Censors, Playing to Packed House Ever Since," *Los Angeles Times,* May 29, 1932, B11.

102  *Ibid.*, B11.

103  Lincoln Quarberg, "New York Censors Pass 'Scarface' to Avoid Lawsuit," undated, Lincoln Quarberg Collection, Scarface Publicity, Academy.

104  Telegram from Howard Hughes to Will Hays, May 11, 1932, Lincoln Quarberg Correspondence 1932, Academy.

105  *Ibid.*

106  Letter from Jason Joy to Harry Buckley, May 16, 1932, Lincoln Quarberg Correspondence 1932, Academy.

107  At that point, the regions that had yet to approve the film were the cities of Chicago and Boston and the states of Pennsylvania and Kansas.

108  Officials in the city of Chicago were weary of all gangster films, especially *Scarface*. With Mayor Anton Cermak vocally condemning the film, the city's censors initially rejected *Scarface* in June 1932. A little over a year later, Hughes hired James R. Quinn, a politically connected Chicago attorney, to see if he could help get the film passed. After speaking with new Mayor Edward Joseph Kelley, Quinn reported that the film would never be approved for exhibition in the city. Hughes tried unsuccessfully to get the film passed in Chicago on several more occasions, but unlike New York, Hughes never threatened to file a lawsuit to force the showing of the film in Chicago.

109  See After Print Costs.

110  Quarberg, "New York Censors Pass."

111  Lincoln Quarberg, "The Truth about Motion Picture Censorship," McCarthy General Caddo 1931 thru 1936, HHC-Film.

112  Quarberg, "New York Censors Pass."

113  Wagoner, Untitled Article.

## Chapter 4

1  Douglas W. Churchill, "The Gilded Lillian," *The New York Times*, February 4, 1940, 123.

2  Will H. Hays, *Progress and Trends of Motion Picture Entertainment* (New York: Motion Picture Producers and Distributors of American, 1935), 22.

3  Ruth A. Inglis, "Need for Voluntary Self-Regulation," *Annals of American Academy of Political and Social Science* 254 (November 1947): 154.

4  Jack Buetel was born Warren Higgins. When he moved to Hollywood, he changed his name to Jack Beutel. He later changed the spelling of his screen name to Buetel, and that is how he was most commonly credited and cited.

5  Jane Russell as told to Sid Ross and Kay Sullivan, "They Sold Me Like a Can of Tomatoes," *Parade*, November 15, 1953, 9.

6  Douglas W. Churchill, "Screen News Here and in Hollywood," *The New York Times*, December 11, 1940, 37.

7  Hawks signed a two-year contract with Hughes Production, which gave him thirty-seven percent of net profits from each picture. Hughes bought out the contract for a sum of $76,000.

8  Douglas W. Churchill, "Hollywood Legend," *The New York Times*, December 15, 1940, 151.

9  Russell, "They Sold Me," 9.

10  Paula Carlesi, "Behind Glamour Queen Jane's Tinsel Façade," *Los Angeles Herald-Examiner*, August 16, 1969, B6.

11  Jane Russell, *Jane Russell: My Path & My Detours* (New York: Franklin Watts, 1985), 58. Russell was a spokeswoman for Playtex in the 1970s and 1980s.

12  The author found no internal corporate documents that discussed Hughes's supposed construction of the bra.

13  *"Pic,"* February 4, 1941, page unknown, found in Outlaw Adv 1940-46, HHC-Film.

14  Letter from Cliff Broughton to Russell Birdwell, January 29, 1941, Hughes Outlaw Misc Matters, HHC-Film.

15  *Ibid.*

16  Letter from Russell Birdwell to Cliff Broughton, February 6, 1941, Hughes Outlaw Misc Matters, HHC-Film.

17  *Ibid.*

18  Letter from Joseph Breen to Howard Hughes, November 27, 1940, The Outlaw (Hughes, 1941 #1), Academy.

19  Re: The Outlaw—Howard Hughes Prod. by Joseph Breen, March 28, 1941, MPAA Production Code Administration Files, The Outlaw (Hughes, 1941 #1), Academy.

20  Letter from Joseph Breen to Howard Hughes, March 28, 1941, MPAA Production Code Administration Files, The Outlaw (Hughes, 1941 #1), Academy.

21  Letter from Hughes Productions to the Motion Picture Producers and Distributors of America and to the Board of Directors thereof, April 28, 1941, McCarthy Outlaw Cen, HHC-Film. If any aspect of a film was deemed unacceptable by the PCA, the decision could be appealed to the MPPDA's board of directors.

22  Letter from Noah Dietrich to R. M. Savini, April 11, 1941, HHC-Film.

23  Letter from R. M. Savini to Noah Dietrich, April 14, 1941, HHC-Film.

24  Letter from Carl E. Milliken to Howard Hughes, May 16, 1941, MPAA Production Code Administration Files, The Outlaw (Hughes, 1941 #1), Academy. Prior to joining the MPPDA, Milliken served as the fifty-first governor of Maine.

25  Telegram from Howard Hughes to Neil McCarthy, May 15, 1941, McCarthy Outlaw Censorship, HHC-Film. One of the lines Hughes was required to change, which the MPPDA thought alluded to an illicit affair, was "You borrowed from me; I borrowed from you." Hughes wanted to substitute "Tit for tat," and in the congratulatory telegram, he admonished McCarthy for not mentioning his proposed replacement to the board.

26  Letter from Joseph Breen to Howard Hughes, May 23, 1941, McCarthy Outlaw Censorship, HHC-Film.

27  Letter from Francis S. Harmon to Neil S. McCarthy, June 3, 1941, McCarthy Outlaw Cen, HHC-Film.

28  Letter from Irwin Esmond to Howard Hughes, July 10, 1941, Department of Education, NY Archives.

29  Appeal from the Action of the Director of the Motion Picture Division in refusing to license a motion picture entitled The Outlaw by Albert I. Lodwick, April 13, 1942, Department of Education, NY Archives.

30  Answer of the Appeal from the Action of the Director of the Motion Picture Division in refusing to license a motion picture entitled "The Outlaw" by Irwin Esmond, April 17, 1942, Department of Education, NY Archives.

31  Letter from Albert Lodwick to Howard Hughes, March 27, 1942, Censorship PA, HHC-Film.

32  Kenneth C. Ray, Ohio Division of Censorship, Certificate of Censorship, June 19, 1942, McCarthy Outlaw Cen, HHC-Film.

33  Letter from Neil McCarthy to Tom Connors, April 14, 1942, Outlaw Re Distribution, HHC-Film.

34 Letter from Tom Connors to Neil McCarthy, May 7, 1942, Outlaw Re Distribution, HHC-Film.

35 "Record Drive for Picture," *The New York Times*, June 17, 1942, 32; "Hughes Defies Censor Nix and Will Roadshow His 'The Outlaw' Pic," *Variety*, June 17, 1942, 2.

36 Telegram from Russell Birdwell to Howard Hughes, July 27, 1942, Outlaw Re Distribution, HHC-Film.

37 Letter from Neil McCarthy to the Honorable Angelo Rossi, January 30, 1943, McCarthy Outlaw Cen, HHC-Film.

38 The shot never appears in the actual film, but it clearly was an allusion to the scene where Billy supposedly rapes Rio.

39 Fred R. Sammis, "The Case Against The Outlaw," *Photoplay*, September 1946, 109-110.

40 The synopsis is based on the version of *The Outlaw* commonly found on DVD, but given all of the changes made, there are various versions. This is compounded by the fact that the copyright on the film was not renewed, and it entered the public domain in 1971. For more information on the film entering the public domain, see David Pierce, "Forgotten Faces: Why Some of Our Cinematic Heritage is Part of the Public Domain," *Film History: An International Journal* 19, no. 2 (2007): 125-143.

41 Edwin Schallert, "'Outlaw' Dubbed Weird Among Movie Experiences," *Los Angeles Times*, February 8, 1943, 22.

42 Alexander Fried, "'Outlaw,' Howard Hughes Film, Opens Run at Geary," *San Francisco Examiner*, February 8, 1943, page unknown.

43 Claude A. La Belle, "Howard Hughes's 'The Outlaw:' Picture is Odd Version of Billy the Kid Story," *San Francisco News*, February 8, 1943, 7.

44 "Hughes's Western," *Time*, February 22, 1943, page unknown, found in Outlaw Adv 1940-46, HHC-Film.

45 Many reviewers also commented on a live stage skit performed by Jane Russell and Jack Buetel after the screening. Much like the film itself, none of the reviewers liked it. Edwin Schallert described it as "one of the mysteries of the evening." See Schallert, "'Outlaw' Dubbed Weird," 22.

46 Schallert, "'Outlaw' Dubbed Weird," 22.

47 La Belle, "Odd Version," 7. La Belle did not think Russell had the electricity of the late Jean Harlow.

48 "Hughes's Western," page unknown.

49 Edwin Schallert, "Drama," *Los Angeles Times*, February 12, 1943, 14.

50 Russell Birdwell, "'The Outlaw' Proves Sex has Not Been Rationed!" *Variety*, February 12, 1943, 10.

51 *Ibid.*, 10.

52 Roman Catholic bishops dominated the organization, which originated as the Catholic Legion of Decency in 1933. The name was changed the following year when an attempt was made to broaden the membership of the organization through the inclusion of many Protestant and even some Jewish clerics. The organization became all Catholic again in the 1960s, and it was renamed the National Catholic Office for Motion Pictures in 1966.

53 "Legion of Decency," *Time*, June 11, 1934, page unknown, found in McCarthy Outlaw Cen, HHC-Film.

54 Memorandum reciting chief points in telephone conversation between Carl E. Milliken in New York and Francis S. Harmon in Hollywood, in re THE OUTLAW written by Francis S. Harmon, March 4, 1943, MPAA Production Code Administration Files, The Outlaw (Hughes, 1941 #1), Academy. In the

memorandum, Harmon reports that he was given access to the detailed reports of the Legion reviewers, and he transcribed many of their comments.

55  Telegram from Russell Birdwell to Neil McCarthy, March 8, 1943, McCarthy Outlaw Cen, HHC-Film.

56  Memorandum reciting chief points in telephone conversation between Carl E. Milliken in New York and Francis S. Harmon in Hollywood, in re THE OUTLAW written by Francis S. Harmon, March 4, 1943.

57  According to the report, Hughes was planning to establish his own theatre circuit in order to exhibit *The Outlaw* throughout the country. If such a plan was considered, it was never implemented, likely as a result of Hughes's acquisition of RKO. See Thomas M. Pryor, "By Way of Report," *New York Times*, April 25, 1943, X3.

58  Letter from Neil McCarthy to Howard Hughes, June 28, 1943, McCarthy Outlaw Cen, HHC-Film.

59  Letter from Robert Savini to Noah Dietrich, September 13, 1943, folder #42, HHC-Film.

60  Letter from Noah Dietrich to Robert Savini, September 17, 1943, folder #42, HHC-Film.

61  Letter from Noah Dietrich to Robert Savini, March 2, 1943, folder #42, HHC-Film.

62  Letter from Neil McCarthy to George Medalie, May 27, 1942, McCarthy Outlaw Cen, HHC-Film.

63  Letter from George Medalie to Neil McCarthy, June 3, 1942, McCarthy Outlaw Cen, HHC-Film.

64  Telegram from Russell Birdwell to Howard Hughes, July 27, 1942.

65  Letter from Gordon S. White to Paul Lazarus, Jr., February 14, 1946, Outlaw Censorship Exh NY, HHC-Film.

66  Will Hays stepped down as president of the MPPDA in 1945 after twenty-four years of leadership. His successor, Eric Johnston, the former president of the United States Chamber of Commerce, changed the organization's name as part of a larger rebranding effort.

67  In the Matter of The Outlaw, Appeal to the President of the Motion Picture Association of America, March 16, 1946, Outlaw MPA v HTCo, HHC-Film.

68  *Ibid.*

69  Hughes even admitted to the MPAA that he altered the film in the aftermath of its San Francisco premiere.

70  Albert Goldberg, "A Horse Opera to End 'Em All—'The Outlaw,'" *Chicago Daily Tribune*, March 14, 1946, 24.

71  Philip K. Scheuer, "'Outlaw' Odd Opus," *Los Angeles Times*, April 4, 1946, A3.

72  "This Week: Jane Russell," *Time*, March 25, 1946, page unknown, found in Outlaw Adv 1940-46, HHC-Film.

73  Hedda Hopper, "Looking at Hollywood," *Los Angeles Times*, March 28, 1946, A3.

74  San Francisco Advertising Campaign, LA-SF Ad Campaign, HHC-Film. The advertisements were used across the country, including a two-week blitz in four San Francisco newspapers that heralded the film's re-release in the city.

75  *Ibid.*

76  Letter from Darryl F. Zanuck to Joseph Breen, April 2, 1946, MPAA Production Code Administration Files, The Outlaw (Hughes, 1941 #1), Academy.

77  "Archbishop Cantwell Hits Film as Offensive," *Los Angeles Times*, April 5, 1946, A9.

78 Letter from the Secretary of the MPAA to Howard Hughes, April 9, 1946, MPAA Production Code Administration Files, The Outlaw (Hughes, 1941 #1), Academy.

79 "Hughes Film Ads Draw M.P.A. Fire," *Los Angeles Times*, April 12, 1946, 1.

80 "Movie Association May Oust Hughes," *The New York Times*, April 12, 1946, 22.

81 Press release from the office of Howard Hughes released by Russell Birdwell, April 22, 1946, Outlaw MPA v HTCo, HHC-Film.

82 *Hughes Tool Company* v. *Motion Pictures Association of America*, United States District Court for the Southern District of New York, April 22, 1946, MPAA Production Code Administration Files, The Outlaw (Hughes, 1941 #1), Academy.

83 *Ibid.*

84 "Bay City Police Close 'Outlaw,'" *Los Angeles Times*, April 25, 1946, 2.

85 *The People of the State of California* v. *Allister Dunn*, Decision on Motion for Instructed Verdict, May 17, 1946, Outlaw Censorship Exh New York, HHC-Film.

86 *Joy Theatres, Inc.* v. *City of Alexandria, et al.*, July 15, 1946, Censorship Louisiana, HHC-Film.

87 *Hughes Tool Company* v. *Motion Pictures Association of America*, United States District Court for the Southern District of New York, June 14, 1946, "Outlaw, The"-MPA vs. HTCo., HHC-Film.

88 Letter from Joseph I. Breen to Howard Hughes, September 6, 1946, Outlaw Censorship MPA, HHC-Film.

89 "Film Code Group Outlaws 'Outlaw,'" *Los Angeles Times*, September 9, 1946, 7.

90 Louis F. Thomann, "Hughes Fight Tightens Administration of Hollywood Code on Advertising," *Printer's Ink*, September 13, 1946, 122.

91 Telegram from Noah Dietrich to Howard Hughes, May 23, 1947, Outlaw Censorship Legion of Decency, HHC-Film.

92 Letter from Noah Dietrich to Monsignor John McClafferty, Catholic Legion of Decency, May 22, 1947, Outlaw Censorship Legion of Decency, HHC-Film.

93 Telegram from Noah Dietrich to Howard Hughes, May 2, 1947, Outlaw Censorship Legion of Decency, HHC-Film.

94 Letter from Gordon S. White to Francis Harmon, July 11, 1949, MPAA Production Code Administration Files, The Outlaw (Hughes, 1941 #1), Academy.

95 Letter from Foreman Rogers (Tuskeegee, AL) to Hughes Productions, September 19, 1946, Outlaw Censorship Exhibit New York, HHC-Film; Letter from B. Bennett (Fort Branch, IN) to Hughes Productions, September 20, 1946, Outlaw Censorship Exhibit New York, HHC-Film.

96 "$16,000,000 Total Gross is Seen for Hughes's 'Outlaw,'" *Hollywood Reporter*, March 13, 1950, 4.

97 See "Analysis of Film Rental & Cost 'The Outlaw,'" March 31, 1950, Re-Release Outlaw-Scarface, HHC-Film. The gross included a total domestic total of $3,028,614 along with $731,953 overseas.

98 Inglis, "Voluntary Self-Regulation," 154.

99 Ruth A. Inglis, *Freedom of the Movies: A Report on Self-Regulation from the Commission on Freedom of the Press* (Chicago: University of Chicago Press, 1947), 142.

100 Inter-office memo from Sidney Schreiber to James S. Howe, April 4, 1947, MPAA Production Code Administration Files, The Outlaw (Hughes, 1941 #2), Academy.

101 Terry Eastland, ed., *Freedom of Expression in the Supreme Court: The Defining Cases* (Lanham, MD: Rowman & Littlefield, 2000), 135. The Supreme Court made the ruling in the case *Joseph Burstyn, Inc.* v. *Wilson*. Burstyn, a distributor, received a license from the state of New York to exhibit the Italian short film *The Miracle* (1948), directed by Roberto Rossellini, but it was rescinded on grounds it was sacrilegious. Burstyn took the case to court arguing, among other things, that it violated freedom of speech.
102 The production code was replaced in 1968 with a film rating system that, with a few minor changes, is still in place to this day.


Chapter 5

1 Letter from Howard Hughes to the Men and Women of Hughes Aircraft Company, undated, Howard Hughes Collection, HHC-Lied.
2 Letter from Neil S. McCarthy to Noah Dietrich, May 16, 1940, McCarthy General Caddo 1941 thru 1942, HHC-Film.
3 Thomas F. Brady, "Selznick to Make Ibsen Film Abroad," *The New York Times*, January 12, 1948, 16.
4 Odlum founded Atlas with his brother-in-law. At the time, he was married to Hortense McQuarrie, who went on to become the first woman president of Bonwit Teller department store in New York. Odlum and McQuarrie divorced in 1935, and a year later, Odlum married noted pilot Jackie Cochrane.
5 Maxine Block, ed., *Current Biography: Who's News and Why 1941* (New York: H. W. Wilson Company, 1941; reprint, New York: H. W. Wilson Company, 1971), 629.
6 "Odlum Denies Chance of Early Sale of RKO," *The New York Times*, January 16, 1948, 34.
7 *Ibid.*, 34.
8 See "Hughes, Odlum in Agreement," *Hollywood Reporter*, January 29, 1948, 1; "Hughes RKO Deal Off," *Variety*, April 8, 1948, 1.
9 Hedda Hopper, "Hughes's RKO Deal Called Off," *Los Angeles Times*, April 8, 1948, 24.
10 Louella Parsons, "Hughes Buys Controlling Share of RKO," *Los Angeles Examiner*, May 3, 1948, 1.
11 Hedda Hopper, "Hedda Hopper Looking at Hollywood," *Los Angeles Times*, May 7, 1948, 19.
12 The other major subsidiary was RKO Pathé which produced newsreels and documentaries.
13 "Hughes's RKO Deal Completed," *Los Angeles Herald-Express*, May 11, 1948, A3. The other offer reportedly came from British film magnate J. Arthur Rank.
14 Besides the undisclosed clause, Odlum also held a significant amount of RKO stock futures.
15 The Little Three objected to their inclusion on grounds that their lack of theatre ownership meant they could not possibly enact the same level of control over the industry. The Justice Department tacitly agreed, and in 1939, the Paramount suit was amended to focus exclusively on the Big Five. A separate suit however was brought against the Little Three alleging unfair trade practices. When the consent decree of 1940 with the Big Five was abandoned and court action resumed, the Little Three were brought back into the case.

16  "Self-Regulation Code No Concern of Gov't," *Variety*, June 14, 1939, 4.

17  "The First Year Under the Consent Decree," in *The 1942 Film Daily Year Book*, ed. Jack Alicoate (New York: Film Daily, 1942), 633.

18  "'We'll Go To Trial'—Biddle for Clark," *Motion Picture Herald*, June 2, 1945, 9.

19  "Film Biz Beats Divorcement," *Variety*, June 12, 1946, 1.

20  "Supreme Court Decision in U. S. Suit Vs. Majors," *Motion Picture Herald*, May 8, 1949, 39.

21  "That Supreme Court Decision: This is What They Say!" *Motion Picture Herald*, May 15, 1949, 13.

22  "Hughes Signs RKO Deal," *Variety*, May 3, 1948, 10.

23  Agreement between Atlas Corporation and Howard Hughes, May 10, 1948, Howard Hughes Collection, HHC-Lied.

24  Letter from Ned E. Depinet, President of Radio-Keith-Orpheum Corporation, to the Stockholders, February 18, 1949, Howard Hughes Collection, HHC-Lied.

25  Agreement between Atlas Corporation and Howard Hughes, May 10, 1948.

26  Thomas F. Brady, "RKO Board Agrees to Split Its Stock," *The New York Times*, October 31, 1948, 79.

27  Herman A. Lowe, "RKO Divorcement Oked," *Variety*, November 2, 1948, 1.

28  Brady, "RKO Board Agrees," 79.

29  Edwin Schallert, "Conte's New Contract Carries Stage Privilege; Author Forms Company," *Los Angeles Times*, November 1, 1948, A6.

30  Thomas F. Brady, "Hollywood Augury," *The New York Times*, November 7, 1948, 5.

31  Hedda Hopper, "Bob Hope to Portray Fight Impresario," *Los Angeles Times*, November 6, 1948, 8.

32  The stipulation on theatre ownership was designed to prevent RKO from having a monopoly on first run theatres in any given area. As a result, the consent decree went beyond just numbers and stated explicitly which individual theatres RKO could acquire.

33  Radio-Keith-Orpheum Corporation Proxy Statement, March 28, 1949, 6, Howard Hughes Collection, HHC-Lied.

34  See Proxy Statement, March 28, 1949, 13, 18.

35  Radio-Keith-Orpheum Corporation Plan of Reorganization for Separation of Theatre Operation From Picture Production and Distribution, February 18, 1949, 2, RKO Reorganization, HHC-Film.

36  "RKO Organization Wins an 80% Okay," *Boxoffice*, April 2, 1949, 12.

37  "New Bid for RKO Circuit," *Variety*, May 4, 1949, 7.

38  "Odlum Threatens Hughes Suit," *Hollywood Reporter*, August 5, 1949, 4.

39  "Hughes Delays Action on Bid for Theatres," *Motion Picture Daily*, August 10, 1949, 1.

40  "Hughes, Odlum Face Showdown Tonight; Legal Action Looms," *Hollywood Reporter*, August 4, 1949, 1.

41  "Hughes Won't Close for RKO Theatre Sale at Present," *Hollywood Reporter*, August 22, 1949, 1.

42  "Decree Extension Aids RKO Theatres," *Hollywood Reporter*, October 4, 1949, 4.

43  "Hughes Calls Off Deal for RKO Theatres," *Motion Picture Daily*, August 23, 1949, 1.

44  Letter from Robert Savini to Noah Dietrich, November 18, 1949, Savini, Robert, HHC-Film.

45  Letter from Robert Savini to Noah Dietrich, May 25, 1950, Savini, Robert, HHC-Film.
46  "Government Checking R-K-O's Compliance with the Consent Decree," *Wall Street Journal*, January 16, 1951, 3. Greene and his relatives only owned 26,450 shares, but Greene claimed to represent the holders of the other 273,550 shares.
47  *Ibid.*, 3.
48  *Ibid.*, 3.
49  "Hughes to Fight Gov't Time Limit," *Hollywood Reporter*, February 22, 1951, 1.
50  "R-K-O Theatres, Less Than a Year Old, to Experience First Stockholder Fight at Annual Meeting Tomorrow," *Wall Street Journal*, December 5, 1951, 5.
51  "Hughes Wins 7-0 Supreme Ct. Victory on Right to Kill Sale Deadline," *Variety*, February 6, 1952, 7.
52  Letter from W. K. Serumgard to Harold G. Cutright, February 8, 1951, RKO Theatre Sale, HHC-Film.
53  Letter from David Greene to Ben-Fleming Sessel, December 26, 1952, RKO Theatre Sale, HHC-Film. Sessel was one of two representatives of the Irving Trust Company, which managed Hughes's stock, on the board.
54  "Capital Gain Angles in RKO Theatres Rate High as Realty," *Variety*, November 11, 1953, 3.
55  List would go on to purchase additional stock, and by the end of 1953, he was the record owner of 943,320 shares.
56  "Hughes Gets More Pix Stock," *Hollywood Reporter*, November 10, 1953, 1.
57  Louella Parsons, "Henreid Buys Rights to 'Stubborn Wood,'" *New York Journal-American*, February 7, 1952, 14.
58  "His RKO Picts. Control Not for Sale—Hughes," *Variety*, June 18, 1951, 2.
59  "Hughes–Stolkin Deal Okayed," *Hollywood Reporter*, September 19, 1952, 1.
60  Hughes's exact number of stock fluctuated at any given moment, as he also bought and sold on the open market. As for the Stolkin deal, RKO president Ned Depinet also agreed to sell his 35,000 shares at $7 per share, so the grand total paid by the syndicate actually came out to be $7,338,940.
61  "RKO Movies' Sale Bared by Hughes," (Los Angeles) *Mirror*, September 23, 1952, 8.
62  "Movies: Exit Hughes," *Newsweek*, October 6, 1952, 83; "Business Milestones," *Wall Street Journal*, September 24, 1952, 8.
63  "Hughes-Stolkin Deal Okayed," 1.
64  Edwin Schallert, "Howard Hughes's Interest in RKO Studios Sold," *Los Angeles Times*, September 23, 1952, 1.
65  Press release, September 23, 1952, RKO Stolkin, HHC-Film.
66  "Sees Success of New RKO Owners," *Motion Picture Daily*, September 24, 1952, 1.
67  "RKO Pictures Control Goes to Stolkin Group," *Motion Picture Daily*, September 24, 1952, 6.
68  "RKO's New Owners: Background on Group Which Now Controls Big Movie Maker," *Wall Street Journal*, October 16, 1952, 1.
69  *Ibid.*, 4. Punchboards are games of chance used for profit making or fundraising. For a designated dollar amount, a person gets to punch a hole on a card (or board) to reveal a possible winning prize. The prizes, which are often cheap, rarely equal the amount paid by the participants.
70  "Movies and Oil: More Background on RKO's New Owners; Saga of the Oilman," *Wall Street Journal*, October 17, 1952, 1. Ryan was only mentioned by last name in Costello's testimony, but Ryan confirmed to the *Journal* that Costello was speaking of him.

71 "RKO's President: How Mr. Stolkin Won a $3 Million Fortune in Eight Busy Years," *Wall Street Journal*, October 20, 1952, 1, 5.

72 "Grant Wins RKO Board Issue," *Hollywood Reporter*, October 23, 1952, 4.

73 "Stolkin, Koolish, Gorman Resign RKO Radio Posts," *Motion Picture Daily*, October 23, 1952, 1. The *Wall Street Journal* received the 1952 Sigma Delta Chi award for distinguished public service in the field of newspaper journalism for their coverage of the Stolkin group.

74 "Stolkin and Koolish Out of RKO," *Variety*, October 23, 1952, 3.

75 "Stolkin Quits as RKO President; He and 2 Others Leave Board," *Wall Street Journal*, October 23, 1952, 1.

76 "Stolkin, Koolish, Gorman Resign," 5.

77 "Hughes, Stolkin Decision Near," *Variety*, December 3, 1952, 10.

78 Letter from Arnold Grant to the Stockholders of RKO Pictures Corporation, November 13, 1952, RKO Stolkin, HHC-Film.

79 "RKO Gets Another Shuffling," *Hollywood Reporter*, November 14, 1952, 1; "Hughes Sued Over R.K.O. Losses; Chairman Quits in Row With Board," *The New York Times*, November 14, 1952, 31.

80 "Grant, RKO Chairman, Quits; Minority Group Asks Receiver for Firm," *Wall Street Journal*, November 14, 1952, 1, 2.

81 "Decision Near," 10.

82 The original agreement between Hughes and the Stolkin syndicate had a joint and several clause that stated that each member of the group was responsible for the payments owed by all five members. The group believed that the clause effectively meant that all of the stock had to be sold together so they requested its removal in an attempt to sell individually.

83 "Stock Sale Limitation Waived by Hughes in Regaining RKO Control," *Wall Street Journal*, December 15, 1952, 1.

84 "Howard Hughes Group Named to RKO Board; Has Apparent Control," *Wall Street Journal*, December 13, 1952, 1.

85 "Drop RKO Receivership Suit; Lawyer Disclaims Special 'Consideration,'" *Variety*, January 27, 1953, 3.

86 "RKO Ownership Back to Hughes," *Variety*, February 9, 1953, 1.

87 A six-month escape clause was another concession Hughes added to the original sales agreement at the urging of the Stolkin group. As a result, the syndicate did not default on the payment but rather exercised their right to return the stock assuming the loss of the down payment.

88 "Stolkin Group Turns Back Control of R.K.O. Pictures Corp. to Hughes," *The New York Times*, February 12, 1953, 35.

89 "Hughes Recovers RKO Plus $998,000 as Stolkin Exits with $1,750,000 Loss," *Variety*, February 11, 1953, 3.

90 Brady, "Hollywood Augury," 5.

91 Letter from Barney Balaban to Stockholders, February 25, 1949, Howard Hughes Collection, HHC-Lied.

92 Thomas Schatz, *Boom and Bust: American Cinema in the 1940s*, History of the American Cinema, ed. Charles Harpole, no. 6 (New York: Charles Scribner's Sons, 1993; reprint, Berkeley: University of California Press, 2008), 14.

93 J. A. Aberdeen, *Hollywood Renegades: The Society of Independent Motion Picture Producers* (Los Angeles: Cobblestone, 2000), 163.

94 Michael Conant, "The Paramount Decrees Reconsidered," *Law and Contemporary Problems* 44, no. 4 (Autumn 1981): 84.

1  Bill Davidson, *The Real and the Unreal* (New York: Harper & Brothers, 1961), 165. Davidson had a long career as a reporter in Hollywood. His book features countless quotes given directly to him over the years.

2  Mitchum was nominated for Best Supporting Actor, but he lost to James Dunn in *A Tree Grows in Brooklyn* (1945).

3  Kirtely Baskette, "Lucky Bum," *Modern Screen*, October 1945, 126.

4  "Mitchum Near Reconciliation," *New York Journal-American*, September 1, 1948, 8.

5  *Ibid.*, 8.

6  "Trap Actor and 2 Girls in Dope Raid," *Chicago Daily Tribune*, September 2, 1948, 1.

7  "Narcotics Arrest Smashes Film Career, Says Mitchum," *Los Angeles Times*, September 2, 1948, 1.

8  "4 'Big' Arrests Due in Movie Dope Case," *New York Journal-American*, September 3, 1948, 1.

9  "Grand Jury Dope Inquiry to be Asked," *Los Angeles Times*, September 3, 1948, 2.

10  "Arrests Due," 1.

11  "Raid May Have Dislodged Millions in Film Money," *Los Angeles Times*, September 2, 1948, 2.

12  "Mitchum's Dope Case Defense Gathers Speed," *Chicago Daily Times*, September 3, 1948, B6.

13  Ruth Brigham, "More Movie Celebrities to Be Named," *New York Journal-American*, September 3, 1948, 4.

14  Hedda Hopper, "Mitchum Case Tough Blow to Hollywood," *Los Angeles Times*, September 7, 1948, A7.

15  Hedda Hopper, "Red Skelton to Play Amateur Cameraman," *Los Angeles Times*, September 4, 1948, 8.

16  "Dope Inquiry," 1.

17  "Defense Gathers Speed," B6.

18  "Mrs. Robert Mitchum Says She'll Stand By," *Los Angeles Times*, September 4, 1948, 1.

19  "Defense Gathers Speed," B6. It was later speculated, but never definitively proven, that Mitchum's former agent Paul R. Behrmann had engineered the marijuana arrest. Behrmann stole money from several clients, including Mitchum, and Mitchum testified against him in court. According to the theory, Behrmann responded by using his connections to Mickey Cohen, the most powerful gangster in Los Angeles who had contacts within the police department, to entrap Mitchum.

20  Jerry Giesler as told to Pete Martin, *The Jerry Giesler Story* (New York: Simon and Schuster, 1960), 1.

21  The White-Slave Traffic Act, or Mann Act, was designed to curtail prostitution and human trafficking, but its ambiguous wording allowed it to be used to prosecute even consensual sexual activity. Notable individuals who were charged under the act, but not necessarily found guilty in a court of law, including boxer Jack Johnson, architect Frank Lloyd Wright, musician Chuck Berry, and cult leader Charles Manson.

22  "Trap Actor," 1.

23  "Mitchum Declines Grand Jury Quiz," *Los Angeles Times*, September 5, 1948, 1.

24  "Mitchum Plea Fails; Narcotics Trial Set," *The New York Times*, September 30, 1948, 24.

25 "Despite Fans' OK on Mitchum, RKO and Biz Recognize a 'Problem,'" *Variety*, September 15, 1948, 3.

26 "Public Response so Sympathetic, RKO Rushing Out Mitchum's Next," *Variety*, September 8, 1948, 1.

27 "Despite Fans' OK," 22.

28 "Reefer Rap No B.O. Deterrent to Mitchum's Lastest Picture," *Variety*, September 22, 1948, 55.

29 "The Screen in Review," *The New York Times*, September 20, 1948, 21.

30 Mae Tinee, "This Sprightly Movie is Good Entertainment," *Chicago Daily Times*, September 27, 1948, A7. Mitchum sang several songs in the film.

31 John L. Scott, "'Rachel and Stranger' Unusual," *Los Angeles Times*, September 24, 1948, 23.

32 "Despite Fans' OK," 3.

33 See "1948-49 Program," Pictures Inventory, HHC-Film.

34 Thomas F. Brady, "Hughes to Start Mitchum's Film," *The New York Times*, December 25, 1948, 11.

35 *Ibid.*, 11.

36 *Ibid.*, 11.

37 Seymour Korman, "Mitchum is Found Guilty in Dope Case," *Chicago Daily Tribune*, January 11, 1949, 1.

38 Vickie Evans failed to appear for trial claiming she was stranded in New York. A bench warrant was issued for her arrest, and she was extradited back to California. She went on trial in March 1949 and was found not guilty by a jury.

39 "Robert Mitchum Found Guilty," *Los Angeles Times*, January 11, 1949, 2.

40 "Mitchum is Jailed for 2-Month Term," *The New York Times*, February 10, 1949, 37.

41 *Ibid.*, 37.

42 "Judge Refuses Mitchum Plea to Postpone Term," *Los Angeles Times*, February 12, 1949, 3.

43 *Ibid.*, 3.

44 "Chance to Leave Jail Makes Mitchum Sad," *Los Angeles Times*, February 16, 1949, 2.

45 "Mitchum Begins Behind-Bars Role," *Los Angeles Times*, February 11, 1949, 2.

46 "Mitchum Returns from Outdoors to Serve Rest of Sentence in Jail," *Los Angeles Times*, March 25, 1949, 17.

47 *Ibid.*, 17.

48 *Ibid.*, 17.

49 Quoted in "Opinions of other Newspapers," *Los Angeles Times*, March 18, 1949, A4. A schottische is a slow polka.

50 "Actor Held 'Built Up' After Narcotic Term," *The New York Times*, June 21, 1951, 18.

51 "Letters to the Times," *Los Angeles Times*, September 10, 1948, B4. The letter came from Mrs. W. O.

52 "Mitchum's Career Safe Despite Jail," *Los Angeles Times*, February 10, 1949, A2.

53 *Ibid.*, A2.

54 *Ibid.*, A2.

55 The arrest was ultimately expunged in January 1951 after Mitchum completed his probation.

56 Lee Server, *Robert Mitchum: "Baby, I Don't Care"* (New York: St. Martin's Griffin, 2001), 424.

57  "Mitchum's Career Safe," A2.

58  The film's Italian title was *Stromboli, terra di Dio* (which translates to *Stromboli, Land of God*).

59  "Life in a Sausage Factory," *Time*, February 7, 1949, 84.

60  Davidson, *Real and Unreal*, 156.

61  Arthur L. Charles, "The Secret Behind the Bergman Tragedy," *Modern Screen*, November 1949, 72.

62  Davidson, *Real and Unreal*, 157.

63  *Ibid.*, 157-158.

64  Bosley Crowther, "'Saratoga Trunk,' with Copper and Bergman, Arrives at the Hollywood," *The New York Times*, November 22, 1945, A42.

65  Davidson, *Real and Unreal*, 160.

66  Roberto Rossellini, "Dix ans de cinema," *Cahiers du Cinéma*, November 1955, quoted in Tag Gallagher, *The Adventures of Roberto Rossellini: His Life and Films* (New York: Da Capo Press, 1998), 310.

67  Laurence Leamer, *As Time Goes By: The Life of Ingrid Bergman* (New York: Harper & Row, 1986), 163. Goldwyn reportedly made the comments to his son the day after meeting with Rossellini.

68  Ingrid Bergman and Alan Burgess, *Ingrid Bergman: My Story* (New York: Delacorte Press, 1980), 193.

69  Gallagher, *Adventures of Roberto Rossellini*, 315.

70  K. Baedeker, *Southern Italy and Sicily*, Handbook for Travelers, Third Part (London: Dulau and Co., 1880), 320. The crusaders returned to France where they implored the monks of Clugny to intercede for the deliverance of these tortured souls, which induced Saint Odilo of Clugny to institute the festival of All Souls' Day.

71  George Weller, "Ingrid's Rossellini," *Collier's*, November 12, 1949, 15.

72  Bergman, *My Story*, 221.

73  Cholly Knickerbocker, *New York Journal-American*, April 13, 1949, quoted in Louis Pizzitola, *Hearst Over Hollywood: Power, Passion, and Propaganda in the Movies* (New York: Columbia University Press, 2002), 427. Cholly Knickerbocker was a pseudonym used by several writers who contributed to the gossip column over the years. At the time of the Bergman–Rossellini affair, Igor Cassini was the writer.

74  "Principles Silent on Ingrid Romance," *Los Angeles Times*, April 20, 1949, 9.

75  Letter from Joseph I. Breen to Ingrid Bergman, April 22, 1949, quoted in Bergman, *My Story*, 225-226.

76  Letter from Sid Rogell to Edward Killy, May 17, 1949, quoted in Richard B. Jewell, *Slow Fade to Black: The Decline of RKO Radio Pictures* (Oakland: University of California Press, 2016), 96.

77  Joseph Henry Steele, *Ingrid Bergman: An Intimate Portrait* (New York: David McKay, 1959), 175. Steele's book features correspondence he shared with Bergman over the years.

78  "Una panoramica de la historia," *Nuestra Cine*, March 1970, quoted in Gallagher, *Adventures of Roberto Rossellini*, 329.

79  Bergman, *My Story*, 221.

80  "The Story of Ingrid Bergman's Love," *New York Post Home News*, September 1, 1949, 2.

81  Hedda Hopper, "Ingrid Tells Hedda Her Troubles," *Los Angeles Times*, August 10, 1949, 1. Production engineer Ludovici Muratori was not so lucky. Overcome by the elements, most notably the toxic fumes, he suffered a heart attack and died.

82 Thomas F. Brady, "The Hollywood Observation Post," *The New York Times*, September 11, 1949, X5.

83 Edgard Macarini, "Sono la prova vivente della brutalita di Hollywood," *Vie Nuove*, February 26, 1950, quoted in Gallagher, *Adventures of Roberto Rossellini*, 347.

84 The synopsis is based on the English version of the film released in America.

85 Hopper, "Ingrid Tells," 6.

86 Steele, *Intimate Portrait*, 256.

87 Bergman's business manager John Vernon supposedly was embezzling from star which led to her tax troubles. Vernon ultimately committed suicide before charges could be brought.

88 Steele, *Intimate Portrait*, 260.

89 *Ibid.*, 260.

90 Louella O. Parsons, "Ingrid Bergman Baby Due in Three Months at Rome," *Los Angeles Examiner*, December 12, 1949, 1.

91 Louella Parsons, *Tell It to Louella* (New York: Putnam, 1961), 59-60, 74.

92 Bergman also believed Hughes was responsible for leaking the pregnancy and attempting to capitalize on it, but she never blamed him publicly. In fact, in her autobiography, she described a supportive letter Hughes wrote to her a few days after her son was born. Hughes said that he was impressed with her "courage, utter simplicity, and lack of guile or subterfuge." He went on to say that he hoped one day Renato would come to realize that his mother was "one of the most brilliant and courageous women of our generation." Bergman never replied to the letter, and when she rediscovered it twenty-five years later, she was taken aback by its kindness. "It was such a dear letter from a man I'd disappointed and brushed off in every possible way," she wrote, "and I felt sad that I hadn't given it the attention it deserved." See Bergman, *My Story*, 194.

93 "Inside Stuff-Pictures," *Variety*, February 22, 1950, 16.

94 Memo from Gordon S. White to Mr. Johnston, February 27, 1950, MPAA Production Code Administration Files, The Outlaw (Hughes, 1941 #2), Academy. The memo also discussed the advertising surrounding the re-release of *The Outlaw*.

95 *Ibid.*

96 *Ibid.*

97 "RKO Orders 800 Prints for Splash 'Stromboli' Openings," *Hollywood Reporter*, February 6, 1950, 1.

98 "'Stromboli' Ban Urged by Bishop," *Los Angeles Times*, February 9, 1950, 19.

99 "Theatre Chain Bans Showing of 'Stromboli' Film," *Chicago Daily Times*, February 4, 1950, 1.

100 "Ban 'Stromboli' in 175 Theatres of 2 State Chain," *Chicago Daily Times*, February 8, 1950, 18.

101 Congressional Record-Senate, Statement of Senator Edwin Johnson, March 14, 1950, 3282.

102 *Ibid.*, 3285.

103 "Beefs No Bar to 'Stromboli' Bookings," *Variety*, February 15, 1950, 1.

104 Bergman, *My Story*, 243.

105 Bosley Crowther, "The Screen in Review; 'Stromboli,' Bergman-Rossellini Movie, Is Unveiled at 120 Theatres in This Area," *The New York Times*, February 16, 1950, 28.

106 Otis L. Guernsey Jr., "On the Screen," *New York Herald Tribune*, February 16, 1950, 19.

107 "The New Pictures," *Time*, February 27, 1950, 87.

108  "Stromboli Erupts Over U.S.," *Variety*, February 16, 1950, 11.

109  See "1949–50 Program," Pictures Inventory, HHC-Film.

110  Barrett McGurn, "'Stromboli' Altered," Rossellini Charges," *Los Angeles Times*, February 16, 1950, 26.

111  "Near Reconciliation," 8.

112  "American Blackball: Roberto Says Business is Real Bad for Ingrid," *Los Angeles Times*, August 7, 1955, A7.

113  Bergman and Rossellini divorced in 1957.

114  "Bergman News Jolts Hollywood Like A-Bomb," *Los Angeles Times*, February 3, 1950, 8.

115  James Robert Parish, *The Hollywood Book of Scandals: The Shocking, Often Disgraceful Deeds and Affairs of More than 100 American Movie and TV Idols* (New York: McGraw Hill, 2004), vii.

Chapter 7

1  Noah Dietrich, *Howard: The Amazing Mr. Hughes* (Greenwich, CT: Fawcett Publications, 1972), 236.

2  "Hughes Clinches $8,825,690 Deal for RKO Stock," *Los Angeles Times*, May 12, 1948, A1.

3  Thomas F. Brady, "Hughes Purchases Atlas's RKO Stock," *The New York Times*, May 12, 1948, 33.

4  "Hughes, Schary in Accord," *Los Angeles Times*, June 9, 1948, 23.

5  "Dore Schary Resigns RKO Post," *Hollywood Reporter*, July 1, 1948, 4.

6  Schary moved to MGM, and he acquired the rights to *Battleground*. Released in 1949, it netted a profit of over $2,300,000 and was MGM's highest grossing film in five years.

7  "Schary Resigns," 4.

8  "RKO Cutting Personnel 75 Pct.," *Hollywood Reporter*, July 9, 1948, 1.

9  Thomas F. Brady, "14 RKO Publicists Dropped by Studio," *The New York Times*, July 10, 1948, 9.

10  "Board Backs Hughes to Hilt," *Hollywood Reporter*, July 12, 1949, 1.

11  "Howard Hughes Elected to Head RKO Production," *Los Angeles Times*, July 12, 1949, A1.

12  "Board Backs Hughes," 1.

13  "Hughes Sets 15 'A' Features on 28-Picture Slate for 1949–50," *Hollywood Reporter*, March 15, 1949, 11.

14  See Radio-Keith-Orpheum Corporation Annual Report for the Year Ended December 31, 1949, 3, RKO Annual Report, HHC-Film. Despite the studio's financial problems, the Radio-Keith-Orpheum Corporation, which had yet to be divested, still recorded a profit both years due to the theatre operations.

15  Sid Rogell, "Outlook at RKO Bright," *Los Angeles Herald-Express*, September 10, 1949, B14.

16  "RKO Skeds 40 for New Season," *Hollywood Reporter*, July 27, 1949, 12.

17  Thomas F. Brady, "Hughes Takes Over Rogell Film Tasks," *The New York Times*, May 23, 1950, 35.

18  "Hughes is Given Confidence Vote," *Hollywood Reporter*, May 26, 1950, 1, 4.

19  "Hughes Hugs Backlog, Loses 100G Monthly; Biz Baffled," *Variety*, October 11, 1950, 3.

20  See Radio-Keith-Orpheum Corporation Financial Statements 1950, 22, RKO Annual Reports, HHC-Film.

21 "New RKO Picture Company Ready to Start: Depinet," *Motion Picture Daily*, December 5, 1950, 1.

22 "30 Films on New RKO Slate," *Hollywood Reporter*, November 21, 1950, 1, 5.

23 See RKO Pictures Corporation Annual Report 1951, 3, 4, RKO Annual Reports, HHC-Film.

24 "Las Vegas Ready for Big Preem," (Los Angeles) *Mirror*, February 12, 1952, 36.

25 Jimmy Starr, "'Las Vegas Story' Premiere is Wild and Wooly Affair," *Los Angeles Herald-Express*, February 13, 1952, B1.

26 Tom Coffey, "Reel Vegas Tamer than Real Town," (Los Angeles) *Mirror*, February 18, 1952, 37.

27 Advertisement, (Los Angeles) *Mirror*, February 14, 1952, 52.

28 Press release from Cleary-Strauss & Irwin, March 31, 1952, HHC-Lied. The release included a letter sent to the membership of the Guild outlining the events surrounding the dispute between Hughes and Jarrico.

29 Special Committee on Un-American Activities, *Investigation of Un-American Propaganda Activities in the United States*, vol. 1 (Washington, D.C.: Government Printing Office, 1940), 1.

30 The "Hollywood Ten," as they came to be known, were screenwriter Alvah Bessie, screenwriter and director Herbert Biberman, screenwriter Lester Cole, director Edward Dmytryk, screenwriter Ring Lardner Jr., screenwriter John Howard Lawson, screenwriter Albert Maltz, screenwriter Samuel Ornitz, producer and screenwriter Adrian Scott, and screenwriter Dalton Trumbo.

31 "Film Industry's Policy Defined," *Variety*, November 26, 1947, 3. The forty-eight included, among others, Louis B. Mayer of MGM, Harry Cohn of Columbia, Spyros Skouras of Twentieth Century-Fox, Nicholas Schenck of Loews Theatres, Barney Balaban of Paramount, Albert Warner of Warner Bros., and MPAA president Eric Johnston.

32 Patrick McGilligan, "A True-Blue Red in Hollywood: An Interview with Paul Jarrico," *Cineaste* 23, no. 2 (1997): 32.

33 Collins and Jarrico worked on three screenplays together, including the drama *Song of Russia* (1944) which was described by critics as pro-Soviet propaganda.

34 Press release from the office of Rep. Donald L. Jackson (R-Calif.), April 9, 1952, Howard Hughes Collection, HHC-Film. The release included Jackson's remarks denouncing Jarrico on the House floor, along with excerpts from HUAC testimony from and about Jarrico.

35 "Howard Hughes Tells Court Jarrico Fired Before Probe," (Los Angeles) *Mirror*, November 20, 1952, 6.

36 "Hughes Takes Responsibility In Jarrico Case," (Hollywood) *Citizen-News*, November 20, 1952, 1.

37 Press release from Cleary-Strauss & Irwin, March 31, 1952.

38 *RKO Radio Pictures* vs. *Paul Jarrico*, Complaint, March 17, 1952, 8, HHC-Lied.

39 *Ibid.*, 12.

40 *RKO Radio Pictures* vs. *Paul Jarrico*, Answer to Complaint and Counter Claim, March 28, 1952, HHC-Lied. As for his refusal to answer HUAC questions, Jarrico's legal team countered that Hughes had displayed "the sharpest and most severe criticism and defiance of a legislative committee of Congress" during his testimony surrounding the inquiry into Hughes's failure to fulfill government contracts during World War II.

41 Letter from Howard Hughes to the Screen Writers Guild, March 27, 1952, as quoted in Lee Zhito, "Picture Business," *Billboard*, April 5, 1952, 2, 67.

42 "SWG Ducks Strike Dare by Hughes," *Variety*, March 31, 1952, 6.
43 "RKO Wins Declaratory Judgment Against Jarrico," (Hollywood) *Citizen-News*, December 18, 1954, 1.
44 W. R. Wilkerson, "Trade Views," *Hollywood Reporter*, March 18, 1952, 1.
45 Letter from John D. Home to Howard Hughes, March 18, 1952, HHC-Lied.
46 Statement by Congressman Donald Jackson, March 18, 1952, HHC-Lied.
47 Statement by Congressman John Stephens Wood, March 18, 1952, HHC-Lied.
48 "Nixon Lauds Hughes for Jarrico Case," *Los Angeles Times*, April 4, 1952, 29.
49 Press Release from Carl Byoir & Associates, "V.F.W. Gives Hughes First Loyalty Award," April 26, 1952, HHC-Lied.
50 American Legion Press Association President's Merit Award, April 26, 1952, HHC-Lied.
51 Address of Howard Hughes, Managing Director of Production, RKO Radio Pictures, Inc., at Hollywood Post #43, April 1, 1952, HHC-Lied.
52 *Ibid.*
53 Howard Hughes Statement on Studio Shutdown, April 5, 1952, HHC-Lied.
54 *Ibid.*
55 Mary C. McCall Jr., "As a Matter of Fact," *Frontier: The Voices of the New West*, May 1952, 11.
56 Thomas M. Pryor, "Court Denies Plea in Jarrico Case," *The New York Times*, May 16, 1952, 18.
57 "SWG Adopts Anti-Red Resolution by 10-1 Vote; Press 'Blacklist' Suit," *Variety*, May 23, 1952, 1.
58 "Petition SWG to Declare Hughes 'Morally Right,'" *Variety*, June 3, 1952, 4.
59 "Robert Mitchum Case Irrelevant to Suit of Scribe Vs. RKO," *Variety*, August 18, 1952, 10.
60 "Jarrico Tells Defi at Probe," *Los Angeles Herald-Express*, November 18, 1952, A2.
61 "Hughes Tells Court," 6.
62 "Hughes Heard in Jarrico Suit," *Los Angeles Examiner*, November 21, 1952, 5.
63 Mosk did get Hughes to confirm the rumor that Hughes never actually set foot on the RKO studio lot on Gower Street. Despite owning and operating RKO, Hughes's base of operations continued to be split between his Romaine headquarters and his office at the Samuel Goldwyn Studios.
64 "Legion Officials Admit Not Knowing Names of Filmites They 'Boycott,'" *Variety*, November 20, 1952, 9. The reference was to screenwriter John Howard Lawson, a member of the original Hollywood Ten.
65 "Press Agent Tells Hughes Order in Jarrico Ouster," (Los Angles) *Daily News*, November 21, 1952, 9.
66 *RKO Radio Pictures* vs. *Paul Jarrico*, Decision of the Court, November 26, 1952, HHC-Lied.
67 Seymour Korman, "Studio Upheld in Refusal to Credit Writer," *Chicago Daily Tribune*, November 27, 1952, 3.
68 "Paul Jarrico Loses Suit Against RKO," *Variety*, November 28, 1952, 6.
69 The elimination of such credits led to blacklisted writers such as Carl Foreman and Dalton Trumbo being removed from movies that went on to win Academy Awards for writing. These injustices were not rectified by the Academy until the 1980s and 1990s.
70 Paul Jarrico, "Hollywood Blacklist: Paul Jarrico," interview by Larry Ceplair, March 13, 1990, Oral History Program, University of California Los Angeles.
71 See "Hughes Tools Up For 90% RKO?" *Variety*, August 12, 1953, 16.

72  "Hughes Sued Over R.K.O. Losses; Chairman Quits in Row with Board,"
    *The New York Times*, November 14, 1952, 34. Russell was under contract to
    Hughes personally through Hughes Tool so RKO paid Hughes Tool for her
    services.

73  "Hughes Wasted $$ on Jane Russell, Says Suit," (Hollywood) *Citizen-News*,
    November 14, 1952, 1.

74  "Those Same Minority Stockholders Slap New Suit on Howard Hughes,"
    *Variety*, December 26, 1952, 4.

75  Harold Heffernan, "Expect Hughes to Flash Green Light at RKO," (Los
    Angeles) *Valley Times*, January 3, 1953, 8.

76  "Grainger Promises Better Future; Tells Stockholders of Huge Losses in Past,"
    *Variety*, May 22, 1953, 1.

77  "$1,000,000 RKO Suit Names Howard Hughes," *Los Angeles Times*, April
    7, 1953, 2. Friedman's suit also included former president Ned Depinet as his
    shares were involved in the failed Stolkin transaction.

78  "Hughes Faces New Suit by Stockholders," (Hollywood) *Citizen-News*, April
    15, 1953, 3.

79  "Stockholders Ask Court to Appoint Receiver," *New York Journal-American*,
    October 13, 1953, 3.

80  William Greaves and Malcolm Logan, "Sue Hughes for Hiring Non-Acting
    Lovelies," *New York Post*, October 13, 1953, 2.

81  "RKO Execs Gang Up to Nip Dissident Stockholders' Suit," *Variety*,
    September 16, 1953, 11.

82  Walt Disney's feature length cartoons were distributed by RKO at that time,
    and Roy reported that RKO had collected $100,000,000 in rentals on the
    films in the last fifteen years.

83  "Renews Demand Court Probe Hughes's 'Collusion' in Stockholder Suit
    'Mess,'" *Variety*, November 17, 1953, 10.

84  Thomas M. Pryor, "Hollywood Dossier," *The New York Times*, November 22,
    1953, 5.

85  *Ibid.*, 5.

86  See "Howard Hughes Seeks to Buy RKO Pictures For $23 Million Cash," *Wall
    Street Journal*, February 8, 1954, 2.

87  "Hughes Tools Up," 3.

88  Letter from Howard Hughes to RKO Pictures Corporation, February 7, 1954,
    RKO Pic Corp-Purchase Assets, HHC-Film.

89  "Motion Pictures: First Round is Hughes's," *Newsweek*, February 22, 1954, 81.

90  "RKO Pictures Stock Rises Sharply on Hughes Offer to Buy Its Assets," *Wall
    Street Journal*, February 9, 1954, 9.

91  "Hughes's RKO Pictures Bid May Avert Long Litigation," *New York
    World-Telegram and Sun*, February 9, 1954, 30; "Hughes Buying Up RKO
    100%," *Variety*, February 8, 1954, 1.

92  "Hughes Seeks to Buy," 2.

93  "Hughes Bids For All RKO Stock," *Hollywood Reporter*, February 8, 1954, 1;
    "Hughes Buying Up," 1.

94  Philip R. Ward, "Howard Hughes—Financial Wizard," *Film Bulletin*, February
    22, 1954, 11.

95  Ivan Spear, "Spearheads," *Boxoffice*, February 27, 1954, 37.

96  Letter from James R. Grainger to Howard Hughes, February 15, 1954, RKO
    Purchase Assets, HHC-Film.

97  Press release from the Executive Offices RKO Pictures Corporation, March
    18, 1954, RKO Publicity, HHC-Film. With Hughes's shares, the percentage of

those voting in favor increased to eight-five percent. Only 73,227 shares voted against acceptance.

98  Bill of Sale RKO Pictures Corporation to Howard R. Hughes, March 31, 1954, RKO Purchase Assets, HHC-Film.

99  "Hughes, With $23,489,478, Stroke of a Pen, Becomes 1st Absolute Boss of a Major Pix Co.," *Variety*, April 1, 1954, 1.

100  "Hughes Now Owns RKO Lock, Stock," (Long Beach) *Independent*, April 1, 1954, 24.

101  Bill of Sale, March 31, 1954.

102  "Nevada Judge Quashes Suits Against Hughes," *Los Angeles Times*, March 31, 1954, 1.

103  Letter from James R. Grainger to RKO Pictures Corporation Stockholders, April 8, 1954, RKO Purchase Assets, HHC-Film.

104  "Stock Surrender Date Extended by RKO Pictures," *Los Angeles Herald-Express*, May 10, 1954, B7; "Hughes Extends Stock Deadline," *Hollywood Reporter*, May 10, 1954, 1.

105  "Surrender Date Extended," B7.

106  "Odlum Disavows Pix Prod'n Aims as Goal of RKO Stock Maneuvers," *Variety*, May 12, 1954, 7.

107  "New Stock Battle Seen Over RKO," *Los Angeles Times*, May 14, 1954, 2.

108  "Hughes Agrees to Sell RKO Pictures to Atlas," *New York Herald Tribune*, September 24, 1955, 3.

109  "Atlas Corp." *Wall Street Journal*, December 16, 1955, 17.

110  W. R. Wilkerson, "Trade Views," *Hollywood Reporter*, April 1, 1954, 1.

111  "RKO Down to Indie Lot," *Variety*, September 23, 1954, 1.

112  Dick Williams, "Layoffs Rock RKO as Top Execs Out," (Los Angeles) *Mirror*, September 23, 1954, 1.

113  W. R. Wilkerson, "Trade Views," *Hollywood Reporter*, September 28, 1954, 1.

114  "'The Conqueror' Was a Stupendous Project," *The Conqueror* Press Book, undated, 20, Conqueror, HHC-Film.

115  "Tremendous is the Word for New Film Hit, 'The Conqueror,'" *The Conqueror* Press Book, undated, 16, Conqueror, HHC-Film.

116  "Critic Isn't Conquered," *Chicago Daily News*, March 5, 1956, 25.

117  A. H. Weiler, "Screen: 'The Conqueror,'" *The New York Times*, March 31, 1956, 13.

118  For examples, see Harry Medvey and Randy Dreyfuss, *The Fifty Worst Movies of All Time* (London: Angus and Robertson, 1971) and John Wilson, *The Official Razzie Movie Guide: Enjoying the Best of Hollywood's Worst* (New York: Warner Books, 2005).

119  After on-location filming was complete, the production moved to the RKO lot in Hollywood. Sixty tons of potentially contaminated dirt was taken from St. George to recreate the desert set indoors.

120  Karen G. Jackovich and Mark Sennet, "The Children of John Wayne, Susan Hayward and Dick Powell Fear That Fallout Killed Their Parents," *People*, November 10, 1980, 44.

121  *Ibid.*, 42.

122  Edwin Schallert, "What is the Real Picture at RKO Studios?" *Los Angeles Times*, February 6, 1955, 1.

123  Thomas O'Neil, "Why I Bought RKO," *Film Bulletin*, August 8, 1955, 9.

124  "RKO Radio Pictures Leases 740 Features, Other Films for TV Use to C&C Super Corp. for $15 Million," *Wall Street Journal*, December 27, 1955, 7.

125  O'Neil, "Why I Bought," 9.

126 "RKO Shift to U Set for Feb. 1; Unions Served Closing Notices; Disney Taking Back 200 Cartoons," *Variety*, January 23, 1957, 3.

127 The RKO name and trademarks have been sold on a few occasions since O'Neil closed the studio in 1957. A few films and stage productions have been produced over the years under the RKO banner, but they have been few and far between, with the last coproduction released in 2015.

128 "Hughes Today Controls RKO," *Hollywood Reporter*, May 11, 1948, 1.

129 "RKO: It's Only Money," *Fortune*, May 1953, 208.

130 Peter Lev, *The Fifties: Transforming the Screen 1950–1959*, History of the American Cinema, ed. Charles Harpole, no. 7 (New York: Charles Scribner's Sons, 2003; reprint, Berkeley: University of California Press, 2006), 86.

131 "Wage Earners Laud Hughes for Stand on Reds," *Los Angeles Times*, April 28, 1952, A1.

132 Richard B. Jewell, *Slow Fade to Black: The Decline of RKO Radio Pictures* (Oakland: University of California Press, 2016), 215; "Hughes Writes $23,489,478 Check for RKO," (Los Angeles) *Mirror*, April 1, 1954, 15.

Epilogue

1 "General Tire Goes Hollywood," *Business Week*, July 23, 1955, 32.

2 Universal-International distributed *Jet Pilot* and all other unreleased RKO productions after the studio closed.

3 Bosley Crowther, "Screen: 'Jet Pilot' Lands; Film at Palace Barely Gets Off the Ground," *The New York Times*, October 5, 1957, page unknown.

4 "The Man in the White Shoes," *Forbes*, April 15, 1957, 21; "Report Creator of HELL's ANGELS, SCARFACE, FRONT PAGE, Discoverer of Harlow, Russell, Muni, George Raft Forming Indie Co." *Hollywood Close-Up*, November 10, 1960, 3.

5 Edwin Fadiman Jr., "Can the Real Howard Hughes…" *Playboy*, December 1971, 258.

6 "Hughes Buys Back 2 Films for 12 Million," *St. Paul Dispatch*, January 6, 1956, page unknown.

7 Rene Chun, "How to Recreate Howard Hughes's Legendary Movie Screening Room," *Wired*, December 17, 2015, accessed September 9, 2018, https://www.wired.com/2015/12/howard-hughess-screening-room/. The basic "facts" surrounding the screening are often in dispute. Whereas *Wired* says it took place in 1948 and lasted four months, biographer Richard Hack says it happened in 1958 and persisted for five months and twenty-two days. See Richard Hack, *Hughes: The Private Diaries, Memos and Letters* (Beverly Hills: New Millennium Press, 2001), 253-255.

# Select Bibliography

ABERDEEN, J. A. *Hollywood Renegades: The Society of Independent Motion Picture Producers.* Los Angeles: Cobblestone, 2000.

ASTOR, Mary. *A Life in Film.* New York: Delacorte, 1967.

BALIO, Tino. *Grand Design: Hollywood as a Modern Business Enterprise 1930–1939.* History of the American Cinema, ed. Charles Harpole, no. 5. New York: Charles Scribner's Sons, 1993. Reprint, Berkeley: University of California Press, 1995.

BANKS, Miranda J. *The Writers: A History of American Screenwriters and Their Guild.* New Brunswick, NJ: Rutgers University Press, 2015.

BARBAS, Samantha. "How the Movies Became Speech." *Rutgers Law Review* 64, no. 3 (2012): 665-745.

BARTLETT, Donald L., and STEELE, James B. *Howard Hughes: His Life and Madness.* New York: Norton, 1979. Reprint, New York: Norton, 2004.

BEARDSLEY, Charles. *Hollywood's Master Showman: The Legendary Sid Grauman.* New York: Cornwall Books, 1983.

BEHLMER, Rudy, ed. *Memo from David O. Selznick: The Creation of Gone with the Wind and Other Motion-Picture Classics—as Revealed in the Producer's Private Letters, Telegrams, Memorandums, and Autobiographical Remarks.* New York: Modern Library, 2000.

BERG, A. Scott. *Goldwyn: A Biography.* New York: Riverhead Books, 1989.

BERGMAN, Ingrid, and BURGESS, Alan. *Ingrid Bergman: My Story.* New York: Delacorte Press, 1980.

BROWN, Peter Harry, and BROESKE, Pat H. *Howard Hughes: The Untold Story.* New York: Dutton, 2004.

CHANDLER, Charlotte. *Ingrid Bergman: A Personal Biography.* New York: Applause Theatre & Cinema Books, 2007.

CONANT, Michael. "The Paramount Decrees Reconsidered." *Law and Contemporary Problems* 44, no. 4 (Autumn 1981): 79-107.

CRAFTON, Donald. *The Talkies: American Cinema's Transition to Sound, 1926–1931.* History of the American Cinema, ed. Charles Harpole, no. 4. New York: Charles Scribner's Sons, 1997. Reprint, Berkeley: University of California Press, 1999.

DAVENPORT, Joe, and LAWSON, Todd S. J. *The Empire of Howard Hughes.* San Francisco: Peace and Pieces Foundation, 1975.

DAVIDSON, Bill. *The Real and the Unreal.* New York: Harper & Brothers, 1961.

DAVIS, Ronald L. *The Glamour Factory: Inside Hollywood's Big Studio System.* Dallas: Southern Methodist University Press, 1993.

DIETRICH, Noah. *Howard: The Amazing Mr. Hughes.* Greenwich, CT: Fawcett Publications, 1972.

DOHERTY, Thomas. *Hollywood's Censor: Joseph I. Breen & The Production Code Administration.* New York: Columbia University Press, 2007.

DROSNIN, Michael. *Citizen Hughes.* New York: Holt, Rinehart and Winston, 1985.

DRUXMAN, Michael. *Paul Muni: His Life and His Films*. Revised ed. Albany, GA: BearManor Media, 2016.

DWIGGINS, Don. *Howard Hughes: The True Story*. Santa Monica, CA: Werner Book Corporation, 1972.

EASTLAND, Terry, ed. *Freedom of Expression in the Supreme Court: The Defining Cases*. Lanham, MD: Rowman & Littlefield, 2000.

EYMAN, Scott. *Empire of Dreams: The Epic Life of Cecil B. DeMille*. New York: Simon & Schuster, 2010; *The Speed of Sound: Hollywood and the Talkie Revolution, 1926–1930*. New York: Simon & Schuster, 1997.

FELDMAN, Charles. *The National Board of Censorship (Review) of Motion Pictures, 1909–1922*. New York: Arno Press, 1977.

FLEMING, E. J. *The Fixers: Eddie Manix, Howard Strickling and the MGM Publicity Machine*. Jefferson, NC: McFarland & Company, 2005.

GALLAGHER, Tag. *The Adventures of Roberto Rossellini: His Life and Films*. New York: Da Capo Press, 1998.

GARDNER, Gerald C. *The Censorship Papers: Movie Censorship Letters from the Hays Office, 1934–1968*. New York: Dodd, Mead, 1987.

GERBER, Albert B. *Bashful Billionaire: The Story of Howard Hughes*. New York: Lyle Stuart, 1967.

GIESLER, Jerry, as told to Pete Martin, *The Jerry Giesler Story*. New York: Simon and Schuster, 1960.

GLANCY, Mark H. "Warner Bros. Film Grosses, 1921-51: The William Schaefer Ledger." *Historical Journal of Film, Radio and Television* 15, issue 1 (March 1995): 55-73.

GOMERY, Douglas. *The Hollywood Studio System*. New York: St. Martin's Press, 1986.

HACK, RICHARD. *Hughes: The Private Diaries, Memos and Letters. Beverly Hills: New Millennium Press, 2001*.

HAMPTON, Benjamin B. *A History of the Movies*. London: Noel Douglas, 1932.

HAVER, Ronald. *David O. Selznick's Hollywood*. New York: Alfred A. Knopf, 1980.

HAYES, WILL H. *The Memoirs of Will H. Hays. Garden City, NY: Doubleday, 1955*.

HIGHAM, Charles. *Howard Hughes: The Secret Life. New York: Putnam's Sons, 1993. Reprint, New York: St. Martin's Press, 2004*.

HOCHMAN, Stanley, ed. *From Quasimodo to Scarlett O'Hara: A National Board of Review Anthology, 1920–1940*. New York: F. Unger, 1982.

INGLIS, Ruth A. *Freedom of the Movies: A Report on Self-Regulation from the Commission on Freedom of the Press*. Chicago: University of Chicago Press, 1947; "Need for Voluntary Self-Regulation." *Annals of American Academy of Political and Social Science* 254 (November 1947): 153-159.

JACOBS, Lewis. *The Rise of the American Film*. New York: Harcourt, Brace and Company, 1939. Reprint, New York: Teachers College Press, 1975.

JEWELL, Richard B. *RKO Radio Pictures: A Titan is Born*. Berkeley: University of California Press, 2012; *Slow Fade to Black: The Decline of RKO Radio Pictures*. Oakland: University of California Press, 2016.

JEWELL, Richard B., with HARBIN, Vernon. *The RKO Story*. New York: Arlington House, 1982.

KAUFFMANN, Stanley, ed. *American Film Criticism: From the Beginnings to Citizen Kane*. New York: Liveright, 1972.

KEATS, John. *Howard Hughes*. New York: Random House, 1966. Reprint, New York: Pyramid Books, 1970.

KENNEDY, Joseph P., ed. *The Story of the Films: As Told by Leaders of the Industry to the Students of the Graduate School of Business Administration George F. Baker Foundation Harvard University*. Chicago: A. W. Shaw, 1927.

KING, Geoff. *American Independent Cinema*. Bloomington: Indiana University Press, 2005.

KOSZARSKI, Richard. *An Evening's Entertainment: The Age of the Silent Feature Picture 1915–1928*. History of the American Cinema, ed. Charles Harpole, no. 3. New York: Charles Scribner's Sons, 1990. Reprint, Berkeley: University of California Press, 1994.

LASKY, Betty. *RKO: The Biggest Little Major of Them All*. Englewood Cliffs, NJ: Prentice-Hall, 1984.

LASKY, Jesse L., Jr. *What Happened to Hollywood?* New York: Funk & Wagnalls, 1975.

LEAMER, Laurence. *As Time Goes By: The Life of Ingrid Bergman*. New York: Harper & Row, 1986.

LEFF, Leonard J., and SIMMONS, Jerold L. *The Dame in the Kimono: Hollywood, Censorship, and the Production Code*. Revised ed. Lexington: University of Kentucky Press, 2001.

LEV, Peter. *The Fifties: Transforming the Screen 1950–1959*, History of the American Cinema, ed. Charles Harpole, no. 7. New York: Charles Scribner's Sons, 2003. Reprint, Berkeley: University of California Press, 2006.

LEVY, Emanuel. *Cinema of Outsiders: The Rise of American Independent Film*. New York: New York University Press, 1999.

LONGWORTH, Karina. *Seduction: Sex, Lies and Stardom in Howard Hughes's Hollywood*. New York: Harper Collins, 2018.

MADDEN, Nelson C. *The Real Howard Hughes Story*. New York: Manor Books, 1976.

MALTBY, Richard. *Harmless Entertainment: Hollywood and the Ideology of Consensus*. Metuchen, NJ: Scarecrow Press, 1983; *Hollywood Cinema*, 2nd ed. Oxford: Blackwell Publishing, 2003.

MATHISON, Richard. *His Weird and Wanton Ways: The Secret Life of Howard Hughes*. New York: Morrow, 1977.

MCCARTHY, Todd. *Howard Hawks: The Grey Fox of Hollywood*. New York: Grove Press, 1997.

MCDONOUGH, John R., and WINSLOW, Robert L. "The Motion Picture Industry: United States v. Oligopoly." *Stanford Law Review*, no. 3 (April 1949): 385-427.

MCGILLIGAN, Patrick. "A True-Blue Red in Hollywood: An Interview with Paul Jarrico." *Cineaste* 23, no. 2 (1997): 32-39.

MCGILLIGAN, Patrick, and BUHLE, Paul. *Tender Comrades: A Backstory of the Hollywood Blacklist*. Minneapolis: University of Minnesota Press, 2012.

MEDVEY, Harry, and DREYFUSS, Randy. *The Fifty Worst Movies of All Time*. London: Angus and Robertson, 1971.

MOLEY, Raymond. *The Hays Office*. New York: Bobbs-Merrill, 1945.

MOORE, Terry. *The Beauty and the Billionaire*. New York: Pocket Books, 1984.

NAVASKY, Victor S. *Naming Names*. New York: Viking Press, 1980.

PARISH, James Robert. *The Hollywood Book of Scandals: The Shocking, Often Disgraceful Deeds and Affairs of More than 100 American Movie and TV Idols*. New York: McGraw Hill, 2004.

PARSONS, Louella. *Tell It to Louella*. New York: Putnam, 1961.

PHELAN, James. *Howard Hughes: The Hidden Years*. New York: Random House, 1976.

PIZZITOLA, Louis. *Hearst Over Hollywood: Power, Passion, and Propaganda in the Movies*. New York: Columbia University Press, 2002.

RANDALL, Richard. *Censorship of the Movies*. Madison: University of Wisconsin Press, 1968.

ROBERTS, Jerry, ed. *Mitchum in His Own Words*. With a foreword by Roger Ebert. New York: Proscenium Publishers, 2000.

RUSSELL, Jane. *Jane Russell: My Path & My Detours*. New York: Franklin Watts, 1985.

SCHATZ, Thomas. *Boom and Bust: American Cinema in the 1940s*, History of the American Cinema, ed. Charles Harpole, no. 6. New York: Charles Scribner's Sons, 1993. Reprint, Berkeley: University of California Press, 2008; *The Genius of the System: Hollywood Filmmaking in the Studio Era*. New York: Pantheon, 1988.

SERVER, Lee. *Robert Mitchum: "Baby, I Don't Care."* New York: St. Martin's Griffin, 2001.

SHULMAN, Irving. *Harlow: An Intimate Biography*. New York: Dell Books, 1964.

SILVER, Alain, and URSINI, James, eds. *The Gangster Film Reader*. Pompton Plains, NJ: Limelight Editions, 2007.

STEELE, Joseph Henry. *Ingrid Bergman: An Intimate Portrait*. New York: David McKay, 1959.

STENN, David. *Bombshell: The Life and Death of Jean Harlow*. New York: Doubleday, 1993.

THOMAS, Tony. *Howard Hughes in Hollywood*. Secaucus, NJ: Citadel Press, 1985.

TINNIN, David B. *Just About Everybody vs. Howard Hughes*. Garden City, NY: Doubleday, 1973.

VAUGHN, Stephen. "Morality and Entertainment: The Origins of the Motion Picture Production Code." *The Journal of American History*, vol. 77 (June 1990): 39-65.

WASKO, Janet. *Movies and Money: Financing the American Film Industry*. Norwood, NJ: Ablex, 1982.

WILSON, John. *The Official Razzie Movie Guide: Enjoying the Best of Hollywood's Worst*. New York: Warner Books, 2005.

# Index